WELLERISMS IN IRELAND
TOWARDS A CORPUS FROM ORAL AND LITERARY SOURCES

Fionnuala Carson Williams

'Proverbium'
this publication has also received support from
An Chomhairle Oidhreachta/The Heritage Council, Republic of Ireland,
under the 2002 Publications Grant Scheme, Foras na Gaeilge and
The Belfast Society

The University of Vermont
Burlington, Vermont
2002

Supplement Series

of

Proverbium
Yearbook of International Proverb Scholarship

Edited by Wolfgang Mieder

Volume 12

The cover illustration is from a woodcut by Percy J. Billinghurst for
A Hundred Fables of La Fontaine Jean de la Fontaine,
John Lane The Bodley Head, London & New York 1900, p. 77.
I thank The Board of Trinity College Dublin for permission to reproduce
the image.

© 2002 Fionnuala Carson Williams

ISBN 0-9710223-2-1

Manufactured in the United States of America
by Queen City Printers Inc.
Burlington, Vermont

CONTENTS

MAP OF WELLERISM PROVENANCES
BY PROVINCE, COUNTY AND CITY

This book is dedicated to Bo Almqvist,
who put wellerisms on the Irish map

ACKNOWLEDGEMENTS

For permission to publish archival material I would like to most sincerely thank the respective Heads of the Department of Irish Folklore, University College Dublin, The National University of Ireland, the Ulster Folk and Transport Museum and the Armagh County Museum, National Museums & Galleries of Northern Ireland, the Eesti Rahvaluule Archiiv/Estonian Folklore Archives and the Lietuviu Tautosakos Rankra_tynas/Lithuanian Folklore Archive. I also thank staff in the Queen's University of Belfast Main Library, especially Florence Gray of Inter-library Loans and, in Special Collections, Mary Kelly, Andrea McCrea and Inez Scott, and staff in the Newspaper and Reference Sections of Belfast Central Library.

I am indebted to all those who contributed examples to my questionnaire, Q 2000. Wolfgang Mieder, besides being an inspiration, kindly sent me the Shaw wellerism (Part A 270) and, in addition, I was alerted to some Irish wellerisms through his diligence on the *Dictionary of Wellerisms* and its *Addenda*. I would also like to thank Raymond Hickey for copies of his CD-ROM of Irish drama, from which Kathleen Quinn expertly helped me locate examples. Thanks, too, are due to 'The John Bennett Show' BBC Radio Ulster, and 'The John Creedon Show' Raidió Teilifís Éireann, for broadcasting appeals for wellerisms.

Ciarán Ó Duibhín made a significant contribution to this project. He extracted wellerisms from *Tobar na Gaedhilge*, his database of Ulster Irish, provided translations and verified the translations of all the Irish material, as well as making numerous suggestions, particularly regarding the presentation of the Irish-language material. Also of great import to the corpus was Bo Almqvist's generous access to the wellerisms which he had collected from his informant and friend Mícheál Ó Gaoithín and of immeasurable assistance was Bo Almqvist's file *Irish Wellerisms* which he had begun shortly after taking up permanent residence in

Ireland. He recently, to my surprize and delight, gave it into my custody.

I would like to warmly thank Bairbre Ní Fhloinn and Ríonach uí Ógáin for all their assistance with several details of Irish manuscript references. Déirdre Hennigan, Ian Lee, Patricia Lysaght, Críostóir Mac Carthaigh, Joseph McMinn and Anne Smyth also helped with aspects of Irish references and I would like to thank Richard Harrison for spotting the 'Jonathanisms' and Tom Clyde for information prior to the publication of his book. My thanks are also due to Maura Pringle who prepared the cover and map.

Help finding versions in other languages was kindly given by Bengt af Klintberg, Kazys Grigas, Caragh Halpin, Johannas Hautsma, Arvo Krikmann, Outi Lauhaukangas, Stanislaw Predota and Udo Steuck, and with translations by Stephanie Bachorz, Ingvill Kristiansen, Annikki Kaivola-Bregenhøj, Catherine O'Rawe, Susan Sinisalo, Elly Taylor, Paul Tempan and staff of the School of Modern Languages, Literatures and Arts, Queen's. Paul also provided generous computer expertise, augmented by Rick Stoops, and Paul suggested contacting 'The John Creedon Show' to appeal for wellerisms. I would also like to thank Jacqueline Simpson for publishing a request in *FLS News*. Other colleagues from abroad who have helped in various ways are my friend of many years, Gyula Paczolay, and a new acquaintance, Vita Ivanauskaitë. The many more who also contributed to completing a fuller picture of wellerisms are acknowledged within.

This publication would not have been possible without the generous financial support from Wolfgang Mieder, *Proverbium*, An Chomhairle Oidreacha/The Heritage Council, Republic of Ireland, Foras na Gaeilge and The Belfast Society.

I would also like to record my gratitude to Brian Walker, Director, Catherine Boone, Catherine McColgan, Gillian McIntosh, Margaret McNulty, Alan O'Day and all my other colleagues in the Institute of Irish Studies, The Queen's University of Belfast, for their encouragement and interest, and last, but certainly not least, to Ruairí Ó Bléine for reading the manuscript.

Fionnuala Carson Williams   Summer 2002

PREFACE

The term 'wellerism' for sayings such as, '"Sour grapes!" says the fox when he couldn't catch the chicken' was created in the nineteenth century and was derived from the name of Charles Dickens characters in *Pickwick Papers* — the Wellers — because they were fond of using them (Mieder 1994, ix–x; Bryan & Mieder 1997, especially 26–28). The catalyst for bringing together a corpus of wellerisms found in Ireland was a re-reading over Christmas 1999 of William Carlton's *Traits and Stories of the Irish Peasantry,* first published in Dublin in the early 1830s. The model is Wolfgang Mieder and Stewart Kingsbury's marvellous *Dictionary of Wellerisms* (1994), while the foundation of my knowledge of wellerisms came from my teacher Bo Almqvist and it was he who had drawn attention to us as students in Dublin in the 1970s, to the wealth of folklore in Carlton (1794–1869).

Since that Christmas of 1999 I have actively been putting together as many wellerisms as possible from oral and literary sources and the catalogue now extends to over 900 versions. Part A of the catalogue consists of those found in English in Ireland while Part B is those in Irish. As regards the oral material, the basis of the catalogue is the Schools' Collection, made from 1938 to 1939 by the Irish Folklore Commission. In 1992 I had published some twenty-five from it from nine counties — Cavan, Dublin, Kildare, Leitrim, Louth, Monaghan, Sligo, Wexford and Wicklow ([Carson] Williams). To those I added a number of variants from the same counties and some more from the Schools' Collection from Counties Donegal and Galway, bringing the total to about thirty-six. The next to be added were about thirty from the Byers Papers, Ulster Dialect Archive, Ulster Folk and Transport Museum. Sir John William Byers (1853–1921), a professor of midwifery at what is now the Queen's University of Belfast, had a strong amateur interest in dialect. Born in China to a Presbyterian missionary minister and a teacher he was brought to Ireland in his first year when his father became ill and, while he was chiefly reared in Belfast, he was also familiar with the speech of his mother's home place, Rathfriland, Co. Down. He collected from various counties in the north of Ireland, loosely provenanced 'Ulster.' Over one in nine of the wellerisms assembled together below, however, come from a questionnaire largely suggested and composed by Bo Almqvist as new head of the new Department of Irish Folklore, which derived from the Irish Folklore Commission. The questionnaire, with four examples, (see Appendix 1) was sent out on an all-Ireland basis in 1973 and is referred to below as Q 1973. There were over ninety returns, although many of these, while replete with sayings of various kinds, did not contain wellerisms. Some of the wellerisms returned date right back over the century to 1900 while some were current at that time. In addition I composed questionnaire (Q 2000, an early version with ten examples and a later with five, see Appendix 1) which I used from January 2000 for practically two years. Almost ninety were obtained through this, including four in Irish. As well as all these from oral tradition which were recently collected or to be found in manuscripts, a number from printed works, such as Henry Glassie's *Passing the Time, Folklore and History of an Irish Community* (1982) have been added. All in all, there is a wellerism or, in most cases, several wellerisms in English from every single county of all thirty-two in Ireland while Irish wellerisms have been located in twelve counties — Armagh, Clare, Cork, Donegal, Galway, Kerry, Londonderry, Mayo, Monaghan, Sligo, Tyrone and Waterford, in six of which Irish is now not spoken. As mentioned in the Acknowledgements, an important source was also very generously made available — Bo Almqvist's *Collection of Proverbs from Mícheál Ó Gaoithín Dunquin, (formerly Great Blasket), Co. Kerry, undertaken between 1966 and 1974* (annotated typescript), the repertoire of a native Irish speaker, and, in fact, the largest collection of wellerisms from any one person in Ireland. Finally, in the expectation of chasing out some current wellerisms, two radio appeals were made, one in Northern Ireland and one in the Republic of Ireland, resulting in about seven.

Turning to wellerisms in literature, the other important personal source mentioned in the Acknowledgements and kindly made available was Ciarán Ó Duibhín's *Tobar na Gaedhilge*, a database of Ulster Irish which is mainly Donegal literature from 1900 to 1950. As well as Carlton in the nineteenth century, I read much of Samuel Lover (1797–1868) and there located several while Jonathan Swift (1667–1745), cited in the *Dictionary of Wellerisms* (Mieder & Kingsbury 1994), henceforth referred to as

DOW, was an earlier user of wellerisms. For the twentieth century Brendan Behan (1923–64) was an important source while Wolfgang Mieder sent me George Bernard Shaw's (1856–1950) only wellerism (Bryan & Mieder 1994) and his *Addenda* (Mieder 1997) yielded one of the Joycean wellerisms, James Joyce (1882–1941). Two from Brian O'Nolan (1911–66) were located by Bo Almqvist and, subsequently, with this lead, others by me. Raymond Hickey's CD-ROM of drama in English in Ireland from the fourteenth century (2000) demonstrated that very few wellerisms occur in plays. Wellerisms used as jokes were obtained from *Pro Tanto Quid*, the student charity magazine, begun in 1927, of the Queen's University of Belfast.

From this it is evident that my catalogue below has a thorough geographical and chronological coverage and represents both oral and literary tradition. There is a very wide range of types and, as regards oral versions, both informants and correspondents appear to have been remarkably open and frank about sharing material. In some wellerisms women and minorities, for example, those physically challenged, are cruelly lampooned and a few base their humour on what would be considered crude and unacceptable by most. Since these are all part of the genre the collection would not be representative without them. The full range, and almost every single example, is therefore available for analysis (four of a sexual kind have been excluded but may be found in *Pro Tanto Quid* 1966 (1), 1971 (2) and 1973 (1)). Although one cannot transpose contemporary judgements, crudity, as would be understood here and now, had long been a feature of wellerisms as some of the oldest extant — those from Sumeria (in present day southern Iraq) which, at their most ancient, belong to the first few centuries of the fifth millennium before the present, show (Gordon 1959). Crudity in modern wellerisms obviously plays an entirely different rôle; for a start, in contrast to ancient Sumeria where they were so acceptable as to have been recorded on clay tablets by a literate stratum, some correspondents were reluctant to put them into written form. On the other hand, trying to evaluate sterile texts out of context is rather hazardous and where one can find similar items in context, they are often much less startling than in isolation.

The Irish-speaking areas in the province of Connacht are the most systematically covered parts of Ireland. For his annotated collection *Sean-fhocla Chonnacht*, published in two volumes in 1948 and 1952, Tomás S. Ó Máille not only gathered from current oral tradition, but also looked at both manuscript and published Connacht material, including some regional fiction. His intensive search included the full runs of many periodicals, and wellerisms turned up in *An Stoc* (1917–32) and *Ar Aghaidh* (1933–), both monthlies published in Galway city, *Gearrbhaile* (Ballynasloe, Co. Galway, 1927–), *Béaloideas* (1927–) and *Irisleabhar na Gaedhilge/The Gaelic Journal* (Dublin 1882–1909). The two last, of course, potentially contain wellerisms from outside the province and, for this catalogue, I looked at all issues of the later, particularly at all the many lists of proverbs, which is where wellerisms tended to be included. I also looked at all the *Béaloideas* references to proverbs in Caoimhín Ó Danachair's *Bibliography of Irish Ethnology and Folk Tradition* (1978). The area in which the most intensive collection has been concentrated is, again, Irish-speaking, this time in the province of Munster, — the Dingle Peninsula. Besides Almqvist's rich vein of wellerisms from a single individual, Flower noted some from the offshore Great Blasket island and those in 'An Seabhac's' (Pádraig Ó Siochfhradha 1883–1964) *Seanfhocail na Muimhneach* (1926), the first publication in which wellerisms from Ireland appeared as a group, also stemmed largely from the Dingle Peninsula, as did much of the material added by Pádraig Ua Maoileoin to the second edition of 1984 (Williams 1986).

The obvious place to continue looking for wellerisms would be in Brian O'Nolan's and Brendan Behan's columns which were written for quality newspapers. Both writers were extremely interested in language and fluent in Irish and English, writing in both; turns of phrase, puns and proverbs themselves are features of their work. Other works of James Joyce, besides *Ulysses*, *Dubliners* and *A Portrait of the Artist as a Young Man* are another potential source. As regards those from oral tradition, there are probably, at a minimum, 50 to 60 more in the sixteen unindexed counties of the Schools' Collection and a few throughout the Main Manuscript Collection of the Department of Irish Folklore, University College Dublin. Tomás S. Ó Máille did use the Main

Manuscript Collection when compiling *Sean-Fhocla Chonnacht* (1948, 1952) but only unearthed the odd wellerism. Since 1973, however, when the profile of wellerisms was raised by the questionnaire more may have been recorded. Although the majority of wellerisms are probably together in the typescript of Byers' essay 'Proverbs and Sayings,' there may be a small number scattered throughout the rest of the extensive Byers Papers, Ulster Dialect Archive, Ulster Folk and Transport Museum. Unfortunately, as mentioned, little is known of their provenance so they can only be designated 'Ulster' (that is, anywhere in one of nine counties). Internal evidence shows Byers did collect in north Ulster and two wellerisms are more closely placed (Part A 47.2 to Coleraine, Co. Londonderry, and Part A 201 to Inishowen, Co. Donegal). It should be remembered that, in addition to noting wellerisms he heard, Byers also wrote down wellerisms (and indeed other material) from printed sources both in English and in translation from Irish and without ascription. As I discovered that wellerisms were incorporated into the Queen's University rag magazine, other rag magazines are a potential source to be explored. I am grateful to Tom Clyde for suggesting all the other likely university magazines of other kinds and for their details *The Varsity Tatler*, Queen's University Belfast (1912) and, also Queen's, *The Northman* (December 1926–32), *The New Northman* (1932–41) and *The Northman* (1942–50), and *The Quarryman*, University College Cork (December 1913–May 1917; March 1929–63; New Series 1965–73).

As regards references to wellerisms in Ireland found in other languages, I have added full references to those in English (in North America and England), Scots and Scottish Gaelic, most English-language and Scots references being from *DOW*. The English references include a sprinkling from India, Australia and New Zealand. I have also tried to indicate other languages in which these wellerisms have been found. Many of the Scandinavian references are from Pirkko Sallinen (1969 & 1970). With other references and languages I have been most generously helped by friends and colleagues whom I heartily thank (see also Acknowledgements). These references to other languages outside English, Scots and Scottish Gaelic, should not be regarded as comprehensive; in particular, more from Dutch and German could be added and I would welcome correspondence in this regard.

Reference to the antiquity of wellerisms has been made elsewhere by Almqvist (1976, 4, in Almqvist 1973–) and Mieder (1994, xii) and it is enthralling to note that material found in modern Ireland is quite in keeping with two in particular of the oldest extant group — those from Sumeria — 'The fox, having urinated into the sea, "the whole(?) of the sea is my urine!" (he said)' (Gordon 1959, No. 2.67, 222–23) and 'The fox urinated into the Tigris, and said: "I am causing the high tide to rise!"' (Alster 1993, 12).

WELLERISMS IN IRELAND[1]

Over the years, collections devoted to wellerisms in various languages have been published[2] but what is known of wellerisms in Ireland? In 1931 Archer Taylor wrote, 'It has *not* been noticed that the Celts employ the Wellerism with evident ease and freedom, ...'[3] Wolfgang Mieder and Stewart Kingsbury, however, were able to include a few from Ireland in their magnificent *Dictionary of Wellerisms* (in the English language) and its *Addenda*.[4] Turning to works on specifically Irish material, all three of the main published collections of sayings in Irish (which are composed of material from the mid-nineteenth century on) include wellerisms, indeed, *Seanfhocail na Muimhneach* ['Proverbs of the Munster People'], dating to 1926, has a special section devoted to them[5] and the very first entry in *Sean-fhocla Chonnacht*[6] ['Connacht Proverbs'] happens to be a wellerism. In the early eighties Bo Almqvist published a detailed study of one wellerism *'"Siúl díreach, a mhic!" mar adúirt an seana-phortán leis an bportán óg'* ['"Walk straight, son!" as the old crab said to the young crab'] which he had collected about ten years earlier from Mícheál Ó Gaoithín of Co. Kerry, 'Siúl an Phortáin, Friotalfhocal agus Fabhalscéal (AT 276)'[7] ['The Crab's Walk, Wellerism and Fable (AT 276)'].

---

[1] The following essay builds on and supersedes an earlier version, published in 2001, 'Quotation Proverbs in Ireland' in *Northern Lights, Following Folklore in North-Western Europe, Essays in honour of Bo Almqvist*, edited by Séamas Ó Catháin (Carson Williams 2001a), and a lecture which I gave on 23rd March, 2001, at the colloquium *Verbal Wit and Verbal Wisdom* jointly organized by the Warburg Institute and the Folklore Society in the Warburg Institute, University College, London.

[2] Mieder & Kingsbury (1994), Bibliography pp. 157–66.

[3] Taylor (1962 fac., 1985 rpt.), pp. 212–13.

[4] Mieder & Kingsbury, *op. cit.*, henceforth referred to as *DOW*, and Mieder (1997), pp. 187–217.

[5] 'An Seabhac' (1926), Section 10 'A ndubhairt siúd' ['they said'], pp. 99–104, lists approximately 40 wellerisms.

[6] Ó Máille (1948), Vol. I No. 1.

[7] Almqvist (1982–83).

The term 'seanfhocal friotail' or, 'friotalfhocal,' is one which, based on 'Sagwort' or, 'quotation proverb,' was created by Almqvist.[8] Unlike the plethora of appellations available in German (as can be seen in the title of Siegfried Neumann's wonderful assemblage from Mecklenburg[9]) there is no indigenous term in Ireland in either Irish or English. 'Wellerism,' despite its cultural specificity, will, however, be used here due to its international acceptance and recognition as the term in English.

Returning to sources, dictionaries, always a fount of sayings, have also, from the twentieth century, included a sprinkling of wellerisms.[10] As regards English-language wellerisms in Ireland, as mentioned in the Preface, I published twenty-five from the late 1930s Schools' Collection Manuscripts.[11] Almost all of them occurred in lists of sayings composed mainly of proverbs. It appears that in the Schools' Collection the frequency of wellerisms is about one in every 300 different proverbs[12] or, in an equally rough calculation, one wellerism in every ten Schools' Collection manuscripts. In reality in speech it is likely that wellerisms were actually commoner than it would seem from the Schools' Collection. A Co. Armagh sheep farmer commented in 1974 that 'earthy or otherwise [they] … run through everyday conversation … where I live.'[13] The Schools' Collection was, however, largely compiled by children. The frequent seemingly flippant tone and brands of humour of wellerisms might not have

[8] Almqvist op. cit., pp. 37–38/English summary p. 59.
[9] Neumann (1996), *Sprichwörtliches aus Mecklenburg: Anekdotensprüche, Antisprichwörter, apologische Sprichwörter, Beispielsprichwörter, erzählende Sprichwörter, Sagte-Sprichwörter, Sagwörter, Schwanksprüche, Wellerismen, Zitatensprichwörter.*
[10] For example, Dinneen (1934, 1970 rpt.) contains almost 700 proverbs in Irish and five wellerisms. A card index compiled by me of all these is deposited in the Department of Irish Folklore, University College Dublin.
[11] [Carson] Williams (1992), new ed. Carson Williams (2000a).
[12] This compares with Smith & Wilson (1970, 1975 rpt.) *The Oxford Dictionary of English Proverbs* where there is approximately one wellerism per 232 proverb types.
[13] Questionnaire 1973(74) Irish Folklore Collection, Department of Irish Folklore, University College Dublin, ms. 1888 p. 66 (Q 1973(74) IFC1888:66).

encouraged informants to pass them on, especially for a scheme which was conducted under the auspices of the Department of Education.[14] Unlike German, Italian and Scandinavian wellerisms, however, and, indeed, ordinary proverbs in Ireland, hardly any that are anticlerical or irreligious have been recorded, but a number do contain four-letter words. Some decades after the Schools' Collection Scheme a whole compilation of wellerisms, this time directly contributed by adults, was added to the Main Manuscript Collection of the Department of Irish Folklore through a questionnaire issued in 1973. This was the first composed by Bo Almqvist on his appointment to the chair there and was no doubt related to his familiarity with the genre in the Nordic languages.[15]

Although a comparatively rare genre, compounded by being tricky to collect, the wellerisms which have been recorded are a fascinating and varied group which has played a lively part, both in oral tradition in its own right, and in relation to various other genres, and in the writings of foremost literary figures at least from Swift in the early eighteenth century to the present era.

The Schools' Collection wellerisms from the counties of Cavan, Dublin, Kildare, Leitrim, Louth, Monaghan, Sligo, Wexford and Wicklow formed my starting point for a catalogue of those in Ireland which now extends to over 530 different *types*, over 90% of which do not appear to have previously been noted outside the island.[16] They are overwhelmingly an oral genre and of

---

[14] See Tóthné Litovkina (1999), especially p. 151 and p. 157 for wellerisms present in Ireland (except for the first on both pages) which either have a sexual content or might have a sexual implication. Others which are scatological also occur eg. Part A 267 & 302.

[15] The questionnaire, titled 'Wellerisms,' (see Appendix 1) was issued in both English and Irish and distributed throughout Ireland. According to recorded dates questionnaires were returned up to 1978. While some of the data is contemporary, some goes back as far as about 1900. The responses are bound in volumes IFC 1888, 1911, 1917, 2027 and 2154 (p. 279 only). There are approximately 150 examples from English but only about twenty-three from Irish.

[16] The catalogue is completely open to comment and further examples. Current data from a questionnaire circulated by me has been included in the catalogue and here it is referred to as Q 2000 (see Appendix I), while the Department's questionnaire is referred to as Q 1973.

the 930 or so versions now assembled, only some forty are from literature. A search through twenty-five of the plays on Raymond Hickey's CD-ROM did not reveal many and, in the compilation of this catalogue, I read several English-language novels, particularly of the nineteenth century, again only finding a few. Likewise, Ciarán Ó Duibhín's *Tobar na Gaedhilge*, which is mainly Donegal literature of the first half of the twentieth century, only turned up a small number. In relation to the many thousands of sayings in the Department's Archive wellerisms form a very small group but one which displays great diversity and richness.

A great number of the wellerisms are humorous. This is often achieved through irony (considered here as humour), a trait which is also present in the oldest wellerisms available anywhere. Humour based on misogyny, black, blue[17] and scatological humour, for instance, '"Take it or leave it," as the crow said when he flew over,'[18] as well as other types, are also to the fore. The humour in one set centres on the speakers, whether human or animal, deliberately swallowing inappropriate food items as in, '"Just to have it to say," said the old man who ate the bit of the dog.'[19] Another set concerns hygiene, especially to do with food preparation, for example, '"Necessity is the mother of invention," as the cook said when she used her nightcap to strain the jelly.'[20] In many the comic effect is heightened by talking animals, even those which are naturally voiceless, for example, fish and flies, like the following, 'As the fly said as it was walking over the mirror, "That's another way of looking at it."'[21] In addition to language, human characteristics and emotions are frequently given to animals; the monkey, in particular, acts as a human substitute. Monkeys can resemble humans in their actions, and even in their facial expressions, but, because they are not human, they are permitted to speak or behave out of turn.

---

[17] For an insight into such wellerisms see Mieder (1982) 'Sexual Content of German Wellerisms.'

[18] Part A 283.

[19] Part A 255.

[20] Part A 212 from the *Cloughherney* [Co. Tyrone] *Presbyterian Church Quotation Calendar 1945*, kindly sent by Morna Gannon, Christmas 2000.

[21] Part A 311.

Play on words or punning also provide or enhance the comedy, for example, '"Excuse haste and a bad pen," as the pig said when it broke out of the stye'[22] and '"Go mba fearr i mbárach thú!" mar dubhairt Colmcille le n-mháthair'[23] ["May you be better tomorrow" or "May you be a man, tomorrow," as Colmcille said to his mother']. Dunne is one of the common personal name used in this connection, as the following demonstrates,'"Well done!" said old Dunne when young Dunne was born.'[24] In a number of cases the humour is at the expense of those physically challenged. '"Luk now!" said the blind man,'[25] in many variants, is a common example and is known not only in Ireland in both languages but widely outside. In Ireland and elsewhere extended versions exist which include the deaf, the lame and the silent. Others in this unkind category, most likely coined and circulating among the able-bodied, include, '"How are you getting on?" said the bus conductor to the man with no legs' and '"I didn't quite catch that," said the man with no hands.'[26] I would suggest, however, that their *raison d'être* is more of a mental challenge to understand the pun, rather than a direct jibe. Taylor is of the opinion that wellerisms containing a pun, such as those just quoted, are more recent than those encompassing a proverb like '"Gach 'n neach mar oiltear é," ars' a' traona ag dul 'sa' neantóig'[27] ["Everyone as he's reared," said the corncrake going into the nettles']. Nowadays, the majority of wellerisms in

---

[22] Part A 119, The Byers Papers. This detailed collection of Ulster words, proverbs, children's, medical and other lore, together with a few songs and photographs, was made in the first twenty years of the 20th century by Sir John Byers, Professor of Midwifery at the Queen's University of Belfast from 1893 until his death in 1920. It is contained in eight library boxes Byers Boxes T1–8 in the Ulster Dialect Archive, Ulster Folk and Transport Museum (NMGNI, UFTM), and remains largely unpublished, although some material from it is included in the Museum's Electronic Database, Ulster Dialect Archive, and in the *Concise Ulster Dictionary* (Macafee, 1997), based on the Electronic Database.
[23] Part B 89.1.
[24] Part A 63.
[25] Part A 259.60 Co. Londonderry; for examples in Irish see Part B 40.
[26] Part A 98 & 36 respectively.
[27] Taylor (1962 fac., 1985 rpt.), p. 8; proverb Part B 78.2 & .3.

14

circulation and being created probably hinge on puns. Occasionally the misunderstanding of another language supplies the humour. Stylistic devices like alliteration, repetition, rhyme and contrast, often in combination, play important parts in contributing to the wit. Humour is also achieved because of the structure of the typical wellerism. This resembles the classic one-line joke where the quotation in the first part can be considered as the build-up to the incongruous speaker and circumstances which constitute the second part and the punch.[28] In all these respects the Irish material resembles wellerisms in other languages and locations.

The speakers fall into four distinct groups — actual people (by far the biggest category), for example, '"May the Lord direct me!" says Tom Malone when he pulled the tail out a th' [= of the] ass,'[29] animals (three times more wild than domestic[30] — and *deliberately* incorporating exotic species) as in '"There's no such thing," as the farmer said when he saw the giraffe,'[31] supernatural or fictitious characters (particularly the devil) like *'"Glór mór ar bheagán olna," mar adubhairt an tÁidhbhirseoir nuair a bhí sé ag bearradh na muice'*[32] ['"Great noise for little wool," as the Adversary [ie. Devil] said when he was shaving the pigs'] and, lastly, inanimate objects, as in the following, *'"Dia linn!" ars' an sac nuair a thuit an pionall'*[33] ['"God be with us!" said the sack when the pack-saddle fell']. In some rare examples the quote is voiced by a group, for example, the Breekers, who were local fishermen, *na Tincéaraí i mBalla* [= the Tinkers in Balla] and eels.

Stock speakers can be added to fixed expressions as a way of imbuing them with reliability and in Ireland we find the simple and widely used 'as the man said,' as well as the more specific *'mar a dúirt an file'* which also occurs in English, 'as the poet said.' Evoking a poet, or an important, or wise person, 'Confucius, he say,' someone else from the past, or even just anyone else apart

---

[28] Norrick (2001), pp. 258–59.
[29] Part A 184.1.
[30] This is unlike proverbs where domestic animals are the norm, Williams (1982–83), pp. 127–32.
[31] Part A 278.
[32] Part B 107.1.
[33] Part B 61.

from the user, is a way of giving reliability to a saying. There does seem to be a liking for ascribing sayings to people and in the wellerism questionnaire returns we find comments to this effect such as, 'Sometimes the person talking does not know who used the old saying and in this case he says "mar adúirt an té adúirt"[34] ["as the one who said it said"].' The same correspondent goes on to explain that in his district there was a wonderful craftsman called Jack McDermot who had left school back in 1895. Jack McDermot was also remembered as being very witty and sayings are still often attributed to him with the phrase *'mar adúirt Jack Sáibhéiridhe'* or *'mar adúirt Jack Mhicín'* ['as Jack Sáibhéiridhe, or Jack Mhicín, said']. In general these have not been included in the catalogue as they can be attached to any saying and do not make them triadic. Other phrases like 'as the actress said to the bishop' are often added by a second person to make an otherwise innocuous saying noticeable, to the consternation of the original speaker,[35] and, again, these are usually excluded. Exceptions are made to texts which make for cohesive, well-rounded wellerisms, such as, 'as the girl said to the soldier' which turns up in both oral tradition and literature and therefore has useful contexts. Exceptions are also made to some sayings of which *'mar dubhairt Colmcille'* ['as Colmcille said'] and *'mar a dúirt Cailleach Bhéarra'* ['as the Cailleach Bhéarra said'] are part since, as well as these figures being noted for their sagacity, the wellerism may also allude to some other attribute or legend attached to them. It is also possible that non-specific speakers from the past as in *'ers' an fear fudó'* ['said the man long ago'], as well as providing credence for sayings, may be substitutes for people no longer meaningful or able to be recalled and so some of these, depending on the rest of the saying, have been included in the catalogue.

What is quoted also displays variety. The most usual sort of quote is a proverb. Most of the proverbs in wellerisms, like 'The more haste the worse speed' and *'Is luachmhar an t-anam,'* the equivalent of 'Life is precious,' are found in common use in Ireland in their own right. Besides the quotation being a conventional proverb it can be a statement like 'That'll be a fire

---

[34] Q 1973 1888:123, see also comment with Part B 169.
[35] Common amongst students in the mid-1960s in Belfast.

when it burns,' a commonplace remark, such as, 'So near and yet so far,' an exclamation, 'You're late!' an interrogative, 'Who knows?' a command, 'Up and at it!' an exhortation, 'Peace be with them!' or a blessing, challenge, curse, insult or salutation. In addition, the wellerism used sarcastically by Jonathan Swift back in 1711 in a letter to his friends about the fewer amount of their replies compared with his number of letters, '"Now we are even," quoth Stephen when he gave his wife six blows for one,'[36] may be related to the current use in children's lore — 'Even Stevens' — to denote that both parties are satisfied. Many wellerisms, therefore, are contexualisations of well-known, fixed sentences which, in turn, themselves become fixed in the longer form. A few wellerisms are reworked riddles or *vice versa*.[37] The actual quotation is variable in length and can even be as short as a single word, such as, 'Right,' and *'Neart!'* ['Strength!']. Indeed, such examples can be of the most effective, '"Land," said Columbus,' being a case in point. In a few instances the quotation is in a language different from the rest, juxtaposing it with the remainder. Macaronic wellerisms, wellerisms and proverbs, and wellerisms and riddles are subjects which will be returned to later. Like the humour, the speakers and what is quoted are in the general European mould. Commonplace utterances become unusual or remarkable because of the fame or infamy of who is speaking and in what circumstances, for example, 'Hame is hamely,' becomes transformed because it is followed by 'as the devil said when he found himself in the lawcourt,' and similarly, 'as Adam said to Eve' transforms the commonplace 'Let's call it a day.'[38] A wellerism particularises a general statement by providing a frame or context of speaker and circumstances.

Most wellerisms, as described, consist of three parts with the quotation, speaker and the circumstances in that order. A few have split dialogue, such as, '"Divil may care," as Punch said when he

---

[36] Swift edited by Harold Williams (1948), Vol. 1, p. 171; context — letter XIV 16/1/1711. Ref. via Mieder, *op. cit.*,

[37] For example, Part A 129. For a note on this sort and further examples, see the section 'Wellerisms & Riddles' below and Taylor (1960), pp. 55–56.

[38] Part A 109 & 55, respectively.

lost mass, "There's more churches nor one."[39] These could usually still work as wellerisms even without the second part of the dialogue; the second part of the dialogue extends the humour. There are, however, also some where both parts of direct speech are essential, as in, '"All his taste," said the critic, "is in his mouth,"' and '"What do you want," said the carpenter, "a big, ugly mortice, or a neat six-inch nail?"'[40] Notice that in these latter types the circumstances are not given. One of the commonest wellerisms, '"I see," said the blind man,' is often extended by such additions as, '"Hear, hear!" said the man with no ears,' and, indeed, sometimes even a third speaker is introduced, '"I'll give you a toe on the behind!" said the man with no legs.'[41] It is not, however, in the same category as those just mentioned because the extensions are introduced to revamp an over-familiar wellerism, rather than being an integral part of it from its inception and, in any case, the first sentence can freely stand alone as a wellerism.

A third variety has an inverted order introducing the speaker and circumstances before the quotation as in, 'As Nelson said at the Battle of Trafalgar, "It's a good job we were there!"'[42] Those with the usual order, where the quotation is placed first, certainly have most impact because a familiar utterance is, at the last minute, unexpectedly transformed; on the other hand, the initial evocation of a well-known figure captures listeners' attention.

To date very few examples with a dialogue between two speakers, a variety which exists in disparate parts of the globe, have been found in Ireland, for example, '"I didn't know you were there," said the bull to the fly when the fly said, "I must be going."'[43] It is likely that more exist because in the collectors' handbook under 'Popular Oral Tradition' Seán Ó Súilleabháin has an entry 'Speech attributed to animals, plants and objects.'[44] Such 'conversation' wellerisms are common in parts of west Africa where animals are frequently the protagonists. They also appear to be common in the Caribbean, possibly because of the African

[39] Part A 60.2.
[40] Part A 285 & 309 respectively, both from the same Correspondent.
[41] Part A 259.33.
[42] Part A 144.
[43] Part A 146.
[44] Ó Súilleabháin (1942, 1962 fac.), Ch. XIII, pp. 652–53.

18

input there, for example, the following from Haiti, *'Gros coq dit, "Moin chanté quand moin vlé"; piti di, "Moin chanté lò moin peu"* [The big rooster says, "I sing when I want to"; the little rooster says, "I sing when I can"].[45] A similar structure was also collected in a totally different environment — from the Cumberland Sound Inuit people in the late nineteenth century by Franz Boas, *'Oxatlarau'nerin   kukiliutiksaquangitutin. Qungase'qdjuaq   tautu'nartoq* [The owl said to the snowbird, "They say you have nothing to pick your teeth with," and the snowbird replied, "And your throat is so wide one can look right through it"].[46]

The circumstances of the use of the quotation fall into two main categories — when it was uttered, 'as the old woman said *when* she turned her shift' or to whom or what it was addressed, 'said the cat *to* the hot milk.' The former category — when it was said — is comoner than the later in which the speaker addresses someone or something. About half of the whole corpus belongs to the former category. There are two wellerisms which actually display variants of both main types, '"He's a coorse [= uncouth] Christian," as the deil said when he stroked the hurtchin' [= hedgehog] and '"You're a very coarse Christian," as the devil said to the hedgehog,' and '"Isn't it great the dust I'm raising?" said the fly as he rode on the carriage axle' and '"What a dust we kick up!" as the fly said to the cart-wheel.'[47]

A secondary sort noted in the group does not need to spell out the circumstances by virtue of whom the speaker is, for example, '"Diamonds for life," said the **cardplayer's** wife,'[48] and, still current and common, '"I see," said the **blind** man.'[49] So, in this secondary sort, all that is necessary is a qualifying adjective. In a few wellerisms, such as, '"Thy complexion is black," says the **raven**,'[50] even a qualifying adjective is unnecessary. Similarly, circumstances do not appear to be required where the speaker is a named historical character whose attributes are familiar to the

---

[45] 'Fayo' (n.d.), No. 1685, p. 190.
[46] Boas (1897); I am grateful to Carl Rubino for this ref.
[47] Part A 39.2, 39.1, 69.2 & 69.3 respectively.
[48] Part A 58.1.
[49] For example, Part A 259.23.
[50] Part A 44.

listener. In these the person speaking can be someone widely known as in the following, '"Better marry than burn," as Saint Paul said,'[51] or a local celebrity as in the case of, '"I doubt it," said Croker of Ballinagarde.'[52] The latter is supposed to be the deathbed rejoinder of Croker, a nineteenth-century Co. Limerick landlord, to the clergyman who told him he was bound for a better place.

In about two-thirds of the wellerisms with named speakers, the speakers are lesser-known people, rather than famous figures.[53] In the majority of the wellerisms which have a lesser-known named speaker it is likely that they were real people and that the wellerism refers to an incident with which they were associated or a saying which typified them.[54] Part of the response from a correspondent to Q 2000, to whom I had sent a preliminary list of wellerisms, runs:

'some I had heard before but the vast majority were totally new to me. The format of the proverb [wellerism] I have heard employed on occasions by speakers who would have a reputation for a ready turn of phrase and whose sayings would be frequently repeated by their listeners, on each occasion with an attribution to the originator of the saying. Most of these would refer to some local character, either living or deceased, but whose name and reputation would be known to the listeners and who would normally have more than one saying to his credit.'[55]

Both people's actual names, like Nancy Carr, Ned Ennis and Walter Brídean, and nicknames, like Pára Ban [sic] and Crochúr a'

---

[51] Part A 195.

[52] Part A 64.2.

[53] As in Ireland, there were fewer well-known named speakers amongst the German material, see Neumann (1996), p. 187.

[54] In a few cases the local speaker is more closely identified, for example: '"Ate your mate and you can't be bate," says Bloomfield the basket maker' and '"I doubt it!" said Croker of Ballinagarde,' Part A 82.2 Co. Cavan, & Part A 642 Limerick city, respectively.

[55] Letter from TC dated 1/8/2000.

Casur, occur.[56] Because people could be identified three names in compromising wellerisms have been disguised.[57] The personal second names are connected with the districts in which the proverbs were collected and seem to be actual rather than stock. Taylor cites Kalén saying, 'Kalén declares that he has been able to trace practically every Wellerism in oral tradition in the Swedish province of Halland back to a definite personal allusion when the Wellerism gives a clue in a proper name.'[58] It is likely, however, that pre-existing turns of phrase were attached to *different* real people from time to time. '"God bless us and save us," said old Biddy Davis, "the sticks might be drier tomorrow,"' for example, was used in Co. Laois 'when something wasn't going quite right' and is even accompanied by a pedigree, 'Biddy Davis [was] a v[ery] old woman who died when I was a child in the late thirties,'[59] but a related wellerism in currency later and containing the same name also exists.[60] Factors in the perpetuation of this particular name are that 'Davis' rhymes with 'save us' and that the metre of the first part 'God bless us and save us' matches that of the second 'said old Biddy Davis,' or, as it is found in another version, 'old Mrs Davis.' Davis is not an unusual name. Exceptions to the real names are, of course, 'Pat,' 'Paddy,' and the surnames 'Lyons' and 'Power,' which occur because of their punning value — 'lines' and 'power' (meaning 'strength'). Tadhg and Máire are often also stereotypical names.

Famous speakers include those with particular contact with Ireland, such as Oliver Cromwell, who campaigned in Ireland from 1649 to 1650, James II, the loser of the throne of Britain and

---

[56] Part A 7, Part A 57, Part B 181, Part A 312.1 & Part B 102 respectively.

[57] Part A 37, 118 & 207.

[58] Taylor (1962 fac., 1985 rpt.), p. 215.

[59] Part A 102 from a Correspondent living in Gowran, Co. Kilkenny, at the time this was submitted (1975), but who recalls hearing this from her grandmother of Stradbally, Co. Laois.

[60] '"Dear bless us and save us," said oul [= old] Mrs. Davis, "I never knew herrins wus [= herrings were] fish."' Part A 103.3 from a Correspondent in her mid-forties who remembers hearing it in Glasgow when she was growing up from her grandmother, who was originally from south Armagh. See also Part A 103.1 & .2.

Ireland to William of Orange at the pivotal Battle of the Boyne in 1690 in Co. Meath, as well as those more widely-known like Napoleon. In addition to those already mentioned which include historical figures with a particular connection with Ireland such as King James (II? 1633–1701)[61] which must at least be variants with a more regional provenance than those related to international types is the following, "'I'll light on you with a scraigh [= shriek]," as the divil said to the ould seceder,'[62] collected in Ulster about the beginning of the twentieth century. An old seceder was one who seceded from mainstream Presbyterianism in 1740; separate congregations were maintained in Ireland until 1840, although the term would have been understood beyond this date.[63]

While the previous example is likely of local origin, a somewhat larger group is that in which the speakers are international stereotypes, for instance, "'Down tools!" said the tailor when he dropped the needle,'[64] fits the notion of the tailor being undersized. In line with the inhabitants of certain parts of a country being regarded by the rest as numbskulls, Connacht[65] and Kerry men are depicted as stupid. Women, especially older women, are often presented as slovenly or foolish, particularly as regards marriage expectations, as demonstrated in the following, "'It's mairg [= a pity] to be dirty," said the old woman when she washed her cap in the potato water,' and "'Youth must have its fling," said the old woman when she jumped over the besom' [= brush].[66] Contrary to prevailing attitudes towards them, Travellers, formally tinsmiths, are not portrayed negatively, but simply take

---

[61] Mentioned in "'Peace be with them!" as King James said to his hounds' Part A 226.

[62] Part A 256.

[63] I am grateful to Stephen Gregory, Librarian of Union Theological College, Belfast, for this information; letter 9/2/2000.

[64] Part A 298; the context reinforces this view, see catalogue.

[65] For example, "'That's her!" as the Connacht man said to the bull' Part A 125.5 collected from a man who was born and reared in Roscommon town but is now living in Dublin. He told me that it was very common in Roscommon, even though that is a Connacht county. It was used to confirm that something was correct.

[66] Part A 191 & 327.

22

their place amongst other craftspeople in the wellerisms.[67] While some crafts and trades people crop up in the Irish material — blacksmith, carpenter, cobbler, tailor, sweep — it is to a much lesser extent than in Neumann's north German material. This probably reflects the difference in the two regions. Unlike Ireland, in Germany there was a very strong guild system and the 'occupational' wellerisms which *are* found in Ireland are probably a response to Continental models. A few examples show a contempt for rural dwellers and may therefore have originated in an urban setting, such as, the common, '"Everyone to his taste," said the farmer when he kissed the cow,' and, '"One good turn deserves another," said a countrywoman as she wound the clock.'[68] However, the majority of those in the catalogue were collected in rural areas and used by farmers and the speaker is simply 'man.' In Neumann's Mecklenburg corpus the commonest speaker is also 'man' but there is, in addition, a very large group attributed to *'Buuer'* [= 'farmer'] which was perhaps circulating amongst townspeople.

From this outline of the Irish material it is obvious that it accords with wellerisms elsewhere and that the remarks about wellerisms in general made by Taylor and Mieder,[69] and even those by Neumann about his regional assemblage,[70] apply very much to it. The main purpose of this work is therefore to present the Irish material, which is little known, while the remainder of this introduction will look at some of its aspects in detail and try to make some contribution to wellerism study.

CATALOGUING

It seems that pre-existing sayings and exclamations generated the majority of wellerisms in Ireland. By and large, these are central to the wellerisms which I have therefore catalogued according to the quotation in them. Some sayings can give rise to different endings. In these the speaker can be the same and the situation different, or

---

[67] For example, '"I wud [= would] rather hev [= have] yer [= your] work nor yer music," as the Tinker say'd to the jackass' Part A 321.
[68] Part A 287.1 & 104 respectively.
[69] Taylor (1962 fac., 1985 rpt.), pp. 200–20 & Mieder (1989), Ch. XI 'Wellerisms' pp. 223–29 respectively.
[70] Neumann (1996), pp. 1–32 & section introductions.

the other was round. The fact that the same conventional proverbs (and other items) can have different speakers and circumstances attached to them indicates the constancy and ubiquity of the quotation. The best illustration of this is Irish *'Cím,'* English 'I see.' It is most productive in terms of what follows the quotation and besides one variant common to both languages, 'said the blind man,' to date over twenty distinct endings (mostly in English) have been identified. It is likely that these display regional characteristics. In another set, certain sayings are associated with specific people. A third set consists of condensed folk narratives while others embody folk motifs. All of these kinds will be looked at later in detail.

It is probable that some of the wellerisms in the catalogue which follows are incomplete. The part most likely to be lacking is the circumstances or the addressee. The reason for this may be that they are familiar, for instance, '"Up and at it again," as the hedgehog said to the hare'[71] has been recorded as many times without an addressee, as in, '"To it again!" says the grainneóg' [= hedgehog][72] as with. It is hard to know whether this should be considered as a new attenuated form which exists in its own right or not. Another reason for the attenuation of wellerisms is for propriety. *'"Is beag an rud nach cuidiú é," arsa an dreoilín nuair a rinne sé a mhúin san fharraige'* ['"It's a small thing that doesn't help," said the wren when he urinated in the sea'], for instance, has also been recorded as *'"Is beag an rud nach cuidiughadh é," ars' an dreolan'* ['"It's a small thing that doesn't help," said the wren'].[73] Phrases such as 'I'm no scholard' and 'Sour grapes,' while possibly even more abbreviated allusions to wellerisms, have, however, not been included.

MACARONIC WELLERISMS

As well as some wellerisms being macaronic with the quotation in a non-host language, such as French and Native American, in the case of English-language ones, and English in the case of Irish-language wellerisms, one invents a pseudo language, 'White bear

---

[71] Part A 5.2.
[72] Part A 5.7.
[73] Part B 22.2 & 22.5 respectively.

24

to black bear, "*Ama pola.*"[74] Regional accents and the accents of
migrants are also employed to create puns or other humour based
on stereotyping. While there are macaronic wellerisms in both
languages Irish/English macaronic wellerisms are almost exclusive
to the Irish language. One which occurs both in Irish and in
English is only macaronic when the background language is Irish,
'"*More light!*" *ars an chailleach nuair a bhí an teach le thine.*' It
is simply all in English when its context is English, '"More light!"
said the hag when the house was on fire.'[75] This appears to be an
international wellerism which is not macaronic elsewhere. It is
difficult to know what extra import being macaronic has in this
particular wellerism. A chief reason for bilingualism in wellerisms
usually seems to be to distance the speaker in the wellerism from
the user of it but, in a few, the humour hinges on their being
macaronic. '"*I'll never play this game of 'An bhfuil agat tá,'*" *ers'
an fear fudó'* ["'I'll never play this game of 'Have you got yes,'"
said the man long ago'] is one example. It is about a man who
loses at cards because he understands only English and does not
know that his companions are exchanging tips in Irish.[76]
Obviously the macaronic versions must date to a comparatively
recent period when both English and Irish were being used side by
side in Ireland.

THE PERFORMANCE OF WELLERISMS
While the impact of macaronic wellerisms in oral tradition can still
be appreciated to a certain extent from the written record other
features of the performance of wellerisms, such as pitch, timing
and facial expression which, no doubt, play a important part in
their successful delivery, are lost because the majority here survive
solely as unannotated texts. In the main wellerisms, like proverbs,
exist within the context of everyday conversation.[77] There is
evidence that an expression introduced by one speaker can be
'wellerised' by a second.[78] There is also some evidence that

---

[74] Part A 238.
[75] Part B 122 & Part A 170 respectively.
[76] Part B 97.
[77] As Kwesi Yankah has pointed out. See, for example, Yankah (1989),
especially p. 167.
[78] See, for example, Part A 182.14.

wellerisms in dialogue were not necessarily articulated in full.[79] Written records of incomplete wellerisms may actually be reflecting how they were used in dialogue.

Other aspects of wellerisms would also be best conveyed if observed in context. In one Irish-language wellerism there is a curious example of the sound of the words approximating to the sound of an action.[80] It runs '*"Raghadsa romhatsa!" adeir an bríste corda*'[81] ['"I'll pass you," as the corduroy trousers said'] which Bo Almqvist heard in the 1970s on the Dingle Peninsula, County Kerry, from Seosamh Ó Dálaigh who explained to him that corduroy trousers make a sound when one leg brushes against the other that could be interpreted as '*raghadh-romhatsa*' ['I'll go before you']. Rev. Patrick S. Dinneen, in his dictionary, also notes a version with the comment, 'from the illusion one wearing such has of being followed.'[82]

One wellerism accompanied by a gesture has also been recorded, '"I feel a right tit," as Napoleon said when he surveyed the carnage of Waterloo.'[83] This was noted in Belfast about 1990 and was sent to me with the comment 'normally said with the left hand held horizontally inside the jacket.' Napoleon is also familiar in Belfast from other local lore.[84]

It is unlikely that these aspects of wellerisms are insular, compare the Jamaican, '*Darg drink water say, "Fe yuh, fe yuh"* [Dog drinking water says, "For you, for you"] (a dog drinks water for himself but Master God is for us all. *"Fe yuh, fe yuh"* is the sound the dog makes when it drinks)'[85] and they might be looked out for in future wellerism research.

---

[79] See, for example, Part A 78.

[80] Birds' calls and animal noises are often features of proverbs in Irish.

[81] Part B 162.2.

[82] Part B 162.1.

[83] Part A 295.

[84] Most evident in the place-name 'Napoleon's Nose' for an eminence on Cave Hill, a landmark visible from much of the city and closely identified with it.

[85] McKenzie (n.d.), n.p. under 'God.'

26

WELLERISMS AND LITERATURE

My catalogue includes wellerisms from both oral and literary traditions. I did not come across any woman writer in Ireland (or, indeed, elsewhere) who includes wellerisms. As mentioned earlier, only some forty versions, representing fewer different types, stem from literature. Oral versions of those used by writers in either English or Irish have, as yet, been found for few of these. There are two main possibilities as regards sources for those in literature and it is, to a large extent, possible to distinguish between them. Undoubtedly the style as known in recent times in Ireland derives from oral tradition which has been adopted into literature for various reasons, primarily to add authenticity to dialogue. This is certainly the case with William Carlton (1794–1869) who uses copious amounts of set sayings exactly as they are in (later) oral tradition. When it comes to his contemporary, the more flamboyant Samuel Lover (1797–1867), in whose popular works eight different wellerisms have so far been located, it may be that he has adapted or even created some new variants on oral models, in addition to transposing oral variants, such as, '"Turn about is fair play," as the divil said to the smoke–jack,'[86] which he employs in a discussion between a king and a bishop in 'The King and the Bishop — A Legend of Clonmacnoise' (a story based on a local legend). '"There's a pair o' ye now," as the divil said to his knee-buckles,' which he uses in an international folktale *The Fox Caught by the Butcher* may derive from '*"Tá beirt agaibh ann," mar deir an gabhar le n'adharca,*'[87] ['"There's a pair of you," as the goat said to his horns'] which was subsequently collected from oral tradition in Irish but not in English. It is obvious from the dialogue in his versions of oral material that he was very much attuned to local expressions. '"That's the cut," said Cutty when he cut his mother's throat' may be modelled on something otherwise lost to Irish tradition but noted by Vincent Stuckley Lean in 1903, '"That's the kick," said Paddy when he kicked his mother into the fire.'[88] Lover uses puns extensively and for this reason alone could

---

[86] Part A 304.1.

[87] Part B 27.1.

[88] Lean (1903) Vol. II, Part II, p. 749.

have been attracted to wellerisms, witness the following from his novel *Treasure Trove*:

> '... the shout of pursuit was heard at the entrance of the "close," [= yard] and the portal was barely shut and barred when the heavy tramp of men was heard rushing past ...The party within made no move till the tramp of the pursuers died away in the distance, then Phaidrig, with a low chuckle, spoke. "Close work," said he, "as the undher millstone said to the upper, when there was no corn."
>
> "'Twould have been grinding work, sure enough, had we been taken," said the stranger.'[89]

This particular example may well be a creation by Lover, especially when one bears in mind that the 'speaker' is a millstone and inanimate objects as speakers are atypical. It is interesting to note that when Lover left Dublin in 1835 he went to London where he, along with Charles Dickens and others, co-founded the literary journal *Bentley's Miscellany*[90] and Lover contributed to the journal during its editorship from 1837 to 1839 by Dickens whose characters, the Wellers, in *The Posthumous Papers of the Pickwick Club*, published serially from 1836 to 1837, used so many of these sayings.[91] In length and referents, however, Lover's wellerisms are much closer to oral tradition than Dickens.'

Like Lover, Brendan Behan (1923–64) was also a master at capturing speech in print and certainly in his autobiographical *Borstal Boy* included a great many conventional proverbs and at least two wellerisms, for example, '"All the better," as the old one said when she was told that there was no tea but only porter,'[92] the most likely source of which would have been his own family and others in Dublin. James Joyce (1882–1941), on the other hand, seems to keep a foot in both camps with some of the wellerisms he

---

[89] Part A 322 Lover (1844), *Treasure Trove: The First of a Series of Accounts of Irish Heirs: Being a Romantic Irish Tale of the Last Century*, p. 19.
[90] Hogan *A–L* (1996), p. 724.
[91] Cooke (1999), p. 41.
[92] Part A 10. Behan's other wellerism, for which see Part A 287.19, is definitely derived from oral tradition.

28

uses in *Ulysses* being popular ones more or less straight from oral
tradition, for example, '"Everyone to his taste," as Morris said
when he kissed the cow,' and others like, '"Assuefaction
minorates atrocities," as Tully saith of his darling Stoics,'[93]
drawing on his own creativity. The wellerisms of Brian O'Nolan
(1911–66), however, are his own creation, a noticeable difference
with some being their greater length compared with most of those
in oral tradition, for example, '"We won't go into that now," as
Evans of the *Broke* wittily remarked to his fellow passengers as
they stood regarding the sea from the deck of the *Bolivar*.'[94]

A third source for those in literature and print may be oral or
literary sources from outside Ireland which, again, may be altered,
or used as in the original, as clearly demonstrated in Declan
McCormack's recent review in a Dublin-based newspaper of the
edited diary (1805–43) of a County Louth customs officer, 'In
many ways this is the diary of a dull nobody, and even a quick
gallop through it brings to mind Sam Weller's remark, '"Vether
it's worth going through so much to learn so little,' as the charity
boy said when he got to the end of the alphabet, is a matter of
taste." It is, actually, but it's a damn close-run thing.'[95] Here, the
style of the nineteenth-century diarist probably put the reviewer in
mind of the Wellers.[96]

The examples in literature, as well as attesting to the presence
of wellerisms in Ireland over several centuries, also give valuable
contexts for this genre and sometimes backgrounds for particular

---

[93] Part A 287.4 & 15a.1 respectively.

[94] Part A 101.

[95] McCormack (2002), 'Joys of the diligent detailed Diary of a Dundalk
Nobody,' by-line 'Future historians will be indebted to a 19th century
gentleman for the diary he kept,' 'Books' page of the 'Living' section of
the *Sunday Independent* 13/1/2002, p. 16.

[96] Charles Dickens' work was read in Ireland from the time it was
published (Cooke 1999, p. 44) and it has continued to be read ever since.
Dickens made three readings tours in Ireland, the first in 1858, when he
read in Dublin, Belfast, Cork and Limerick as part of his first
professional readings. The second was in 1867 when he included 'Trial
from Pickwick,' and read in Dublin and Belfast. The last was in 1869, in
Belfast, Dublin and Belfast again, and, once more, included 'Trial from
Pickwick' see Cooke (1999), p. 1 ff, p. 166 ff & p. 191 ff.

types which the other sources generally lack, for instance, Lover uses '"You're late," says Boyce' in the dialogue of a short story and then also supplies a derivation for it in a footnote.[97] In addition, in many cases, it seems that literature preserves versions or variants from oral tradition which would otherwise be lost. One must also bear in mind the likely influence that those in literature, particularly throughout the nineteenth century, had, in turn, on the oral tradition.

Included in the catalogue are also up to a dozen wellerisms from printed sources, the immediate origin of which is likely England or America. They are included because they occur in Irish contexts and can thus throw light, particularly on the transmission of material, but also on its use. Some of those published in *The Dublin Journal of Temperance, Science and Literature* of 1842 are probably taken from the Philadelphian *Alexander's Weekly Messenger* (1839) while at least one, and maybe more, could be from the London-based magazine *Punch*.[98] The origin of three others, all in *P.T.Q.,* two because of their use of 'shall' in places where 'will' would colloquially be used, and one with the loss of a final 'r' ('pola' for 'polar'), which are both features of many accents in England, also point to a non-local source. *No place is an island* but, obviously, English–language material is the most likely of any other language to turn up in Ireland, moreover, movement in this direction — to Ireland than from it — is more likely, with this genre at any rate.

THE OLDEST WELLERISMS
Archer Taylor states that 'Allusions to a well-known or readily imagined scene represent perhaps the oldest form of the Wellerism.'[99] There are a number of this sort in the catalogue in both English and Irish, for example, '"That's not a good fit," as the serpent said when he swallowed a buck goat, horns and all' and *'"Sin é an t-iasc, ach ca bhfuil an salan?" a nduirt an fear, nuair a dh'imig an túin as an saighne'* ['"There's the fish, but

---

[97] See Part A 157.1.
[98] Part A 160, 223 & 248 respectively. I was alerted to the possibility of *Punch* as a source through *DOW*.
[99] Taylor (1962 fac., 1985 rpt.), p. 8.

30

where's the salt?" said the man when the bottom fell out of the seine net'].[100] While this form, as far as can be told from what has survived, is the oldest, it has been popular over a long period and wellerisms on this model may still be being created.

WELLERISMS AND PROVERBS

Wellerisms containing a proverb make up almost a quarter of the total in my catalogue. Proverbs are also the largest category of any type of quotation in it and one might assume that wellerisms developed from conventional proverbs had we not seen in the preceding section that Archer Taylor, while noting that those containing a proverb, as far as is recorded, are an older type than those with puns, pointed out that there is a type pre-dating both. Nevertheless, wellerisms containing proverbs which are international must have been a key type in the perpetuation and dissemination of the genre. As mentioned earlier, the proverbs are usually ones that are well-known in their own right and I have tried to give some indication of this in the notes after catalogue entries. Three wellerisms even manage to squeeze in two proverbs each, including an extended proverb, "'Everyone to his taste," said the husband of the very plain woman, "for, you know, <u>Love is blind and lovers cannot see</u>"' and "'A shut mouth catches no flies," said the trout to the spider: "Watch it, bullet eyes, all that flutters is not flies,"'[101] the later being a parody of 'All that glitters is not gold.' In a third, "'A rolling stone gathers no moss," said the sitting duck'[102] the second part is likely compressed from the proverb 'A sitting hen never grows fat.' These two proverbs have also been combined elsewhere, but not as a wellerism, 'A rolling stone gathers no moss an' a clockin' hen never grows fat.'[103] This phenomenon has not as yet been noted in Irish-language wellerisms although, as in English, pairs of ordinary proverbs occur. There is one wellerism which is an adapted medical proverb, "'It wants to be swimming dead and alive," as the man

---

[100] Part A 86 & Part B 113 respectively.
[101] Part A 287a.1 & 205 respectively.
[102] Part A 247.
[103] Byers Papers as cited in the Electronic Database, Ulster Dialect Archive, UFTM; cf a version in Smyth & Wilson, p. 682, from the south of England and published in 1917.

said when taking a long drink of water after he had eaten the fish.'[104]

Some of the proverbs in question are the same as those which occur in Wolfgang Mieder and Anna Tóthné Litkovina's *Twisted Wisdom, Modern Anti-Proverbs*. In many cases outside Ireland they have not only been found extended into wellerisms but as other adapted types. This, to a lesser extent, has been noted within Irish material, for example, 'Time and patience will take a snail to Jerusalem,'[105] which has also been recorded in Irish,[106] has not only been found as a wellerism, '"Time and patience," as the snail said when it reached America,'[107] but as 'Pains and patience would take a snail to America'[108] and 'Patience and perseverance won a wife for his reverence.'[109] Wellerisms often mock conventional proverbs and convention itself. The respectable premise that 'Age is honourable' is debunked by the ending 'as the man said when he hoisted the creel [= basket] on his father.'[110]

Most conventional proverbs are metaphorical or can be applied metaphorically. Wellerisms frequently turn this assumption on its head by opting for the literal meaning, as we see in the following, *"Is iomaí sórt rud a leanas an peacadh," mar a dubhairt an fear agus an gandal ina dhiaidh*'[111] ['"Many things follow the sinful," as the man with the gander after him said']. Despite their rarity, especially in Irish, conventional proverbs which are personifications are particularly prone to becoming wellerisms, for example, '"Youth must have its fling!" said the farmer as he threw the bonhams [= piglets] from the [cart] rail' and '"Time flies," as the woman said when she threw the clock at her husband.'[112] It is also interesting to note that, although

---

[104] Part A 281.

[105] For example, IFC School mss. (IFCS) 929:138, 933:244 & 934:249, all Co. Monaghan.

[106] Ua Muirgheasa (1907), No. 332 Co. Armagh.

[107] Part A 293 Co. Mayo, a county from which there remains extensive migration to North America.

[108] IFCS 949:103 Co. Monaghan.

[109] IFCS 942:74 Co. Monaghan.

[110] Part A 6.

[111] Part B 155.2.

[112] Part A 325 & 294.

wellerisms, like conventional proverbs, portray a misogynist stance this particular one is the opposite, which may fit in with the general tendency of wellerisms to turn conventional proverbs on their heads. A closer look at proverbs with personification should provide a *terminus anti quem* for this type of wellerism. Proverbs are, in the main, international and it would be interesting to examine to what extent the same proverb repertoire shows up in wellerisms internationally. Again, I have attempted to indicate these connections in the corpus. *'"Is deas an rud an ghlaine,"* mar a dúirt an bhean nuair a thiontaigh sí a léine i ndiaidh seacht mbliana'[113] ['"Cleanliness is a fine thing," as the woman who turned her shift after seven years said'], for example, as well as being found in English in Ireland, occurs in at least eight other languages, such as German, *'"Reinlichkeit is de Hauptsak," seggt de oll Fruu un kihrt tau Pingsten ehr Hemd üm'*[114] ['"Cleanliness is the most important thing," said the old woman when she turned her shift at Whitsun']. At the present stage of compilation, however, there are more wellerisms containing proverbs which have been noted only in Ireland (in either English or Irish) than those found both in either of these languages and also in others outside the island. Within areas where wellerisms are established, certain proverbs, such as 'Age is honourable' tend to become 'wellerised,' however, these proverbs can be different in different regions.

Overall, a surprizingly low number of proverbs are, in fact humorous, or even witty; in a corpus of five hundred from oral tradition, for instance, only two were found. Wellerisms containing proverbs, therefore, seem to act very much as a foil to conventional proverbs.

WELLERISMS AND RIDDLES

It has been noted by Archer Taylor that some wellerisms, if rephrased, can become riddles or *vice versa* and a few of those in the catalogue — ten in English and two in Irish — have also been identified as riddles in Ireland or elsewhere. Bo Almqvist located two, and indeed, collected one, and after a search of (mainly)

---

[113] Part B 103.1.

[114] Neumann (1996), Q. Die Geschlechter No. 634 & similar variants.

children's riddle and joke books which had been published in the United Kingdom of Great Britain and in the United States of America, I turned up others. A potential source — the Schools' Collection in the Department of Irish Folklore — was not extensively examined so more examples may emerge. While nearly every wellerism could be turned into a riddle this patently does not happen. Of those that do they are almost always of the type where the speaker is addressing someone: 'as D said to E,' rather than the commonest type of wellerism where circumstances are included: 'as D said when …' One of the Irish-language versions, however, is more complex and runs *'"Níl aon tsólás ná go leannan a dhólás féin é," fé mar dubhairt an mongcaidhe nuair a thug sé póg do'n ghrainneóig*[115] ['"There's no joy without its sorrow," as the monkey said when he kissed the hedgehog' (published in 1930) with a related riddle being collected by Bo Almqvist from Mícheál Ó Gaoithín between 1966 and 1974, which, in English translation, runs, 'What did the ass say to the hedgehog long ago when he kissed her in the bush? Well, there's no joy without its sorrow.'

Even within this kind of wellerism, 'as D said to E,' only a few also emerge as riddles. Furthermore, the wellerisms which do also occur as riddles have the less typical non-human speakers, for example, the flea, and some are inanimate, which are also atypical as speakers in wellerisms. As Ed Cray noted, the speaker and addressee, if not two of the same thing, are similar and this is evident in the Irish material, for example, one strawberry addressing another, or a scarf addressing a hat, and so on. The kind of riddle concerned is also atypical; in one collection of a thousand assorted riddles only twenty-four were of the type in question.[116] It is known as the joking question and is usually based on a pun. So, in summary, a small number of atypical wellerisms interact with a small number of atypical riddles.

Currently, most wellerisms circulate amongst adults (as was probably always the case) and most riddles circulate amongst children. The wellerisms which also emerge as riddles may be at some sort of interface of adult/child lore and it is more likely that

---

[115] Part B 183.
[116] Brandreth (1980) [UK].

such wellerisms were converted by adults into riddles for the enjoyment of children, as a familiar way of communicating their content, rather than the other way round. They would then be taken up and circulated amongst children. Given the antiquity of both wellerisms and riddles, and the attested long-term use of riddles by children, it is likely that joking questions converted from wellerisms have been in existence for a considerable time. One of those in Irish was collected in 1942, which predates the marked rise in the 1960s of this sub-genre mentioned by Annikka Kaivola-Bregenhøj,[117] however, by 'a considerable time' I am thinking of centuries rather than decades. Such riddles are not 'true riddles' and can often be found in joke books. Other wellerisms are related to jokes of other kinds. *"'Críostaidhe thú? ars an sagart le fear. "Ní headh," ars an fear, "ach Ultach"'*[118] ['"Are you a Christian?" said the priest to the man.' "No," said the man, "an Ulsterman"'] has resonances with '... an Englishman who was travelling through the Highlands ... came to an inn near a village. Seeing nobody around he knocked on the door, but received no reply. So he opened the door and walked in. He spied a man lying on a bed and asked him, "Are there no Christians in this house?" Whereupon the man replied, "No, sir, none. We are all Camerons."'[119] Wellerisms and longer jocular narratives will be discussed below.

WELLERISMS AND FOLK NARRATIVE
While it can only be surmised that certain wellerisms refer to historical events and people, and to reminiscences or incidents connected with these real people, we can be sure that others refer to or are condensed international narratives. These are, in particular, animal tales and anecdotes, for example, '"Farewell, bad company!" as the fox said when he dhroundet [= drowned] the last of the flays [= fleas] on his back by duckin' his head in the river' and '"Great cry and little wool," as the man said when he

---

[117] Kaivola-Bregenhøj (2001), pp. 57–62.

[118] Part B 51.1 Co. Mayo.

[119] Irving (1969), pp. 51–52, with another version on p. 51, and one from Ireland (ref. not recorded).

clipped the sow.'[120] Several refer to Aesopian fables, such as, *'"Nach mise a thóg an ceo?" mar dúirt an chuileog i ndiaidh an chóiste'*[121] ['"Didn't I raise the dust?" as the fly behind the coach said']. In the catalogue, of the twenty or so wellerisms which have so far been identified as being related to international folk narrative, approximately three-quarters are connected to animal tales. This is of some significance, considering that most wellerism speakers are human rather than animal. Collections of Aesopian fables were published in Ireland, extensively in English, but also to some degree in Irish. Inexpensive versions in English were being sold throughout the countryside by itinerant chapmen from at least the eighteenth century.[122] The fables remained popular for generations. One collection,[123] for instance, was almost simultaneously published in the 1840s in Belfast and Dublin by three different companies.[124] Peadar Ó Laoghaire's later Irish-language versions *Aesop a Tháinig go hÉirinn* ['Aesop in Ireland'],[125] published in Dublin from 1900, were also widely read, particularly in schools and language classes and, of course, collections published in English outside Ireland circulated here and still do. Even some of the earlier collections were illustrated, thus, the one published in 1841 contains over a hundred wood engravings.[126] No doubt, all exercised some influence on the tradition of wellerisms.

Among the few wellerisms connected with international narratives which are not to do with animals are '"Sure I don't know myself, mother!" as Seán na Scuab said'[127] which is related to AT 1383 *Electing a Mayor* and *'"I'll never again play this game of 'An bhfuil agut tá,'" ers' an fear fudó'*[128] ['"I'll never again play this game of 'Have you got yes,'" said the man long

---

[120] Respectively Part A 16.1 cf Aarne & Thompson (1973), henceforth AT, AT 60, & Part A 47.3 cf AT 1037.

[121] Part B 71.2.

[122] See Adams (1987) p. 43, p. 50, p. 183 & p. 187.

[123] Aesop (1841).

[124] See Adams (1987), p. 193, p. 194 & p. 200.

[125] Ó Laoghaire (1900–02 & 1903).

[126] Aesop (1841).

[127] Part A 149, where an example of the narrative can be seen.

[128] Part B 97, where an explanation can be seen.

ago'] which comes under the umbrella of AT 1699 *Misunderstanding Because of Ignorance of a Foreign Language.* International folk narratives like *The Fox's Fire* and *The Fox Climbs from the Pit on the Wolf's Back,* and others, occur in Ireland both as wellerisms and also in extended narrative form as confirmed by *The Types of the Irish Folktale.*[129] The presence of a wellerism in Ireland, however, does not necessarily mean that there will also be a related folktale, nor does a folktale that is well-known in Ireland and known to have a related wellerism elsewhere, signal that that wellerism will be found in Ireland. To the contrary, a related rare tale and rare wellerism can occur together as Almqvist's investigation shows.[130] With *Hare and Tortoise Race: Sleeping Hare* knowledge of one seems to go with the other. On the other hand, *Fox and the Sour Grapes* is not commonly known but the wellerism and the phrase 'Sour grapes' certainly are.

Insular referents and dialect may obscure the internationality of others, for example, '"Cowl wi'out," [= cold outside] as the madman said when he hid behind the winnle straw' [= withered stalk of grass],[131] recorded in Ulster, was collected as follows in Estonia in 1965, '"Poor man who has to stay in the rain while I have a shelter over my head," said a fox and sheltered under an upright harrow' and, as Arvo Krikmann pointed out, may be descended from the international folktale AT 71* *Hare Vainly Seeks Shelter From Reed.*[132] Indeed, a version much closer to the tale, collected in Leinster, '"You can't beat the shelter," as the hare said when he sat behind the tráinín' [= withered stalk of grass] has subsequently emerged.[133] As a narrative it is not in *Types of the Irish Folktale.*

---

[129] Ó Súilleabháin & Christiansen *op. cit.*,

[130] Almqvist *op. cit.*

[131] Part A 47.

[132] Email from Arvo Krikmann 8/3/2000. The quotation proverb is from the Pärnumaa district and is RKM II 206, 226 (1) Eesti Rahvaluule Arhiiv/Estonian Folklore Archives in the Riiklik Kirjandusmuuseum/ State Literary Museum.

[133] Part A 47.3 Co. Kilkenny; 'tráinín,' <Irish 'tráithnín,' more usually rendered 'thraneen.'

A hybrid of local speaker and international narrative AT 67** *The Fox Caught by the Butcher* seems to be represented in the following, '"You wouldn't do that to your match," as Mick Sheedy said to the fox.'[134] The story continues immediately after the wellerism, 'Mick Sheedy the gamekeeper had a hut in the woods ...' and has been collected many times in Ireland as a tale rather than a wellerism. The same story has also been collected in Irish, but with a different wellerism, *'"Fágaim geárrtha 'gat é," ars' Crochur Á Chasuir leis a' mada ruadh'*[135] ['"I'll curtail you!" said Crochur Á Chasuir to the fox'].[136] While different wellerisms in different languages (English and Irish) for the same narrative might not be so unexpected, it is more difficult to account for two different wellerisms in Irish referring to the same narrative, something which is also demonstrated in one case in the catalogue. The wellerisms are *'"A' lorg mná," a ndubhairt an gabhar'* ['"Looking for women," said the goat'] and *'"Abhaile má fhéadaim!" a ndubhairt an gabhar'* ['"Home, if I'm able," said the goat'][137] which both refer to the story of the billy goat seeking a nanny goat.

Other wellerisms, while not encapsulating entire narratives, clearly refer to tales, such as, *'"Arú! Nach tú an fear agam?" a ndubhairt an madaruadh leis an mbairneach'*[138] ['"Wow! Aren't you some man?" said the fox to the limpet'], an Irish by-form of AT 105 *The Cat's Only Trick*, which is reasonably well-known as

---

[134] Part A 196.1 Patrick Weston Joyce (1910, 1988 ed., 1991 rpt.), pp. 117–18 and see and Part A 196.2 O'Farrell (1980, 1983 rpt.), p. 60, for another version of the story and wellerism with the similar name of Sheedy. The surname 'Sheedy' is common in east Galway, while the similar-sounding 'Sheehy' is common in Munster generally. The (earlier) Sheedy version would seem to have been collected in Limerick while the other version was most likely collected in the midlands.

[135] Part B 102.

[136] In total 96 versions are mentioned in *TIF*. Lover *Legends and Stories of Ireland.* [?2nd Series] (New Edition n.d.), p. 145 includes a version of the story with yet another wellerism (Part A 224) but his wellerism is spoken by the fox which is quoting the devil and is not a reduced version of the narrative.

[137] Part B 139 & Part B 1 respectively.

[138] Part B 87.2.

38

a tale in Ireland having being noted 71 times in *Types of the Irish Folktale*. In many cases where a wellerism and a folktale are connected the quote in the wellerism is a set sentence like 'Up and at it!' which is well-known apart from the wellerism.

As with the riddles, where only a small proportion of wellerisms were found to have riddle parallels, only a small proportion of wellerisms in the catalogue are related to international narratives. Again, as with the riddles which were linked to atypical wellerisms, the majority of wellerisms linked to tales are atypical as they have animal, not human, speakers thus the majority of tales connected with wellerisms are not ordinary folktales but animal tales. It might be added that the body of animal tales in Ireland, compared with other countries, is small, which may be a factor in the sparcity of the wellerism genre here. Pack Carnes and others have investigated the close connection of ordinary proverbs and fables.[139] From their findings, one might expect a higher number of wellerisms (and possibly, as an outcome of this, of wellerisms in general) with animals as speakers in regions with large stocks of animal tales.

WELLERISMS AND INTERNATIONAL FOLK MOTIFS
While I have only been able to identify a small proportion — about two per cent — of the wellerisms in the catalogue as having links with folk narrative, a further number embody international folk motifs. These include lack of knowledge of animals, for example, *MI* J 1905 *Absurd ignorance about milking animals* "'It's all a cod," as the woman said when she went to milk the bull,'[140] and *MI* J 1880 *Animals or objects treated as if human—miscellaneous*, as in, *"'Gluais, a mhála, is go n-éirí an t-ádh leat!" mar adúirt an bacach ar maidin'* [141] ["'Get going, bag, and good luck!" as the tramp said in the morning'] both of which motifs are common. Motif *MI* J 1790 *Shadow mistaken for substance* as in *"'Seo chút mé, a dhiail!" ers' an chailleach fudó is í á' rith i ndiaig a scáth'*[142] ["'Here I come, you devil!" said the

---

[139] See Carnes (1991) & Carnes, Editor, (1988) *Proverbia in Fabula. Essays on the Relationship of the Fable and the Proverb.*
[140] Part A 41.1.
[141] Part B 132.2.
[142] Part B 146.2.

hag long ago when she was running after her shadow'] is also present. Yet others portray comic concepts commonly found throughout oral tradition, such as carelessness about gender, as in "'Good boy yourself," said the woman to her daughter.'[143]

INFORMANTS AND COLLECTORS

Unless published elsewhere, the names of almost all informants are shown as initials only. Three names in the wellerisms themselves have been disguised. Informants, collectors and questionnaire correspondents were from many walks of ·life, including a number of clergy from various denominations, and a nun. With the exceptions of Bo Almqvist, Robin Flower (1882–1946) and Henry Glassie, collectors seem to have been Irish, frequently from the very district in which they were collecting. The people who contributed wellerisms varied in age from children of about ten to the very elderly, although only a tiny number of the informants were either children or the very elderly.

The Q 1973 correspondents acted as both informants and collectors. Usually the distinction between whether they were acting as informants or as collectors is unclear, hence the word 'correspondent' here can mean either 'informant' or 'collector.' Many of the correspondents were teachers. Despite the fact that two-thirds of the network of questionnaire correspondents at any time was men, many of those in the pool who were women participated in this questionnaire.[144]

Four questionnaire correspondents supplied wellerisms in both English and Irish. These were never the same wellerisms. Some informants use wellerisms more than others and it would be interesting to know whether, with bilingual speakers, this extends to both languages. Bo Almqvist assembled forty-two wellerisms (including three variants) from Mícheál Ó Gaoithín, which is by far the greatest number ever collected from one individual in Ireland. Not only is it an impressively extensive repertoire as far as Ireland is concerned, it is numerically on a par with any

---

[143] Part A 29.
[144] For a history of the questionnaire system in Ireland and some comments on its correspondents, see Ní Fhloinn (2001), especially pp. 222–23.

individual's anywhere in Europe. Neumann mentions repertoires of forty-five. When one considerers that the people he refers to are in a heartland of wellerisms — northern Germany — this makes Mícheál Ó Gaoithín's stock, from a periphery, all the more significant and remarkable.

While Mícheál Ó Gaoithín, in addition to the wellerisms, had a huge store of proverbs and other sayings, and was a very active tradition bearer, it does seem that certain people, as passive tradition bearers, have a knack for recalling wellerisms. IK, a woman living in Co. Kilkenny, contributed thirteen to Q 1973, at least one from her grandmother, who had died aged 80 in 1942 in Stradbally, Co. Laois, and also some from Co. Kilkenny, including one with the comment, 'used by a workman on a farm in Clifden, … near Gowran, 20 or more years ago. Hers was the largest set to Q 1973 from an individual. **TC**, a man in his 60s, originally from Kilkeel, Co. Down, now living in North Belfast, is another with this ability. He remembers where and when he heard most of the ten that he contributed to Q 2000 and they ranged from the 1970s to the present.

THE FREQUENCY OF INDIVIDUAL WELLERISMS
The vast majority of wellerisms in the following catalogue have only been recorded once, however all the stylistic devices mentioned in the opening remarks — alliteration, and so on, — helped to establish whether or not texts were wellerisms. Symmetry is especially important in this because what is quoted is usually balanced equally with the remainder, in other words the quote has the same number of stressed and unstressed syllables as the remainder. Many wellerisms have been noted twice, not necessarily in the same locality, or even neighbouring counties, signalling that they were actually commoner. *'"Is mór an ní an neart!" arsa an dreoilín nuair a chaith sé chiaróg leis an bhfaill'*[145] ["Strength's a great thing!" said the wren when he threw the beetle over the cliff'] is probably the wellerism most typical of Ireland as it has been recorded frequently in both languages (fifteen times in English and twelve times in Irish). One

---

[145] Part B 143.1, see the rest under this number and Part A 277 for the English-language versions.

variant is even bilingual. It is usual for proverbs like *'Is mór an ní an neart!'* ['Strength's a great thing!'] to carry on in their accustomed language even after another language has become more dominant. Indeed, to compound the matter, the proverb in the wellerism is common in Irish but not in English, nevertheless, the usual English-language version of the wellerism simply has the word 'Strength!' The bilingual version, however, maintains the *proverb* in Irish 'When the wren threw a beetle against the wall [?it said], *"Is mór an nidhe an neart!"'*[146] Although this wellerism is macaronic it is so for a very different reason from the other macaronic wellerisms. The wellerism *'"Is beag an rud nach cuidiú é," dúirt an dreolán nuair a rinn sé a mhún san fharraige'* ['"It's a small thing that doesn't help," ie. "Every little helps," said the wren when he urinated in the sea'] is also common in both languages.[147] '"That will be a good fire," said the fox when he wet in the snow and saw the steam,' noted nineteen times in English and twice in Irish, has been found in all four provinces over an extended period.[148] '"Everyone to his taste," said the woman when she kissed the cow,' has been widely recorded, too, over a long period.[149] It also occurs in Swift and Joyce, a further indication of its popularity, but despite all this has not been recorded in Irish. '"Hard lines!" said the monkey when he sat on the railway track,' '"It won't be long now," said the monkey when he got the piece off his tail' and '"Great cry and little wool," as the man said when he clipped the sow,'[150] are common in English, with the two latter also having been collected in Irish and being quite common in that language.[151] The most frequently-collected wellerism in Irish is, however, *'"Chonaic mé cheana thú!" mar adúirt an cat leis an mbainne te'*[152] ['"I've seen you before!" as the cat said to the hot milk'] which has been recorded eleven times. It also occurs in

---

[146] Part A 277.14.

[147] See Part A 180 & Part B 22.

[148] See Part A 83 & Part B 189.

[149] See Part A 287.

[150] Respectively Part A 173.1, 182.1 & 48.1 for these particular variants.

[151] For versions in Irish, see Part B 81 & 107.

[152] Part B 41.2. There are 10 versions in all, half with 'bruite' [= 'seething'] rather than 'te.'

42

English but to a much lesser extent.[153] Others such as *'"'S iomdha gléus ceoil a bhíonns ann,"* arsan fear a raibh an trumpa maide aige'[154] ["There are many kinds of musical instrument," said the man with the imitation trump'], *'"Fill oram!" adeir an droghnú,'*[155] [' "Come back to me!" says the botched job'] and *'"Is luachmhar an t-anam,"* mar aduairt an táilliúir agus é ag rith ón ngandal'[156] ["The soul is a valuable thing," as the tailor said, running from the gander'] are exclusive to Irish, where they are quite common. '"I see," said the blind man,' and its diverse variants is easily the commonest in English, appears perennial[157] and is one of the few used by children. In at least one case it has become attached to a local person — Jansy 'an old blind boatman on the Killarney lakes' in Co. Kerry.[158] It has been recorded in Irish, but is not common and versions lack a personal name.[159] The commoner wellerisms in Ireland, whether connected with folk narrative, or distinct from it, tend to show up internationally.

SOME COMPARISONS
In the catalogue which follows there are about 340 different wellerisms in English and 198 in Irish. Taking into account some obvious factors, such as the much greater proportion in recent times of English speakers to Irish speakers, and allowing for the greater concentration of collection in Irish-speaking districts, the figures indicate that wellerisms, throughout the twentieth century and for the later part of the nineteenth, were as common in Irish as in English. Only about twenty wellerisms out of a total of over 530 are common to both languages.[160] Twelve wellerisms which are

---

[153] See Part A 254. It has been recorded twice in English and in different provinces from the Irish.
[154] Part B 106.3. Seven versions in all have been recorded.
[155] Part B 92.4. Seven versions in all have been recorded.
[156] Part B 11.5. Six versions in all have been recorded.
[157] To date 60 versions have been gathered together in the catalogue. These range in date from Jonathan Swift 1738, up to press; see Part A 259 and cf Part A 15.
[158] Part A 259.55 Co. Kerry.
[159] See Part B 40.1–.3.
[160] This is in sharp contrast to proverbs themselves where there is a very close overlap between those in Irish and those in English see Carson

common to both languages are also international. Broadly speaking, those in Irish are from an older era than those in English. The majority of those in Irish were collected before 1952, whereas the majority of those in English were collected from 1973. This might indicate that most wellerisms have a very short currency and that many of those in Irish never passed into English. The main reason for their short currency might be their local creation and application. A correspondent to Q 2000 commented that some of those which referred to a local character, either living or dead, 'would be remembered for years, others would be repeated for a month or two and then be forgotten. Some of them would not have much currency outside a particular locale, many being a type of in joke in fairly close knit communities.'[161] This is another aspect which could be pursued.

While the Irish and English-language wellerism repertoires do not overlap to any great extent, the quotations, speakers and situations are all very much alike. Irish-language wellerisms, as a whole, appear to be less international than those in English; less than eight per cent are international, whereas for those in English the percentage is nearer to thirteen. As in English, there is a large proportion which has not been located anywhere else. Similarly in both languages there are a few which are related to fables and other genres of narrative as well as many which do not appear to be.

While word puns would vary between languages, some double meanings carry through in both languages. This applies to the commonest wellerism in English 'I see...' but, although it does occur in Irish, it is rare.

Wellerisms where the speaker is an indigenous saint or hero, such as Columcille and Conán, mythological figures, such as the Cailleach Mhuigheo and figures from folklore, such as An Sotach, are found in Irish but do not seem to occur in English. Irish-language wellerisms also differ from those in English in that they do not include international figures. While the monkey has been recorded once as a speaker in an Irish-language wellerism, it may be that, in Irish-language wellerisms, the goat fulfils a similar role

---

Williams (2000b), p. 429.
[161] Letter from TC dated 1/8/2000.

44

to that of the monkey.[162] Another discernable difference is that Irish place-names, although rare in all wellerisms, are more than twice as frequent in the Irish-language wellerisms than in the English-language ones. Places are mentioned in very few English-language wellerisms. One of these, '"It's nothin' when ye're used to it," as the eels at Toome said when they were being skinned alive' has been noted outside Ireland without the place-name.[163] Another wellerism with a place-name could certainly be envisaged with other names. All the rest need the place-names in question since they depend on puns. The following is a typical example 'As the man said, "That's like Rostrevor, it's beside The 'Point."'[164] None of the wellerisms in Irish containing place-names are puns.

Dialogue wellerisms seem to be more frequently used in Irish but, once again, we are dealing with small numbers. Some of the conventional proverbs used as quotes in wellerisms in English, such as, 'Youth must have its fling,' are less common or absent from the Irish-language record and this explains their absence there as wellerisms and indicates that the presence of a conventional proverb in a wellerism presupposes its currency at some stage in the same location.

While the vast majority of wellerisms in oral tradition in both English and Irish are symmetrical with the same number of stresses in the part quoted as in the remainder, a number of those in oral tradition in Irish have much longer second parts, for example, '"Chití, mara bhfuil tuilleadh mine agat, beidh do bhrothchán lom," mar dubhairt an fear fadó le n-a mhnaoi nuair

---

[162] See Part B 81 for the monkey wellerism and Part B 1 & 139 for goat wellerisms.
[163] See Part A 217.2 for the version including the place-name Toome. Eels have been caught at Toome, Co. Antrim, where the Lower Bann river leaves Lough Neagh, since the mesolithic period. Versions from Great Britain without any place-name can be found in *DOW*, No. 887. NB Jonathan Swift in … *Polite Conversation* … (1738, 1963 ed.), simply used: ''Tis nothing when you are used to it.'
[164] Part A 250 'As the man said, "That's like Rostrevor, it's beside The 'Point."' 'The 'Point' is Warrenpoint; it and Rostrevor are neighbouring County Down towns. (The wellerism was collected in Co. Tyrone, which is not an adjacent county.)

thuit an sac mine sa lán mara air[165] ["'Cití, unless you have some more meal, your porridge is going to be thin," as the man long ago said to his wife when he let the flour sack fall into the sea'].

THE USES OF WELLERISMS

Most wellerisms are humorous and most circulate orally in everyday conversation amongst adults. Wellerisms come to life in dialogue, which is probably where they originated. They are mini-narratives within dialogue. Their humour spices up dialogue and makes commands and admonitions more palatable. While some wellerisms could only be imagined in use by men there appear to be some favoured by women. As mentioned earlier, wellerisms act as a counterblast to the wise sayings in tradition. 'An Seabhac' and Ó Máille give many instances of when wellerisms would be employed. Q 1973 is also very valuable for such details. From his fieldwork in the 1970s in Fermanagh Henry Glassie describes how 'Clever chat becomes "crack" through the logical, free play of wit. Crack snaps with humorous figures of speech. The convention of attributing proverbs generally bids, and particularly eases Wellerisms into talk. At last comprehending: "I see, said the blind man, You're a liar, says the dummy, Give him a kick in the arse, says the cripple.'"[166] Several were used to take the wind out of a person's sails or as a reaction to minor misfortunes. Some very specific uses are given, such as, "'Down!" said the fowler when he shot the duck' which was heard in the mid-thirties in a card school, 'The expression would be used by a person having the fall of play when he would be beating a player who had fought into him.'[167] Others were used as put-offs to children, or to pacify them, and to excuse impoliteness. Some, such as, "'Land," says Columbus'[168] are euphemisms. In this case it was used to imply that a person was being attentive to his elderly neighbour in the hope of eventually acquiring his farm. At least one, "'When that kindles it'll be a fire," as the fox said when he wet on the snow,'[169] was used both in its straightforward meaning, when a fire was not

---

[165] Part B 138.
[166] Glassie (1982), p. 276.
[167] Part A 66.
[168] Part A 154, Co. Kerry.
[169] Part A 83 & Part B 189.

46

taking light, as well as metaphorically, for instance, to quash gossip. It is more likely, however, that most wellerisms had various applications, although perhaps not as many as proverbs, and, as a result of this, the transmission of wellerisms in comparison to proverbs is curtailed.

Although wellerisms are usually spread through oral channels they sometimes occur in print in joke books and similar publications.[170] An example of this is *Pro Tanto Quid*, later known as *P.T.Q.*, the student rag magazine, of Queen's University, Belfast. It has been published annually since 1927 and is sold in order to raise money for charity. When first published it claimed to be the only local joke book. In 1929 ten thousand copies were distributed, probably mainly in Belfast. In the 1960s university colleges in Derry city and Coleraine were included in the production, and distribution extended to many towns. In 2002 *P.T.Q.* had its first female editor and this was also the first year that a professional distributor was used. All of the issues from 1929 to 1973 (with the exceptions of 1933, 39, 42, 43, 48, 52 and 72 which were missing) were read. *P.T.Q.* varies in length from 50 to 70 pages and, from the beginning, contained, among other things, cartoons and jokes. These sometimes have the form of wellerisms and almost all of the wellerisms have been included in the catalogue below. By the 1970s wellerisms in *P.T.Q.* grew less frequent and I ceased to read later issues. I did read the current (2002) issue and it did not contain any wellerisms. Since the late 1990s some material from the Internet has been included rather than just that which is circulating orally locally. In all, thirty-one wellerisms were located (thirty different) and all except four (detailed in the Preface) are included in the catalogue. As might be anticipated, a few refer to university life with professors and students as mainstays. The referents are mostly of a general, European nature, rather than being specifically tied into place, and they occasionally relate to things of topical interest such as beatniks (1967)[171] and the growing awareness of minorities

---

[170] Previously noted in California by C. Grant Loomis, Loomis (1955), p. 229.
[171] Part A 192.

(1971).[172] Even after 1969, however, at a period of increasing conflict, when political jokes were rife, only one refers directly to life in Northern Ireland, 'Pilot to passengers coming in to land at Belfast, "Fasten your seat belts and turn your watches back fifty years."'[173] Two, for example, 'As the physiology professor said, "Two's company, three's a deformity,"' are based on common proverbs.[174] Some, like 'As one Chinese stamp-collector said to the other, "Philately will get you nowhere,"'[175] are probably derived from oral tradition as they hinge on (mis)pronunciation. Others seem to work both in print and verbally but were probably also drawn from oral tradition. Lack of context and lack of details of origin are a drawback to this source. Five of the wellerisms in *P.T.Q.*, for example, 'Said one flea to another, "It's about time we went home — shall we walk or take a dog?"' have turned up elsewhere as joking questions.[176]

IRISH WELLERISMS AND THOSE IN OTHER LANGUAGES
This brings us to a consideration of which of the group can be found in other languages and in English outside of Ireland. Taylor identified wellerisms as being very popular in northern Germany and Scandinavia.[177] The search for versions in other languages, with the aid of colleagues,[178] was concentrated in Europe. In addition, *DOW*[179] and its *Addenda*[180] which include North American English, that is of both Canada and the USA, and

---

[172] For example, the Chinese community, see Part A 229.

[173] Part A 258.

[174] Part A 43 which is, of course, based on the proverb 'Two's company, three's a crowd.'

[175] Part A 229.

[176] Part A 307.1, *P.T.Q.* 1958, with another version, Part A 307.2, published in *P.T.Q* in 1970. This occurs as a joking question in Hegarty *Amazing Animal Jokes*, published in London in 1987, n.p.

[177] Taylor (1962 fac., 1985 rpt.), p. 208; see also p. 204.

[178] Bengt af Klintberg (Swedish), Kazys Grigas and Vita Ivanauskaitë (Lithuanian), Caragh Halpin (Spanish), Johannes Hautsma (Dutch), Arvo Krikmann (Estonian), Outi Lauhakangas (Finnish), Gyula Paczolay (Hungarian), Stanislaw Predota (Dutch and Polish) and Udo Steuck (German).

[179] *op. cit.*

[180] Mieder (1997).

comparative works such as Champion's *Racial Proverbs*,[181] which includes less mainstream languages such as Breton and Romany were combed. One can say straight away that the following languages yielded a version or versions matching those in the English of Ireland. Synonyms, of which there were also many, have not been included in the following list. The languages are placed in descending order of versions obtained: American English (35), English in Great Britain, German and Scots all (14), Swedish (10). Estonian and Norwegian both had (7), while Dutch, Finnish and Scottish Gaelic had (6). Five or less were located in Danish, French and Spanish. One matching version was located in the Arabic of Egypt and of Morocco, Frisian, Greek, Icelandic, Italian and Lithuanian.[182] In addition, two in the English of India and two in the English of New Zealand were found, as well as one in the English of Australia and one in the English of Canada. In all only fifty wellerisms from Ireland (about ten per cent) were found in other languages or in English around the world. Discounting varieties of English, they were in almost twenty different languages, mainly European, but some Asian. While wellerisms do occur in Russian, it, and the Southern Slavonic languages, are languages which I was not able to investigate to any great extent. As mentioned, twenty are to be found in Ireland in *both* English and Irish and, out of these, eight have not as yet been found in any other language. This, small as it is, is significant as it is the biggest overlapping group.

It should be borne in mind that printed collections of sayings are not an infallible guide as to whether or not wellerisms exist or existed in any particular language. As Wolfgang Mieder has pointed out, historically proverbs (which are associated with wellerisms) were usually assumed to have to have a didactic function therefore wellerisms, which often mock conventional proverbs and convention itself, are not likely to have been

---

[181] Champion (1938).
[182] Besides the Frisian, which was obtained from Taylor (*op. cit.*, 1962 fac., 1985 rpt.), and the Icelandic, many of these last versions were obtained from Paczolay (1997).

considered as proverbs.[183] It should also be borne in mind that there is disparity between countries in the number of wellerisms which do succeed in making their way into printed collections.

Let us take a closer look at what is available in the printed collections closest to Ireland — those covering Great Britain. This will help to put a balance on the figures above. First and foremost, *DOW* and its *Addenda* include wellerisms from England and Scotland. These are from printed sources, with those from England being from literature and those from Scotland being from both literature and from collections of sayings from oral tradition. In order to be able to make comparisons with material in Ireland and to gain an impression of what is circulating *orally* in England, I published an appeal in the newsletter of the Folklore Society, *FLS News*, of June 2001.[184] While there was no response at all to it, it cannot mean that there are no wellerisms, however, no notion of which was obtained. Practically every printed collection of sayings from Scotland contains a few wellerisms, giving the impression that they are common there, however, there has been a great deal of borrowing from one collection to the next and the variety and size of the pool is much smaller than a cursory look indicates. As regards the Celtic languages, wellerisms from oral tradition do turn up in the Scottish Gaelic collections, although to a lesser extent than in the Scots. On the other hand, printed collections of sayings in Welsh only contain the occasional wellerism and their sparcity in older collections probably mitigates against their inclusion in new collections, whether or not they are present in oral tradition. Turning to Manx, I have not found a single wellerism either in print in any of the collections of sayings or dictionaries, or through enquiries to the Manx Museum, Douglas, which has a comprehensive archive. In Great Britain, least is known of wellerisms in Wales where much of the population is bilingual Welsh/English-speaking and, if one can take it that wellerisms are commoner in English than in any other language in Great Britain, Wales must be the place with the most potential for

---

[183] Mieder (1989), p. 223. This attitude, however, seems to have been different as regards Scots wellerisms and, of course, once some get into a collection, subsequent collectors also tend to include them.
[184] Carson Williams (2001b), p. 15.

overlap and influence. With assistance, I have instigated a small project to collect wellerisms in Wales. In summary, there is less published material from English oral tradition than from literature and less from both traditions in Welsh to compare with Ireland than from some other languages, such as Dutch or Finnish, which are further afield.

WORLD DISTRIBUTION

Taylor says that wellerisms comprising a story are the oldest type. Looking at the far-flung distribution of these — such as parts of West Africa, Europe — it is likely that this type at least developed independently in different areas. It seems that the transmission of wellerisms is akin to legends in that the majority only have a local circulation but that there are also what might be termed 'migratory wellerisms' which are found in several different places with shared historical or cultural connections, in different languages, for example, within Europe, or, in West Africa and the Caribbean. These may stimulate the popularity, or give rise to the development of wellerisms in the new environment, as in Haiti. There also appear to be what might be called 'assertive' wellerisms which are adopted in 'unwellerised territory' but do not, in turn, trigger locally-created wellerisms. *'"Ez a hét is jól kezdoedik," mondta a Cigány, amikor hétfön reggel akasztani vitték'* ['"This week, too, is beginning well," said the Gypsy when he was being taken to be hanged on Monday morning'], one of the few occurring in Hungarian,[185] is such an example. '"Thy complexion is black," says the raven,' and its synonyms,[186] which are to be found in many languages, may be another.

As regards the influence of Irish printed material on wellerism dissemination, all of the Irish-language books containing wellerisms were published within Ireland, customarily in Dublin. Many of the English-language books were published outside Ireland, particularly in London, with a few in the USA and *Ulysses* being first published in Paris. Those in Irish had largely a home market while those in English had both a home market as well as circulating elsewhere.

---

[185] Email from Gyula Paczolay 28/4/2000.
[186] See Part A 44 and also Part A 20, 30, & 92 & Part B 8.

HISTORICAL DEPTH IN IRELAND

The oldest recorded wellerism in Ireland, first disclosed by Lean, is in Raphaell Holinshed's *Chronicles of Ireland* which were published in Dublin in 1577. The *Chronicles* proved so popular that, only ten years later, a second edition was published. They give a history of Ireland in three books, with the first two written by Holinshed, and the third book, which includes the wellerism, written by Richarde Stanyhurst. According to Stanyhurst the wellerism was in Irish but, sadly, he does not give the full text. From what is available in Irish, and his English translation, '"Too late!" quoth Boice,' it might be surmised to have been, *'"Antragh!" adúirt Boice,'* or the like. This is an ironic reference to late repentance. Stanyhurst was born in Dublin in 1547 and died in Brussels in 1618. The wellerism must have been current when he was writing the *Chronicles* while the event it commemorates — the betrayal of the castle of Maynooth, which belonged to the Earls of Kildare — occurred over forty years earlier in 1535. Stanyhurst had a personal link with the Kildare family as he had taught the children of one of the earls. It is very much in keeping with contemporary sixteenth century wellerisms in England and Stanyhurst recognises it as a saying, calling it a proverb and equating it with 'Beware of "Had I wist [= realized]!"' 'After meat mustard,' 'You come a day after the fair' and 'Better done than said.' This tantalising reference is by far the earliest to wellerisms found in Ireland. It may have had a long currency as it crops up again, in English, in the early nineteenth century in a story by Samuel Lover.[187] It is possible that published accounts of the betrayal of the castle of Maynooth in the intervening period helped to keep this wellerism in circulation. It is also mentioned by John J. Marshall in the 1930s, however, there it is unclear whether his source was contemporary and oral, or historical. To my knowledge no further wellerisms in Irish were written down until Robert Mac Adam's 'Six Hundred Gaelic Proverbs Collected in Ulster,' published in parts in the *Ulster Journal of Archaeology* from 1858 to 1862.[188] His collection includes three wellerisms,[189] with a

---

[187] Part A 157.1.
[188] Most easily accessible in Hughes (1998).

further two which he did not publish.[190] All five are reckoned to have been collected from living tradition and written down about 1830.[191] On the other hand, Jonathan Swift's writings take us back to 1711 for clear examples in English in Ireland.

Bo Almqvist states that 'from our present knowledge the lack of wellerisms in older Irish sources is striking' and sees the immediate inspiration for the genre as being those in the English-language tradition of Ireland.[192] Whether or not, '"Too late," quoth Boice' occurred in Irish (there is, as yet, nothing to collaborate Stanyhurst), at least a five hundred year long tradition of wellerisms in Ireland has been established.

CONCLUSION

Although rare in Ireland, as they perhaps always were, wellerisms are still current here today. It would seem that, despite models in oral tradition and in print, coinciding with the rise in popularity of the wellerism during the sixteenth century in neighbouring countries, the genre was never prevalent and was not committed to Irish-language manuscripts (in which it was the custom, right up until the nineteenth century, to list sayings of various kinds).

Wellerisms give us an insight into what was considered humorous at various periods and they immortalise small and great alike. While local characters will continue to be featured it is likely that, because of mass communication, world figures may come to occupy a greater place in them. The genre, particularly in English, is producing new types as witnessed by those referring to such novelties as the Dublin Point Theatre, opened in 1996 — '"I must get to the point!" as the pop-star said to the taxi driver.'[193] Despite the fact that wellerisms are in short supply in Ireland, vital information about the diffusion of and the interaction between different genres can be gleaned from them.

---

[189] Part B 78.1, 96 & 106.1; cf Hughes *op. cit.*, No. 437.
[190] Part B 179 & 181.
[191] Ó Tuathail (1933b), p. 204.
[192] Almqvist *op. cit.*, p. 42/p. 60.
[193] Part A 236. The wellerism was heard in about 2000 on the radio.

THE CATALOGUE

GUIDE

Each wellerism is shown in bold. In order to best convey their oral nature and dialectal features they are given as in the original, both those in English and those in Irish. This includes any non-standard spelling and grammar. Words not written in full eg. **'a–'** which may stand for 'arse' or 'ass'='posterior' and words with initial capitalisation in the original, eg. **'Christian,' 'Devil'** and **'Wren,'** have been left as such. Punctuation, particularly as regards to inverted commas, has been silently standardised. Any words or letters in round brackets were in the original while any words or letters added by me for clarification are in square brackets.

On the line below each wellerism is its provenance and date of usage, if known. Wellerisms are provenanced to county except for those from the cities of Belfast, Derry, Dublin, Galway and Limerick. Unless a city is named, it can be assumed that the wellerism came from a rural area. In some cases only a province or part of a province is known. Many wellerisms from printed general collections of sayings and from literary works could not be closely provenanced. The line below this shows the source. Those from the Department of Irish Folklore, University College Dublin, are indicated by IFC, if from the Main Manuscript Collection, and by IFCS, if from the Schools' Collection. The manuscript number follows and is separated from the page number by a colon. This is followed by 'C m' or 'C f' indicating that the Correspondent, 'C,' was male or female, if this is known. A plus sign '+' indicates that there was more than one wellerism from that Correspondent. An 'i' indicates 'informant' and the informant's initials, if known, follow, again with 'm' or 'f' for 'male' or 'female,' if known. A plus sign '+' after those indicates that there was more than one wellerism from that informant. '[E & Ir]' after a Correspondent's or informant's initials indicates that that person supplied wellerisms in both English and Irish. 'Q 1973' indicates that the wellerism was obtained through the questionnaire sent out by the Department of Irish Folklore in 1973, while 'Q 2000' indicates that the wellerism resulted from my collection drive from January 2000. Those from most of the principle printed collections of sayings, dictionaries, language studies, and similar works, are referred to by author without title. For those from literature the title of the work is included with a short indication of oeuvre, such as, 'autobiography,' 'play,' and so on. The earliest date of publication is used where possible but, if this varies from the edition available, an attempt has been made to include the original date and place of publication. Almost all of the original manuscript records of oral versions, and most other sources mentioned, have been seen by me. In the few cases where this was not possible this is indicated by 'as cited in ...,' and the source named. 'Ref. via' means that I was alerted to the reference by the authority named and that the source was then examined ('as cited in ...' and 'ref. via' are also used in the same way with regard to other sources.) Any explanation or context with the wellerism, whether from an oral or printed source, then follows. Some from Irish-language literature are lacking. Any place-name mentioned in the explanation or context will be in the same county as the wellerism provenance unless otherwise stated. English-language wellerisms are catalogued in Part A while wellerisms in Irish are in Part B and any that occur in both languages are cross-referenced. In a few cases only English translations for Irish-language wellerisms were available, however, there was always an Irish-language version of the same wellerism and so all the translations could be catalogued with the relevant Irish-language type. They are indicated by 'Irish lacking' with the translations in square brackets beneath.

Each wellerism appears under a key word, as it appears in the text, in the quoted part, separated by a slash '/' from the speaker eg. 'long/monkey.' This also applies to wellerisms in which the quotation comes after the speaker. The wellerisms are arranged alphabetically according to the key words. Where more than one wellerism has the same key word the speakers are arranged alphabetically so 'know/man' will be before 'know/woman.'

All the versions of any one wellerism type appear under the same number. Where there are two versions the earlier will appear first and be '.1' and the second '.2.' Where there are more than two versions, similar variants are grouped together with the commonest variant first. Any key words or speakers that vary are shown in round brackets after the key word and speaker of the .1

variant, and these are also cross-referenced. Attenuated versions appear after the full versions. References to related items such as riddles and folktales follow each wellerism type, as do my notes. Unless otherwise stated, the references to fables are to Aesop, the 1954 edition, 1973 reprint, translated by S. A. Handford. A wellerism that seems to have some connection with any other in the catalogue will be followed by 'see also' and its catalogue number.

If the wellerism has been found anywhere outside Ireland this is shown on the line above the wellerism, along side the heading of key word and speaker. The references to those outside Ireland are in abbreviated form in alphabetical order — 'Am Eng'=American English, 'E Eng'=the English of England, 'Fin'=Finnish, and so on. Most of these references are from printed collections. Most of the versions in other languages not located by me have been verified by me. Where the language is in italics, eg. *'Est,'* this indicates that the reference is not from a printed source but from, for example, an archival source. Any such non-printed sources are given in full after the wellerism type. Where the language has 'cf' in front of it this means that it is a variant of the one in the catalogue and variants are also given in full below the wellerisms in question. Where versions outside Ireland are found for those which occur in both English and Irish these are only cited in Part A but the Part B wellerisms are referenced back to these in Part A.

Also after each wellerism type, but preceding the non-published versions and the variants, are exact references to the same type in English, Scots and Scottish Gaelic. If the wellerism is in *DOW*, the *DOW* number is given, and this covers the English and Scots references as explained in *DOW*. Smith & Wilson (1970, 1975 rpt.) references falling outside *DOW*'s remit follow. Any English and Scots references outside *DOW*'s and Smith & Wilson's remits are also given here. With regard to the Scots references in particular it should be noted that all are listed irrespective of whether or not they are original or republished from a previous collection.

A complete list of abbreviations and symbols can be found on pp. 279–82 and of sources on pp. 287–93.

56

Initials in bold in the catalogue are those of some informants and staff members of the Department of Irish Folklore.

INFORMANTS: Those who have contributed one, or a few items, are detailed with their respective contributions. Many others, particularly to Q 1973, contributed several wellerisms but it was not usually possible to distinguish whether they were collectors or informants. Below are some details of informants who are known to have contributed a greater number of items.
IC Ian Coalter (b. 1945) b. & r. The Moy, Co. Tyrone, civil servant, a son of **MC** and a brother-in-law of FCW;
MC f (b. 1913) b. & r. Sandhills, Co. Tyrone, on a farm, mother of IC;
TC m (60s) from Kilkeel, Co. Down, now living in North Belfast;
JG m (b. 1947) b. & r. Roscommon town, now living in Dublin, professional;
MÓG Mícheál Ó Gaoithín (1901–74) b. & r. on An Blascaod Mór/The Great Blasket Island, Co. Kerry, later Dún Chaoin/Dunquin, fisher-farmer.

STAFF: Below are listed those mentioned in the catalogue who are or were full-time Department of Irish Folklore staff members. **BA**; **CB** (1905–76); **AB**; **LC** (1929–92); **JD** (1916–2000); **BNíF**; **MJM** (1913–96); **SÓC(i)** (1915–65); **SÓC(ii)** & **SÓD** (1909–92). With the exception of **AB** and **BNíF**, all are men.

GLOSSARY

Most words are explained where they occur but the following occur frequently and are only glossed here.

auld, oul, oul', ould, owl=old
de'il, De'il, deil, divil=devil
gráineog, graineoig, grannog, grannóg, grainnog
   <Ir gráinneog=hedgehog
say'd, sayd=said
t'=to
ye, ye'll, ye're=you, you will, you are

PART A: WELLERISMS IN ENGLISH

A

actor/student

A 1.1 'Female student, "I knew an actor once, or was it twice?"'
P.T.Q. 1971 Belfast p. 41.

adore/mademoiselle

A 2.1 'Amorous mademoiselle to soldier, "Je t'adore."
Soldier to mademoiselle, "Shut it yourself."'
Kane [b. Belfast, 1908] *Songs and Sayings of an Ulster Childhood.* 1983 Dublin, p. 188 in final chapter 'Where the Alleyman [<Fr <u>Allemand</u>] Won't Catch Me,' which contains reminiscences, songs, rhymes etc., about the First World War: 'Long after the war, we continued to sing of the Yanks [= North Americans] and their part in it: *Mademoiselle from Armentières, parlez-voo?* --- [a very popular First World War song] And Daddy [Hugh Smiley Kane, b. *c.* 1875, Larne, Co. Antrim, mariner] said: *Amorous mademoiselle to soldier ... yourself.* The next disaster to strike was The Flu.' [influenza, 1918]. In 1921, when Kane was a girl of 13, the family migrated to New Brunswick, Canada.

again/bull Part B 16

A 3.1 '"Again to it," said the bull to the butcher when he was overcharging for beef.'
County Longford
Q 1973 IFC 2027:162 C f+

.2 '"Again to it," said the Bull to the Butcher.'
County Cork current when Q 1973 was returned
Q 1973 IFC 1917:40 C m+: 'well-known and frequently used'

Note: the above [as **.2**] was used as one of the four examples on Q 1973, see Appendix 1.

again/girl

A 4.1 '"Well," as the girl said to the soldier, "here we are again."'

Behan *The Quare Fellow*, a play first performed Dublin 1954, 1978 ed. p. 115, Act II, the prison yard, time 1954: 'As the prisoners march off, the hangman comes slowly down the steps.

Warder Crimmin. Is this ...

Warder Regan. Himself.

Hangman. It's Mr Regan, isn't it? Well, as the girl said to the soldier "Here we are again."

Warder Regan. Nice evening. I hope you had a good crossing.

Hangman. Not bad. It's nice to get over to old Ireland you know, a nice bit of steak and a couple of pints as soon as you get off the boat ...'

see also Part A 204.

again (up)/grannóg (hedgehog, grainneog & similar)   Ger

A 5.1 '"To it again," said the grannóg when he raced with the hare in the furrow.'

County Roscommon

Q 1973 IFC 1888:144 C m+: 'used when a person doesn't want to admit defeat. --- I have heard these [this and Part A 37, 68, 85, 125.1, 130.1, 173.6, 182.10, 222, 235.4, 259.40 & 277.8] used over the years in the locality'

.2 '"Up and at it again," as the hedgehog said to the hare.'

County Louth

IFCS 672:265 in a list, mainly of proverbs. Published in [Carson] Williams 1992 p. 67/2000a p. 67 [*sic*]

.3 '"Up and at it," says the hedgehog to the hare.'

County Louth

IFC 1622:36 in a folktale collected by **MJM** from JL m in 1963: 'The Hedgehog races the Hare. Did you ever know the way the hedgehog won the bet from the hare? They were to run a race and the hedgehog said he would win. So the hare took him on. The race took place in priddy-drills [= potato drills], a drill that was moulded after being riz [= raised]. And there was one hedgehog at the top of this drill and another at the bottom. So when the hare would run to the top he'd see a hedgehog before him, and when he'd get to the bottom the hedgehog was there before him; he didn't know there was two in it. "Up and at it," says the hedgehog to the hare. Between them anyway they killed the hare (by exhaustion).'

Published in Michael J. Murphy/**MJM** *Now You're Talking, Folktales from the North of Ireland.* 1975 Belfast p. 144, No. 125

.4 '"Here we go again," says the hedgehog to the hare.'
County Louth
IFCS 674:143 in a folktale titled 'The Hedgehog and the Hare' about a hare racing a hedgehog up and down potato drills. At the end of the first drill: 'They agreed to run again but this time the hedgehog won again. At [the] end the hedgehog would say, "Here we go again," but always won. The result was that '"Here we go again,' says the hedgehog to the hare," has become a familiar phrase locally'

.5 '"At it again," as the grainneog said to the hare.'
County Galway
Q 1973 IFC1888:156 C m

.6 '"To it, and at it again," as the gráineog said to the hare.'
County Kilkenny
Q 1973(75) IFC1917:78 C f+

.7 '"To it again!" says the grainneóg.'
County Meath
Q 1973(75) IFC1917:54 C f+ followed by: 'One might say this when it was time to start working again after a short break for a rest, or for tea etc. The grainneóg challenged the hare to a race in adjoining drills in a plowed field. When the hare got to the far end he saw the gráinneóg already rolled up at the end of his drill. He did not guess that it was another grainneóg. The gráinneóg said "To it again!" and the hare turned and raced back only to find — as he thought — the same grainneóg already there. The race kept on like this till the hare admitted defeat'

.8 '"To it again!" says the grainneog.'
County Westmeath
IFC1917:64 letter 1973, collected by **JD** from PJ m: 'I have thought of another wellerism which I heard with PJ. It comes from the story of the two grainneogs who got the hare to race against them in parallel furrows, one remaining at one end of the furrow while the other remained at the other end. They had the hare running up and down the furrow until he was exhausted. Each grainneog would say when the hare arrived at his end of the furrow "To it again!" The hare would think that the grainnneog was here before him. I remember PJ said it to me one day and we resuming recording, which we had discontinued for some reason or the other. He said "'To it again,' said the grainneog." PJ told me the story

of the grainneogs and the hare long ago. I never heard it from anyone else but him'

.9 '"Here we go again," said the graineoig.'
County Wexford
IFCS 889:76 folktale title

.10 '"At it again," said the gráinneóg.'
County Galway
IFCS 77:414 folktale title, repeated in the text, written down by a schoolboy from his father: '… Ever afterwards when a person fails to do something at the first attempt he is encouraged to persevere by saying to him '"At it again,' said the gráinneóg."'

.11 '"At it again," says the graneóg.'
County Cork
Q 1973 IFC 2027:16 C m. This is the only wellerism that the Correspondent had ever heard

cf Co. Cavan IFC not indexed 1974 collected by **MJM** — note in Michael J. Murphy 1975 p. 175

cf the fable Aesop 66; AT 257A *Hare & Tortoise Race: Sleeping Hare,* 'missing in *IT [TIF]* though tale is fairly common in Ireland' — comment by **BA** on p. 175 of Michael J. Murphy 1975

Notes: There are extremely few saying, in either English or Irish, referring to hedgehogs, no doubt because of its late arrival in Ireland. The earliest evidence for the hedgehog in the country is 13th century; I am grateful to Finbar McCormick for this information. One of the other sayings refers to the hedgehog's spines: '*he would shake hands with a hedgehog*=an effusive, insincere person' Paterson *Armagh Miscellanea* 1920s– ts Vol. XVIII p. 33, in a list titled 'Proverbs.'

age/man Ger
A 6.1 '"Age is honourable," as the man said when he hoisted the creel on his father.'
creel=basket
County Cavan
Q 1973(74) IFC 1888:88 C m+

cf 'Age is honourable, hoist the sack on my father' in the same list as Part A 6.1

cf 'Age is honourable, put the creel on your father' Co. Monaghan IFCS 935:122

cf 'Age is honourable, put the load on my Father' Co. Cavan Q 1973 IFC 1888:83, with the comment: 'most of these [this is one of three] are used with the prefix "as the Fella says"'

Note: the proverb 'Age is honourable' is fairly common in English and also occurs in Irish.

agra/Nancy Carr
A 7.1 '"Well, agra," said Nancy Carr, "It's many's the crush the poor get."'
agra <Irish *a ghrá* (voc.)= *love, a term of endearment*
County Louth
IFCS 665:410 in a list, mainly of proverbs, with the comment: 'meaning the poor are subject to misfortune and may [= should] not be surprised when it comes.' Published in [Carson] Williams 1992 p. 79/2000a p. 75

Notes: Carr — a common personal name in Oriel [which includes Co. Louth], Mayo, Limerick & Donegal, see MacLysaght, but may be a nickname <Ir *cár=grimace* see Ó Muirithe; *crush=bread made from potato starch in place of flour* see Macafee. This may have been a cheaper kind, alternatively, 'crush' may be a mis-spelling of 'curse.'

ahead/scarf   Am Eng
A 8.1 '"You go on ahead and I'll hang around," as the scarf said to the hat.'
Dublin City, South-west
Q 2000 'The John Creedon Show' RTÉ Radio 1, a response from H m of Walkinstown, a variant of which was broadcast on 16/1/2002 to the radio appeal of the same day. See Appendix 2

DOW 1021

cf the riddle published in children's books in the UK and the USA: 'What did the scarf say to the hat? You go on ahead. I'll hang around' Benny *et al* 1998 New York 'Say it Ain't So!' Section I, p. 8, 'necktie'; Brandreth 1980, 1982 rpt. [UK] p. 28, but more usually 'What did the hat say to the scarf? You wrap up and I'll go on ahead' as in Rodgers 1987 London p. 122. Alternative answer 'You hang around while I go on ahead,'or similar, as in Wood *et al* 1986 [UK] n.p.; Girling 1998, London, i WM f p. 40; 'Zig + Zag' 1996, London p. 301, 'space helmet.'

all/cobbler
A 9.1 '"That's all," as the cobbler said when he hit his wife with the last.' [?]
County Tyrone current
Collected in Aug. 1993 from **IC** by FCW in response to the Electronic Database printout, Ulster Dialect Archive, UFTM, entry: 'that's what the cobbler killed his wife with — the last.' **IC**'s words may be slightly different; he commented 'heard now and again.' The Electronic Database entry is from Traynor where Traynor's comment is: 'said when referring to the remaining portion of anything.' The Electronic Database also cites a similar version from the Byers Papers with Byers' comment: 'said when finishing a job of work'

cf '"That is what the cobbler killed his wife with" (the last)' Co. Louth Q 1973 IFC 1917:49 'After finishing work country people would say ...'

cf 'That's what the cobbler threw at the wife, the last.' Q 2000 **IC** who recalls his mother **MC** using it, also Co. Down Q 2000, similar collected in 2001 by FCW from WW 70s retired primary school headmaster

cf *c*. mid-1980s, in a bar during a singsong, the bar man said 'That's the last' AJH's Uncle T. retorted 'Ah, that's what the shoemaker hit the wife with.' Q 2000 Belfast North from AJH in telephone call, later sent in email 17/2/2002

see also Part A 155.

all/old one
A 10.1 '"All the better," as the old one said when she was told that there was no tea but only porter.'
old one= elderly woman
Behan *Borstal Boy*, autobiography, originally published serially from Sept. to Oct. 1956 in the Ireland ed. of the *Sunday Dispatch*, and first in complete form in 1958, 1980 ed. p. 77: 'Maybe it [the book the prison librarian had for him] was one of those banned books by Joyce or one of those fellows, in which case all the better as the old one said when she was told that there was no tea but only porter.'

all sorts/Old Etonian
A 11.1 '"You get all sorts from everywhere," as the Old Etonian said to the Wykehamist, both being con-men.'
Wykehamist=pupil of Winchester, an English public school

Behan *Brendan Behan's Island: an Irish Sketch-book*. 1962 London, Pt. 3 'The Bleak West' p. 115: 'The people of Galway are very proud of being from Galway though, personally, I think that it is silly enough [= quite foolish] being proud of being from anywhere in particular. You get all sorts from everywhere, as the Old Etonian said to the Wykehamist, both being con-men. But proud and all as the Galwegians are, there are pubs where they won't be admitted.'

amphitheatre/gladiator
A 12.1 'One gladiator to another, "A funny thing happened to me on the way to the amphitheatre tonight ..."'
P.T.Q. 1960 Belfast

Note: 'A funny thing happened on the way to the theatre' was a stock introduction used by stand-up comedians. The USA film *A Funny Thing Happened on the Way to the Forum* was not released until 1966.

anyone see *know/old woman*

anything (nothing)/woman
A 13.1 '"Anything is better [than] nothing," as the woman said when she had the small child.'
County Roscommon
Q 1973 IFC 1888:147 C m+

.2 '"Better than nothing," said the woman when she had the small child.'
County Westmeath
Q 1973 IFC 1917:61 C m+ with the comments: 'I have heard them all [this and the others he lists, Part A 83.12. 90.1, 127.1, 173.2, 277.5 & 306.1] locally from time to time. I feel sure there are others which I cannot recall to mind.'

arse/Pat
A 14.1 '"His arse is out," as Pat said when he slept in the narrow bed.'
County Roscommon
Q 1973 IFC 1888:149 C m+.

ass (get up)/cripple   Part B 40
**A 15.1 '"Kick him in the ass," said the cripple.
"Curse him to hell," said the dummy.'**

County Fermanagh current 1972
On a card filed in Almqvist *Irish Wellerisms* 1973– File, with the comment that the wellerism was addressed to a goat eating orange lilies. Collected 1972 by X from Y, who heard it in the parish of Z, Fermanagh, 1972

.2 '"Get up before I kick you out!" said the cripple.'
Belfast North 1940s
Q 2000 i NW f Woodvale Road

see also Part A 259.

assuefaction/Tully
A 15a.1 '"Assuefaction minorates atrocities," as Tully saith of his darling Stoics.'
assuefaction minorates atrocities=accustomed to hardship that hardship is thereby diminished; Tully, Marcus Tullius Cicero [106–43 BC]
James Joyce *Ulysses*, a novel, 1922 Paris, 1986 ed., Part II, Episode 14, p. 322, lines 383–84: 'The tenebrocity of the interior, he proceeded to say, hath not been illuminated by the wit of the septuagint nor so much as mentioned for the Orient from on high Which brake hell's gates visited a darkness that was foraneous. Assuefaction minorates atrocities (as Tully saith of his darling Stoics) and Hamlet his father showeth the prince no blister of combustion.' I am grateful to Estelle Sheehan for help with this.

B

bad company/fox
A 16.1 '"Farewell bad company!" as the fox said when he dhroundet the last of the flays on his back by duckin' his head in the river.'
dhroundet=drowned; flays=fleas; duckin'=ducking
Ulster
Byers Papers Box T4 'S & P' ts T-4-6 p. 69, possibly owing to Hume

.2 '"Farewell to bad company!" as the fox said to the flees.'
flees=fleas
Bigger 'Famous Hillsborough Scholar, Cleric and Antiquary Canon Abraham Hume LLD.' [1814–80] *Belfast News-letter*, 3/8/1926 p. 5: 'He [Hume] also produced for several years *Billy M'Art's Olminick* [*sic*], which raised many a laugh and often applause around the snug firesides

on a winter's evening in "My own County Down" [a song written by Hume, alias 'Billy M'Cart']. Its humour was quaint. "Farewell to bad company, as the fox said to the flees," or "the dark days of December are like Molly Clarke's sweetheart, short and dirty.'"

cf the folktale *TIF* 63 *The Fox Rids Himself of Fleas* [48 versions] and similar motif *MI* K 921 *Fox rids himself of fleas*

Notes: Hume gives a version of the folktale culminating with '"Farewell bad company," siz [= says] he,' which he heard *c.* 1840 from an old man, in *Poor Rabbin's Ollminick [= Almanac] for the toun o' Bilfawst [= Belfast]... 1861...* introduction & p. 25, but not the actual wellerism.
Parody on a formal, for example, deathbed, valediction.

bad man/old maid
A 17.1 'Says the old maid, "A bad man is better than no man."'
old maid=unmarried woman
County Sligo
Q 1973 IFC 1888:112 C f+: 'from the neighbours.'

bad taste/convict
A 18.1 '"I think it is very bad taste using those heavy black caps," as the convict said to the trial judges.'
'O'Brien' *The Best of Myles.* 1968 London, a selection from 'Cruiskeen Lawn' a regular column in a quality daily newspaper, at first in Irish, in *The Irish Times* 1939–66, p. 334: 'I CANNOT stand or understand the sort of typographical shouting that goes on in the hierofrantic sheet, my income tax form, --- This sort of thing "If you are a MARRIED MAN and your wife is living with you …" I think it is very bad taste using those heavy black caps, as the convict said to the trial judges ---'

baird (beard)/fox   Part B 90
A 19.1 '"He has more baird nor brains," as the fox said of the goat.'
baird=beard; nor=than
Ulster
Byers Papers Box T4 ts T-4-5 p. 50. A comment in the same box, p. 64, with a slightly different version runs: 'said of a man who presumes a good deal; without having any real position'

.2 '"More beard than brains," as the fox said of the goat.'

County Leitrim
IFCS 219:83 in a list, mainly of proverbs

cf the fable Aesop 7; *TIF* 31 *The Fox Climbs from the Pit on the Wolf's Back* [45 versions].

balls see *cod*

bastard/parrot   cf Part B 8 also *cf E Eng, †cf Hun
A 20.1 '"You are a square-faced bastard," as the parrot said to the owl.'
County Fermanagh current in 1974
Q 1973(74) IFC 1888:69 C m+: 'common in Fermanagh'

*cf E Eng '"Clipped arse," quoth bunty, (a hen without a rump). Spoken, as several others, when a man upbraids us with what [he] himself is guilty of.' Kelly p. 48 No. 15
†cf Hun 'Bagoly mondja verébnek, hogy nagyfejü' ('The owl tells the sparrow that her head is big.') Paczolay No. 63 p. 319

see also Part A 30, 44 & 92.

beard see *baird*

bed/strawberry   Am Eng
A 21.1 'First strawberry to second strawberry, "If we hadn't been in the same bed we wouldn't have been in the same jam."'
P.T.Q. 1946 Belfast n.p.

DOW 663

cf the riddle published in the UK and the USA 'What did one strawberry say to the other strawberry? If you weren't so fresh you wouldn't be in this jam.' Cray, p. 116 No. 12 collected between 1959 and 1960 from a 6 year old boy. 'What did the mother strawberry say to the baby strawberry? Don't get into a jam' Brandreth 1980, 1982 rpt. [UK], p. 16. 'What did the big strawberry say to the little strawberry? I'm sorry to have got you in this jam.' Rodgers 1987 London, p. 20.

beggars/tramp
A 22.1 '"Beggars can't be choosers," as the tramp said when he found the two left shoes.'
County Roscommon
Q 1973 IFC 1888:148 C m+

Mieder & Tóthné Litovkina p. 49 [but no wellerism]

Note: the proverb 'Beggars can't be choosers' is currently common in English eg. a version noted 19/10/2001 by FCW from LH 60s, retired senior civil servant from Mid-Antrim, who used it when he discovered that supper was not homemade.

belles/vicar
A 23.1 '"The wedding belles were wringing," as the vicar remarked when relating to his wife how a heavy rainstorm had come on just as the party left the church.'
County Leitrim
IFC 1888:105. In response to a broadcast on folklore mentioning wellerisms in 1976 on RTÉ, WS, writer, address 'The Rectory,' so possibly a Church of Ireland clergyman, wrote to DIF and included 18 wellerisms which he had composed [IFC 1888:101–07]. Nine [this and Part A 32, 54, 62, 112, 175, 179, 317 & 319] are included here.

belly (stomach)/hungry man (hungry child)   Fin
A 24.1 '"My belly thinks my throat is cut," as the hungry man said.'
County Wicklow
IFCS 912:50 + in a list, mainly of proverbs. Published in [Carson] Williams 1992 p. 15/2000a p. 22

.2 'As the hungry child said to his mother, "My stomach thinks my throat is cut."'
County Antrim
Q 1973 IFC 1888:33 note that this [.2] appears to be one of several composed for Q 1973 by school children; it is the only one which has been included here

cf Q 2000 'I'm that hungry my belly thinks my throat's cut.' **IC** who recalls his mother **MC** using it, also Q 2000 Co. Down, similar collected in 2001 by FCW from WW 70s, retired primary school headmaster.

bite/toothless dog
A 25.1 '"You bite and I'll bark," said the toothless dog.'
County Cork
Q 1973 IFC 1917:32 + [E & Ir]: 'this is said when you are asked to take part in something while your partner gets all the credit'

Mieder & Tóthné Litovkina p. 7 [but no wellerism].

blin'/needle
A 26.1 '"If 'am blin' 'am na blunt," as the broken needle said to the tailor when he sat on it.'
'am=I'm; blin'=blind; na=not
Boyce ['Paul Peppergrass' b. Donegal 1810, d. Massachusetts 1864] *Shandy M'Guire; Or Tricks Upon Travellers in the North of Ireland*, a novel in the English of Co. Donegal, 1848 New York, 1853 ed., p. 18: '"Ha! Ha!" chuckled the widow at the depth of her penetration; "Ha! My bouchal [= boy], I guessed there was something in the win' [= wind] — if 'am blin' 'am na blunt, as the broken needle said to the tailor when he sat on 't; an' [= and] tell me, Frank, is it the same one [girl he is to marry] still, — Mary Connor?"' Cited in Traynor under 'blind': 'Phr. "If I am blind I am not blunt," I am not totally ineffective, or completely dense. If 'am blin' 'am na blunt," as the broken needle said to the tailor when he sat on it ...'

blowed/bellowses
A 27.1 '"I'll be blowed," as the bellowses said, "if I do that."'
bellowses=bellows
Ulster
Byers Papers Box T4 'S & P' ts T-4-6 p. 76.

bolder/pebble
A 28.1 'As one pebble said to the other on the beach, "Can't you be a little bolder?"'
P.T.Q. 1962 Belfast n.p.

Note: This wellerism, no doubt, links with the proverb 'There's more than one pebble on the beach' and the expression 'S/he's not the only pebble on the beach' and meaning that the person is not the only potential partner. Both proverb and expression are currently common.

boy/woman
A 29.1 '"Good boy yourself," said the woman to her daughter.'
County Cork
Q 1973 IFC 1917:32 + [E & Ir]: 'this is used when anybody, especially a young person, in attempting something, makes a mess or a bad job of it.'

buck/cat   cf Part B 8
A 30.1 '"You're a right buck," as the cat said to his father.'
County Cavan
Q 1973 IFC 1888:86 C m+

see also Part A 20, 44 & 92.

bulls/old man
A 31.1 '"Wee bulls carry high tails," as the old man said on Show Off Sunday when the 5' 2" [five feet two inches] groom marched up the chapel avenue with his 6' [six feet] tall bride.'
wee=small; Show Off Sunday, also *Showing Sunday [Co. Armagh]=the Sunday following a wedding when the bridal party attend the church in which the wedding took place.* Def. from Paterson *Armagh Miscellanea* 1920s– ts Vol. XVIII 'Fews Dialect' p. 129; 6' is approximately 2 metres
County Fermanagh
Q 1973(74) IFC 1888:71 C m+.

business/electrician
A 32.1 '"A shocking business!" as the careless electrician said when he got things mixed.'
County Leitrim
IFC 1888:104 informant/creator WS m+. For note see Part A 23; others from him are Part A 54, 62, 112, 175, 179, 317 & 319.

business/plumber
A 33.1 '"A grand business, if you've a taste for it," as the plumber said.'
Seamus Murphy [1907–75] *Stone Mad,* autobiography of a monumental sculptor, 1966 London, 1977 rpt. p. 185: 'What blinded me ould fella [= father] to put me at [= apprentice me to] this drudgery first day? "'Tis a grand business," says he," all you need to do is cut away what you don't want and the job's finished." Finished is right! You'd want the patience of Job to make anything outa [= out of] this cantankerous bitch of a stone. --- As far as I can see the stopping pot is as indispensable to us as

the glue-pot is to the carpenter … "A grand business, if you've a taste for it," as the plumber said …'

butter/old woman
A 34.1 '"Butter to butter's no kitchen," as the old woman said when she kissed the cow.'
kitchen=a small quantity of well flavoured food added to plain food to make it more appetizing
County Antrim 1960s
Q 2000 i LL f 40s b. & r. near Bushmills

Note: 'Butter to butter is no kitchen' is a common proverb in English and is also found in Irish.

C

care see *paint*

careful/big toe   Am Eng
A 35.1 '"Be careful!" said one big toe to the other, "there's a couple of heels following us."'
Q 2000 'The John Creedon Show' RTÉ Radio 1, email dated 17/1/2002 from the programme's researcher listing all the 5 broadcast responses and 4 others to the appeal which was broadcast on 16/1/2002. See Appendix 2

cf the riddle 'Two toes were walking, what did one say to the other? I think there's a heel following us.' Lynch p. 60, collected from a 12 year old Co. Wicklow girl between 1977 and 1978, also collected in GB: 'What did the little toe say to the big toe? There's a big heel following us.' Rodgers 1987 London, p. 84

DOW 462.

catch/man
A 36.1 '"I didn't quite catch that," said the man with no hands.'
County Londonderry
Q 1973? IFC 1888:27.

chance/'S'

A 37.1 '"I'll chance it," said 'S' to the fart when he shit in his pants.'
County Roscommon
Q 1973 IFC 1888:145 C m+: 'Used when somebody is going to take a chance at doing something.' For Correspondent's additional comment see Part A 5.1

Note: 'S' substitutes for the surname given.

change (clane)/old woman (man) Part B 103 also Dan, Dut, *Est, Fin, Ger, Nor, Scots, Swe
A 38.1 '"Nothing like a change of linen," as the old woman said when she turned her shift.'
shift=undergarment
County Wicklow
IFCS 912:50 + in a list, mainly of proverbs. Published in [Carson] Williams 1992 p. 111/2000a p. 97

.2 '"There's nothing like a clane thing," as the man said when he turned his shirt after seven years.'
clane=clean
County Meath
Q 1973 IFC 1917:54 C f+

DOW 203; 'Cheviot' p. 4; Hislop p. 2
Est '"Hea, kui jälle puhas pesu ihu peal," ütles vanamutt, kui musta särgi pahupidi pööras ja uuesti selga pani.' ('"So good to have clean linen on your body again," said the old woman when she turned her dirty shift and put it on again.') Heard but not recorded by Arvo Krikmann email attachment to FCW

Note: the proverb 'Nothing like a change' is currently common.

chimney see *red chimney*

Christian/Devil (Deil, Divil)
A 39.1 '"You're a very coarse Christian," as the devil said to the hedgehog.'
coarse=uncouth
County Tyrone
Patrick Weston Joyce 1910, 1991 rpt., Ch. 5 'The Devil and his "Territory"' p. 60

.2 '"He's a coorse Christian," as the deil said when he stroked the hurtchin.'
coorse=coarse, uncouth; hurtchin=hedgehog
Ulster
Byers Papers Box T4 ts T-4-6 p. 69

.3 '"He's a coorse christian," as the divil said to the hurchin.'
hurchin=hedgehog
County Donegal
Traynor 1954 under 'hurchin': 'saying (McD)' ie. Canon McD, parish priest

cf '*Boys-a-dear but you're the coorse Christian,*/ quo' she,/ An' me, only a cub, admiring the cut of her.' Opening of the poem 'Johnny-3-Tongues' Co. Antrim, McGuckian 2002, p. 57

Notes: 'first part common' [as in **.2** & **.3**], a comment collected in Feb. 1994 by FCW from **IC**. For an example of 'a coorse Christian' in context in dialogue see 'Tullyneil' 1940, p. 52.

Christian/priest see *Part B 51*

Christmas/girl
A 40.1 '"You won't feel it now till Christmas," as the girl said to the soldier.'
Dublin City late 1930s
Q 1973 IFC 1917:15 C m+: 'The following [this and Part A 163, 173.7, 218.1, 294.1 & 329] were all heard in Dublin in the late 30s in an all male office in the civil service and were all used more for slang than for anything else'

Note: 'Christmas/girl' is immediately followed by 'Lent/girl' Part A 163.

clane thing see *change*

cod (balls)/woman
A 41.1 '"It's all a cod!" as the woman said when she went to milk the bull.'
IFC 1917:98 on a sheet written in 1986 by SMcR f+, DIF student from the USA
.2 '"It is all a balls," said the woman when she milked the cow.'

County Cork
Q 1973 IFC 1917:32 + [E & Ir]

cf the motif *MI* J 1905 *Absurd ignorance about milking animals.*

commander-in-chief/Lord French
A 42.1 '"Well," as Lord French says, "what's the use of being Commander-in-Chief if you can't appoint your own staff?"'
Gogarty *Rolling down the Lea: a pageant of legendary Irish people and places.* 1950 Great Britain, 1982 ed., p. 17: used in response to encountering a quick-witted explanation

Note: Lord French=John Denton Pinkstone French [1852–1925] field marshal and commander-in-chief to the British Expeditionary Force in France and Belgium 1914–15, who resigned after being criticised as indecisive. He then became commander-in-chief of the Home Forces and subsequently Lord Lieutenant of Ireland 1918–21, when he again resigned.

company see *bad company*

company/physiology professor
A 43.1 '"As the physiology professor said, "Two's company, three's a deformity."'
P.T.Q. 1970 Belfast p. 51

Mieder & Tóthné Litovkina p. 221 [but no wellerism].

complexion/raven   cf Part B 8 also Sp & *cf Geo, †cf Scots,
    ‡cf Wel, §cf Mediaeval Dan etc.
A 44.1 '"Thy complexion is black," says the raven.'
O'Donoghue *The Humour of Ireland.* 1894 London, p. 420, in a list titled 'Selected Irish Proverbs, Etc.,'— most items are proverbs

*cf Geo ('One raven tells the other, "You croaker!"') Paczolay p. 321
†cf Scots '"Black arse!" quoth the pot to the cauldron.' Kelly p. 43 No. 97. Cited in Walker p. 40
‡cf Wel '"Tinddu!" meddai'r fran wrth y wylan, a hithau yn dinddu ei hunan.' ('"Black-bottomed!" the crow said to the seagull and she herself being black-bottomed.') Paczolay p. 321
§cf Mediaeval Dan etc. '"Wee wordhe teg so sort tw æst," sagde grydhen til kædhelen ("Woe unto you, so black you are," said the pot to the

74

kettle.)' Kjær p. 580 No. D 1079 with a comment that it is found in European mediaeval tradition outside the Danish source. For others with cooking utensils see Paczolay No. 63

Note: 'The pot calling the kettle black,' meaning one person is as bad as the other, is currently common and cf 'It is a case of the pot calling the kettle black face' Co. Westmeath Q 1973 IFC 1917:60

see also Part A 20, 30 & 92.

contention/Michael Mulally
A 45.1 '"Contention is better than solitude," mused Michael Mulally, taking a wife to him at five-an'-fifty.'
MacManus [c. 1868–1960] *Heavy Hangs the Golden Bough*, a collection of Donegal folktales and legends retold with a saying, usually a proverb, after every one headed 'The Old Word,' ie. a literal translation of the Irish word for proverb 'seanfhocal,' 1950 New York, p. 198. The book contains one other wellerism, also misogynist, see Part A 296.1

Note: the proverb 'Strife is better than loneliness' is common in English and Irish.

corner/wall   Am Eng, ?E Eng
A 46.1 '"So long, see you at the corner," as one wall said to the other.'
Q 2000 'The John Creedon Show' RTÉ Radio 1, a response, a variant of which was broadcast on 16/1/2002, to the radio appeal of the same day. See Appendix 2

cf the riddle: 'What did one wall say to the other wall? Meet you at the corner.' Lynch p. 60, collected from a 12 year old Co. Wicklow girl between 1977 and 1978, also collected in GB see Opie 1959 p. 81, and in the USA see Cray 1964 p. 116 No. 14

DOW 817.

cowl' (coul, shelter)/madman (hare)   *Est,* Ger, Nor &
   †cf Am Eng
A 47.1 '"Cowl' without," as the madman sayd when he hid behine the winnel-sthroe.'
cowl' without=cold outside; behine=behind; winnel- cf *winnle sthroe=a dry, thin, withered stalk of grass* [def. Byers Papers], *solitary straw accidentally left uncut after reaping*

'M'Cart' [Canon Abraham Hume 1814–80] *Poor Rabbin's Ollminick [= Almanac] for the toun o' Bilfawst [= Belfast]... 1861 ...* , a pastiche, n.d. [1860 or 61] Belfast; Dublin, under Jan. Cited in Patterson

.2 "'Coul wi'out," as the madman said when he hid behind the winnle sthroe.'
coul wi'out=cold outside
County Londonderry
Byers Papers Box T4 'S & P' ts T-4-6 p. 69. Published in Carson Williams 2001a p. 14

.3 "'You can't beat the shelter," as the hare said when he sat behind the tráinín.'
tráinín <Ir tráithnín=a straw
County Kilkenny
Q 1973 IFC 1917:78 C f+

*Est 'Vaene mees, kes vihma käes, ma ikka olen ulu all," ütles rebane, kui läks püstilükatud äkke alla vihmavarju.' ('"Poor man who has to stay in the rain while I have a shelter over my head," said a fox and sheltered under an upright harrow.') EKM ERA, RKM II 206, 226 (1) 1965
†cf Am Eng '"How I pity the poor fellows whose business requires them to be out on a night like this," said the policeman, looking out from the side door.' *DOW* 952

cf the Sc Gae retort 'Ho! Ho! Thug mi 'n car asad an tràths'! (Ho! Ho! I've cheated you this time!) (Uist) The saying of a fool who sheltered from a shower of rain in a doorway.' Meek No. 534

cf the folktale AT 71* *Hare Vainly Seeks Shelter From Reed.*

cry (noise, nize)/Deil (man, butcher, De'il, Devil)   Part B 107 also
    Am Eng, Dut, E Eng, **Est*, Fin, Ger, †*Lit,* Nor, Pol, Scots,
    Sc Gae, Swe, ‡*Lat* or *Rus*
A 48.1 "'Great cry an' little wul," as the Deil said when he pluckt the pig.'
wul=wool; pluckt=plucked
Ulster current 1854

'H' 'Rustic Proverbs Current in Ulster.' *Ulster Journal of Archaeology,* 2 (1854), p. 129. Probably the version cited in Byers 1904 Belfast p. 41 [sole wellerism]: 'When a man makes great boasting of what he is going to do, but in the end accomplishes little the Ulsterman says "'Great cry … the pig."' This publication is a fuller version of a lecture Byers delivered to the members of The Belfast Natural History and Philosophical Society [now known as The Belfast Society] 1/12/1903

.2 '"Great cry and little wool," as the man said when he shaved the pig.'
Fyvie Mayo *Old Stories & Sayings of Great Britain & Ireland.* n.d. but early 20th century, London, p. 50 where 'man' is glossed as 'devil'

.3 '"Great cry and little wool," as the man said when he clipped the sow.'
County Cavan
IFCS 968:64 in a list, mainly of proverbs

.4 '"Great cry and little wool," as the butcher said when he shaved the pig.'
Ulster
Byers Papers as cited in the Electronic Database, Ulster Dialect Archive, UFTM

.5 '"Great cry but little wul," as the De'il said when he plucked the pig.'
wul=wool
Anon. *National Proverbs: Ireland.* 1913 London, p. 65

.6 '"Big cry and little wool," as the deil said when he clipt the pig.'
clipt=clipped
Ulster
Byers Papers as cited in the Electronic Database, Ulster Dialect Archive, UFTM

.7 '"Great noise and little wool," as the devil said when he was shearing a pig.'
Patrick Weston Joyce 1910, 1991 rpt. Ch. 5 'The Devil and his "Territory"' p. 61

.8 '"Great nize an' little wull," as the deil said when he pluckt the pig.'

nize=noise; wull=wool
Ulster
Byers Papers Box T4 'S & P' ts T-4-6 p. 65

.9 '"Great nize an' little wull," as the deil said when he shaved the pig.'

Ulster
Byers Papers Box T4 'S & P' ts T-4-6 p. 65

.10 '"But you're all noise and little wool," as the man said shaving the pig.'

O'Farrell 1980, 1983 rpt. in Ch. titled 'Fights and Threats' p. 58

cf 'Like the fellow that was clipping the sow, "Great tears but no wool"' County Cavan IFCS 993:105–06 in a list, mainly of proverbs

cf 'Great Cry & Little Wool (a Tithe Romance)' Leinster. Context: title of account about a way of avoiding paying tithes [= taxes to the establishment episcopalian church, against the paying of which there was 19th century agitation]. The rector accepted a cow in lieu of cash but failed to sell it. Kennedy p. 147

cf '"Great cry and little wool"' used as an epithet to an introduction of a *scena* about Dublin street criers titled 'New Potatoes, An Irish Melody. "*Great cry and little wool.*" Old Saying.' The book's frontispiece is an engraving by the author of Katty, the potato seller whose unfortunate story is the subject of the piece. Lover, 1831 p. 166. Also Lover same title [?2nd Series] n.d. New Edition, London: Ward etc., p. 353, the final words of the introduction to a very full version, which mentions the Bog of Allen, of the folktale 'Little Fairly.' 'So I shall conclude this little introduction, which I only thought a becoming flourish of trumpets for introducing my hero, by placing *Little Fairly* before my readers, and I hope that they will not think, in the words of another adage, that I have given them *great* cry and *little* wool.'

cf 'Great cry and little wool' Co. Sligo IFCS 172:152 in a list, mainly of proverbs, some of which have a literary ring
DOW 260–62 & 880; *Addenda* 33; Kelly p. 29 No. 301; Ramsay p. 7; 'Cheviot' p. 244; Henderson p. 132; Murison p. 92; Nicolson p. 319 No. 10
*Est '"Palju kisa ja vähe villu," ütles vanatühi, kui siga niitis.' ('"Much cry and little wool," said the ogre/devil when he sheared the pig.') EKM ERA, H[folklore collection (1860–1906) of Jakob Hurt] III 7, 201 (12) 1889 and four others up to 1969

78

†*Lit* '"Daug riksmo, mazai vilnos," pasake venikas kirpdamas kiaule.'
('"Much cry, little wool," said the devil when he shore the pig.'
') Kazys Grigas has seen this in LTR, email from Vita Ivanauskaitë 24/5/2000
‡*Lat* or *Rus* variant with 'cat' rather than 'pig' p.c. from Lilija Kudirkiene in same email from Vita Ivanauskaitë 24/5/2000

cf the folktale AT 1037 *The Ogre Shears a Pig* 'instead of sheep' and the related motif *MI* K 171.5 *Deceptive division of animals for shearing* 'the trickster shears the sheep; the dupe the pig'

Note: '"Great cry and little wool," as the devil said when he was shaving the pig,' was used as one of the ten, later five, examples on Q 2000. See Appendix 1.

cut/Cutty   *cf ?E Eng, †cf Ger
A 49.1 '"That's the cut!" says Cutty, when he cut his mother's throat.'
Lover *Rory O'More, A National Romance*, first published as a play and a novel in 1837 in London [which followed Lover's popular song *Rory O'More* composed in 1826] 1898 ed. Westminster p. 37. The wheel of the coach had broken, leaving the passengers stranded by the roadside:
'"Up wid [with] you now on the grey, Hoolaghan, your sowl [= soul], and powdher [= powder] away like shot!"
"What's that he's saying, sir, about powder and shot?" said the lady in alarm.
"He's only giving directions to the coachman, madam," said the young traveller.
--- "The horses 'ill [= will] stay quiet enough while you're gone," said Rory; "here, gi' [= give] me your fut [= foot] — I'll lift you on the baste [= beast]." ---
"There now," said Rory, "you're up! And away wid you! Jist [= just] be into town in no time, and back in less. 'That's the cut! Says Cutty, when he cut his mother's throat.'"
"What's that he's saying, sir, about cutting throats?' said the lady.
"Nothing, madam, I assure you, you need be alarmed at," said the traveller.
"Indeed you need not make yourself onaisy, [= uneasy] ma'am, in the laste [= least]," said Rory, after he had placed Hoolaghan on horseback.
"It will be all over with you soon now."
The lady shuddered at the phrase, but spoke not.' Also in Mair p. 65, but probably a citation from Lover
*cf ?E Eng '"That's the kick," said Paddy when he kicked his wife into the fire.' *DOW* 668

†cf Ger 'Das war getroffen, sagte der Jung, da schmiss er seiner Mutter ein Aug aus dem Kopf.' ['"That was hit," said the boy as he knocked an eye out of his mother's head.'] Simrock No. 10645.

cut/surgeon
A 50.1 'As one surgeon said to the other who was operating, "May I cut in?"'
P.T.Q. 1961 Belfast n.p.

cutbacks/butcher
A 51.1 '"We'll have to make some cutbacks," as the butcher said when he cut off his rump with the chopper.' [?]
Q 2000 i RÓB m+ as he recalls hearing it the week before he told FCW, in mid-April 2002, on RTÉ in a literary piece read on the radio by a man.

D

dab/Daniel
A 52.1 '"Dab!" says Daniel.'
'A Real Paddy' [Pierce Egan 1772–1849] *Real Life in Ireland*, a novel set in Ireland, 1820 London, 4th ed. 1829 Ch. 15, p. 165: 'You must lay, said the jolly *first luff*, bread and butter fashion, or as we sailors have it, *dab says Daniel*. We never apologise on board a man of war, our means of accommodating a friend are always rough and ready, though they may be small, so make the best of your birth.' [= berth] Cited in Partridge p. 41: 'was a nautical c[atch] p[hrase] of *c.* 1790–1860 applied to "lying bread and butter fashion" in bed or bunk.'

dam/assistant
A 53.1 '"One dam thing after another," said the assistant as he followed the professor out the door.'
P.T.Q. 1929 Belfast p. 71

Mieder & Tóthné Litovkina pp. 127–28.
dash/Samuel Morse
A 54.1 '"Dash it all!" as Samuel Morse said when he invented the telegraph code, but he was a bit dotty anyway.'
County Leitrim
IFC 1888:107 informant/creator WS m+. For note see Part A 23; others from him are Part A 32, 62, 112, 175, 179, 317 & 319.

day/Adam
A 55.1 '"Let's call it a day," as Adam said to Eve when he saw the first sunrise.'
County Donegal
Q 1973(75) IFC 1888:23 C m+: 'I had difficulty in finding any worthwhile wellerisms in the district. Most people drew a blank when the matter was raised …'

dead see *stone dead*
Dear see *God/Old Mrs Davis*
dear see *me/monkey*

deeper/geologist
A 56.1 'Geologist, closely examining rock formation high up a cliff, as he steps over the edge, "I must go deeper into this."'
P.T.Q. 1929 Belfast p. 4.

devil/Ned Ennis
A 57.1 '"You are a devil, my dear," says Ned Ennis to the goat.'
County Dublin
IFCS 794:467 in a list with the comment: 'Long ago if the old people had trouble with cattle or anything they would say, "You are … the goat."'
Published in [Carson] Williams 1992 p. 32/2000a p. 40

Note: the personal name Ennis is found in Counties Meath and Westmeath, see MacLysaght.

Devil/skull see *hands*

diamonds/card player's wife
A 58.1 '"Diamonds for life," said the cardplayer's wife.'
County Leitrim
IFCS 222:493a in a list, mainly of proverbs. Published in [Carson] Williams 1992 p. 96/2000a p. 88

.2 '"Diamonds for your life," says the cardplayer's wife.'
County Cavan
Q 1973 IFC 1888:90 C m+ the first in a short list titled : 'Playing card games:-'.

Dick/Cordry
A 59.1 '"Elegant Dick," said Cordry.'
County Cork
Q 1973(75) IFC 1911:72 C f+ [E & Ir], a nun.

divil (way)/Punch
A 60.1 '"Divil may care," says Punch when he lost mass, "I'll be in time for church."'
Lover *Rory O'More: A National Romance,* first published as a novel and play in 1836–37 [which were shortly preceded by a song] all London, 1898 ed., p. 252: '"Forgot! — I suppose you forgot to go to mass! — ho, ho, ho! What a loss you are to the flock this day! — what'll Father Kinshela do without you?"
"None o' your humbuggin,' Sol," said Regan.
"Is it me humbug?" said the tinker with a sneer, as if rejoicing in the power he affected to disclaim. "Come along, man; we're late enough. Never mind chapel today; chapel will wait till next Sunday. Don't you know what Punch said? — 'Divil may care,' says Punch when he lost mass; 'I'll be in time for church.'" And so saying, the tinker led the way to the valley, and Regan followed in silence.'
Note: Sol=Solomon, a tinker. A Punch and Judy show at a fair is mentioned earlier on p. 167

.2 '"Divil may care," as Punch said when he lost mass, 'There's more churches nor one.'"
Lover *Handy Andy: A Tale of Irish Life*, a novel, the earliest edition of the novel was 1842 but it was previously serialised in *Bentley's Miscellany*, both London. In the novel Murtough Murphy was an attorney and friend of the squire's with whom Furlong the agent was staying. n.d. 'Cheap Illustrated Edition' Charing Cross, p. 38: '"Well, now for a start to the river, and won't we have sport! You English-taught gentlemen have only one fault on the face of the earth — you're too fond of business — you make yourselves slaves to propriety — there's no fun in you."
"I beg pawdon [= pardon] — there," said Furlong, "we like fun in good time."
"Ay [= yes]; but there's where we beat you, " said Murphy, triumphantly; "the genuine home-bred Irishman makes time for fun sooner than anything else — we take our own way and live the longer."
"Ah! You lose your time — though — excuse me; you lose your time indeed."

82

"Well, 'divil may care,' as Punch said when he lost mass, 'there's more churches nor one,' says he, and that's the way with us," said Murphy. "Come, Dick, get the fishing lines ready; heigh for the salmon fishery!'

.3 '"That's the way to do it!" said Punch when he lost mass and was in time for church.'
County Laois pre-1942
Q 1973(75) IFC1917:78 C f+: 'a common one with my own grandmother, who lived in Stradbally, [Co.] Laois, died *c.* 1942 aged 80. Used it frequently when we did anything she wanted done but maybe took our times at it. (Had it any connection with the *Punch* magazine, I wonder?)'

cf '"The devil a bit," says Punch' Partridge p. 42: 'very approximately 1850–1910'

Note: in the puppet show, after Punch's being hung, the devil arrives for him

see also Part A 190.

done/blacksmith
A 61.1 '"Well done, mother!" says the blacksmith when the tooth was out.'
Patrick Weston Joyce 1910, 1991 rpt., p. 193: '"Well done, mother!" says the blacksmith when the tooth was out. This is how it was pulled. He tied one end of a strong string round the tooth, and the other end to the horn of the anvil, and made the old woman keep her head back so as to tighten the string. "Asy [= easy] now mother," says he. Then, taking the flaming horseshoe from the fire with the tongs he suddenly thrust it towards her face. Anyone can finish the story.'

done/cook
A 62.1 '"Couldn't be done," as the cook said sticking a fork in the joint.'
County Leitrim
IFC 1888:105 informant/creator WS m+. For note see Part A 23; others from him are Part A 32, 54, 112, 175, 179, 317 & 319.

done/Old Dunne (Auld Dunne, Ould Dunne)
A 63.1 '"Well done!" said old Dunne when young Dunne was born.'
County Cavan

Q 1973 IFC 1888:87 C m+ from same Correspondent as 'power/old Power' p. 86 [Part A 241.8]

.2 as .1
County Roscommon
Q 2000 **JG** who also on the same occasion in Sept. 2001 contributed a version of 'power/Old Power' [Part A 241.2]

.3 '"Well done!" said Old Dunne when young Dunne was born.'
County Roscommon
Q 1973(74) IFC 1888:69 C m+ i PH m+, the same informant as for 'power/Old Power' [Part A 241.5] which immediately precedes 'done/Old Dunne'

.4 '"Well done!" said auld Dunne when young Dunne was born.'
County Tipperary current in 1978
Q 1973(78) IFC 2027:166 C m+ same Correspondent as 'line/auld Lyons' p. 167 [Part A 171] 'still very popular in the Thurles area; it is quoted when a task has been completed or when something prais [*prais* <Ir *pras?=quick*] has been accomplished'

.5 '"Well done!" said ould Dunne when young Dunne was born.'
County Meath late 1930s
Q 2000 EO'B m 70s, retired primary school teacher: 'This is one which just came to mind when I was writing [the list to send to me, and which I then asked for details of] — I haven't heard it for 50 or 60 years. I was at national school [as a pupil] when I heard it last, so we are talking about 1938 or 1939. Isn't it amazing that it should come to mind after all those years? My recollection of its use is that it was just an emphatic way of saying "Well done." And, do you know something? I think there's another similar one at the back of my mind …' FCW suggested that it might be 'power/old Power,' which it was, see Part A 241.6

doubt/Croker (C. of Ballinagarde)
A 64.1 '"I doubt it," said Croker.'
County Cork
Q 1973 IFC 1911:72 C f+ [E & Ir], a nun. This follows the wellerism: 'Croker was a Protestant living in Ballinagarde. When the minister was consoling him that he was going to a better land (when he was dying) he said "I doubt it!"'

.2 '"I doubt it," said Croker of Ballinagarde.'
Limerick City mid-1920s
Q 1973 IFC1917:12 C m+: 'Croker was a landlord in Co. Limerick who had lived a gay [= rakish] life … As he lay dying his parson told him that he was going to a better place, to which Croker rejoined as above'

Notes: his story was given in the *The Irish Times*, Sept. 2000. For the Croker lineage see 'Croker of Ballynagarde' Burke ... *Landed Gentry of Ireland*, pp. 149–50. Ballynagarde is near Grange, in the west of the county, and the Croker in question is likely John Croker [1784–1858] about whom there is other folklore, such as that his ghost is seen, p.c. from Dáithí Ó hÓgáin 30/9/2002, who also told FCW that it is said that, when he was dying, Croker was taken outside so that he could see his pleasant estate and that the wellerism is current and well-known in west Co. Limerick and is used when one wishes to show that one is querying the truth about anything. See also Ó hÓgáin 2001, footnote 18, pp. 130–31.

dough/monkey   Am Eng
A 65.1 '"It all runs into dough," as the monkey said when he pissed in the till.'
dough=American slang for money but familiar in Ireland at least since 1914
County Down 1999
Q 2000 **TC**: 'said of someone with the ability to make money from the most unlikely of projects. Lurgan area.' For his further comments see Part A 118

DOW 840; *Addenda* 97

Note: the use of American English slang 'dough' for 'money' may indicate the immediate origin of this wellerism, although the word 'dough' has been used here for some time outside set expressions.

down/fowler
A 66.1 '"Down!" said the fowler when he shot the duck.'
Q 1973 IFC 1917:14 C m+: 'Heard in Dublin city in the mid thirties in a card school where all the players were from outside Dublin. The expression would be used by a person having the fall of play when he would be beating a player who had fought into him.'

drilling/woodwork teacher

A 67.1 '"Drilling is a bit boring," said the woodwork teacher to the class.'
Q 2000 'The John Creedon Show' RTÉ Radio 1, a response to the radio appeal made on the previous day on the envelope of a letter from PJ m. which was broadcast on 17/1/2002. It seems that there were several from this Correspondent; see Part A 305 and Appendix 2.

drop see *little/woman*

duck/goose
A 68.1 '"Duck!" said the Goose.'
County Roscommon
Q 1973 IFC 1888:145 C m+: 'used when someone knocks their head against a low door frame.' For Correspondent's additional comment see Part A 5.1

cf the warning 'Duck or grouse' painted above a low archway in Whitby, Yorkshire, noted 2001.

dust/fly   Part B 71 also Am Eng, E Eng, Fr, Ger, Swe &
    ?*Classical Greek
A 69.1 '"Isn't [it] I can raise the dust?" said the fly behind the coach.'
County Galway
IFCS 768:158 + in a list, mainly of proverbs, written down by a schoolgirl

.2 '"Isn't it great the dust I'm raising?" said the fly as he rode on the carriage axle.'
County Donegal *c.* 1935
Q 1973 IFC 1888:17 C m+: 'heard in parish of Glenfin … about 1935'

.3 '"What a dust we kick up!" as the fly said to the cart-wheel.'
County Sligo
IFCS 172:157–58 in a list, mainly of proverbs, some of which have a literary ring. Published in [Carson] Williams 1992 p. 75/2000a p. 73

DOW 346–49
*Classical Greek, Aesop — see Taylor 1962 fac., 1985 rpt., p. 213.

E

ears/radio
A 70.1 '"It'll take ears to give you a look-in," said the radio to the blank TV screen.'
Q 2000 'The John Creedon Show' RTÉ Radio 1, email dated 17/1/2002 from the programme's researcher listing all the five broadcast responses and four others to the appeal which was broadcast on 16/1/2002. See Appendix 2.

earth/sun
A 71.1 '"What on earth are you looking at?" said the sun to the moon.'
Q 2000 'The John Creedon Show' RTÉ Radio 1, email dated 17/1/2002 from the programme's researcher listing all the five broadcast responses and four others to the appeal which was broadcast on 16/1/2002. See Appendix 2.

eggs/hungry hen
A 72.1 '"I am not born to keep on laying eggs when given no corn," said the hungry hen.'
County Donegal
Q 1973 IFC 1888:20 C m+.

en'/man
A 73.1 '"Well, that's the en' of that," as the man said when the bottom fell out of the wee pot.'
en'=end; wee=little
Ulster
Byers Papers Box T4 'S & P' ts T-4-6 p. 76

cf the proverb ' *'Sé críoch an phoitín a thóin do thuitim as'* ['The pot's fate is for its bottom to fall out'] Dinneen under 'poitín.'

end/old maid   Dan, *Est*, Fin, Nor, Swe
A 74.1 '"That'll be the end of us all," as the old maid [said] when she saw the wedding.'
old maid=unmarried woman
County Louth
IFCS 672:265 in a list, mainly of proverbs. Published in [Carson] Williams 1992 p. 12/2000a p. 105

cf "''Tis before us all," like Johanna Carroll said about getting married'
Co. Kerry Q 1973 IFC 1917:18 C m+: 'Johanna was still a spinster! I
heard my father say it — the lady was local'

cf 'That could be the end of us all' Q 2000 **IC** whose mother **MC** uses it
if, for instance, listening to the news

*Est '"Seda teed peame kõik käima!" ohkas vanatüdruk pulmarongi
nähes.' ('"We'll all have to take this road once!" sighed a spinster
watching a wedding procession.') EKM ERA, RKM II 84, 467 (5) 1959
and two others.

even/Stephen
**A 75.1 '"Now we are even," quoth Stephen when he gave his
wife six blows for one.'**
Swift *Journal to Stella*. 1766–68, 1948 ed., Vol. I, p. 171, context: letter
XIV, dated Jan. 16, 1711: '... coming down the Mall, who should come
towards me but Patrick [a servant], and gives me five letters out of his
pocket. I read the superscription of the first --- of the fifth and last ... this
is our MD [letter from Mrs Esther Johnson 'Stella' and her companion
Mrs Rebecca Dingley] and it began the most impudently in the world,
thus: *Dear Presto* [ie. Swift]*, We are even thus far*. Now we are even,
quoth Stephen, when he gave his wife six blows for one. I received your
ninth four days after I had sent my thirteenth. ...Why did you not recant
at the end of your letter when you got my eleventh, tell me that huzzies
base, were we even then, were we, sirrah?' ref. via *Addenda* where it is
cited under 44

cf primary school children's retort 'Even stevens' used to acknowledge
that a wrong has been redressed, Ballymoney, Co. Antrim, 1950s
[personal observation and use]; same used in same way in Cork city
among primary school children in the 1970s Informant: GMcI, f. b. 1970
Cork city, and reared there, academic [collected 10/1/2000]. The same
currently used among primary school children in Belfast when two
players or teams score equally. Informant FCW's younger son FC-W b.
1989, collected 6/1/2000; 'Even stevens' also said after something had
been evenly divided or distributed by school children in the 1990s in
Belfast. Informant FCW's daughter CW b. 1980 collected 6/1/2000.
IC as self [ie. FCW] 'You said it if you done something back' [at
primary school]. All collected by FCW.

everyone (man)/ass (bull)   Am Eng, E Eng

A 76.1 '"Let everyone mind themselves," as the ass said when he leaped into a flock of chickens.'

Patrick Weston Joyce 1910, 1991 rpt., Ch. 7 'Grammar and Pronunciation' p. 89: 'The distributive *every* requires to be followed by pronouns in the singular but this rule is broken, even by well-known English writers 'Everyone for themselves' occurs in Robinson Crusoe and in Ireland plurals are almost universally used. *"Let every one mind themselves* as the ass said when he leaped into a flock of chickens."'

.2 '"Every man for himself," as the ass brayed and he leppin' into the flock of hens.'

leppin '= leaping

O'Farrell 1980, 1983 rpt., in Ch. titled 'Fights and Threats' p. 59

.3 '"Everyone for himself," said the bull when he jumped into the flock of goslings.'

County Tipperary

Q 1973 IFC 1917:42 C m+

DOW 168 & 800; *Addenda* 20

Mieder & Tóthné Litovkina p. 81.

everything see *little/woman*

eye/farmer

A 77.1 '"Every eye forms its own beauty," said the farmer when he kissed the cow.'

Q 2000(02) i FH m+ 60s, who heard his father PH [b. 1899] using it. PH owned a pub in Chapleizod, Co. Dublin, and was originally from Co. Sligo

see also Part A 287.

eye/man

A 78.1 '"Better out than your eye," as the man said when he ...' [broke wind]

Q 2000 **JG** who, in telling FCW the wellerism, did not complete it

see also Part A 134.

F

false promises/sober man
A 79.1 '"You don't get many false promises or handshakes over a plate of porridge," said the sober man.'
County Monaghan
Q 1973 IFC 1888:73 C m+, customs and excise officer: 'This saying I heard as a child on the borders of Monaghan and Fermanagh. Recently I heard it again as an indictment of the insincerity that comes out of excessive drinking. A sober observer reminded me of this quotation after attending a wedding party at which the "wine" flowed freely, and with it all the false promises and friendship. Local usage is in the Threemilehouse, Tydavnet areas of Co. Monaghan. Really an indictment of drink in excess. Author unknown.'

fancy see *taste/farmer*

far/man
A 80.1 '"So far so good," as the man was heard to say when he jumped off the skyscraper.'
Belfast area *c.* 1980
Q 2000 **TC**: 'I believe I may also have heard this [Part A 137] used in an American film although "cactus bush" replaced "bed of nettles" and the other ['far/man'] which may also have originated in a film.'

far/passenger
A 81.1 'Male passenger to young, attractive conductress on a bus, "How far can I go for fourpence?"'
P.T.Q. 1970 Belfast p. 51.

fill (mate)/Blind Dan (Bloomfield the basket maker)
A 82.1 'As Blind Dan used to say, "Ate your fill and you'll never be bate, and it's nobody's business how much you ate."'
ate=eat; bate=beaten
County Down *c.* 1933
Q 1973 IFC 1888:45 C m+: '... other [see also Part A 121] expressions of opinion or words of wisdom quoted from characters of the past "As Blind Dan used to say ... you ate" said to encourage a shy eater to dip in! All these I heard about forty years ago but they are not much used here nowadays. I can't think of any such expressions attributed to birds or animals'

.2 '"Ate your mate and you can't be bate," says Bloomfield the basket maker.'
County Cavan
Q 1973 IFC 1888:89 C m+.

fire (one)/fox (monkey, tod)   Part B 189 also Am Eng, E Eng, Ger, Scots
A 83.1 '"That will be a good fire," said the fox when he wet in the snow and saw the steam.'
County Cork
Q 1973(74) IFC 1917:31 C m: 'something that is not going well'

.2 '"When that kindles it'll be a fire," as the fox said when he wet on the snow.'
County Meath
Q 1973 IFC 1917:54 C f+: 'one would say this to someone making a very bad job of lighting the fire — all smoke and no blaze'

.3 "That will be a good fire when it kindles," said the fox said when he p–d in the snow.'
County Roscommon
Q 1973 IFC 1917:55 C f+: 'said on looking at fire that shows no sign of kindling (before the days of firelighters)'

.4 "That will be a good fire when it kindles," as the fox said when he peed in the snow.'
County Cavan
McKieran *By Claddagh's Banks, A History of Swanlinbar and District from earliest times.* n.d. [*c.* 2000] [?local], Ch. 12 'Our Colourful Speech,' p. 92: 'When someone wanted to quash a rumour and felt it was insulting to his intelligence, he had a crushing ready-made weapon: "That will be a good fire ... in the snow.' I thank Ciarán Ó Duibhín for this ref.

.5 '"That'll be a fire when it kindles," as the fox said when he shit in the snow.'
County Cavan
Q 1973 IFC 1888:89 C m+

.6 "That'll make a fine fire," as the fox said when he pissed on the snow.'
County Roscommon

IFC 1771:11 collected by **JD** from WR m [d. 1973]

.7 'As the fox said when he pissed on the snow, "That'll make a fire if it lights."'
County Fermanagh 1970s
Glassie *Passing the Time, Folklore and History of an Ulster Community.* 1982 Dublin, p. 276: 'Clever chat becomes "crack" through the logical, free play of wit. Crack snaps with humorous figures of speech. The convention of attributing proverbs generally bids and particularly eases Wellerisms into talk. At last comprehending: "I see, said the blind man, You're a liar, says the dummy, Give him a kick in the arse, says the cripple." [Part A 259.30] Starting a fire: "As the fox said … lights."'

.8 'As the monkey said when it pissed in the snow and looked back, "That'll be a great fire when it lights."'
County Tyrone
IFC 1888:56 collected in 1974 by **SÓC(ii)** from PÓD m+
Note: all seven [this and Part A 83.8, 173.10, 174, 182.3, 250 & 311] from this informant are inverted

.9 '"That'll be a good fire when it kindles," said the fox after he had liquidated on the top of a mountain on a frosty morning.'
County Cavan
Q 1973 IFC 1888:86 C m+

.10 '"It'll make a good fire if it gets time," as the fox said when he pissed on the heap of stones.'
County Roscommon
Q 1973 IFC 1888:147 C m+: 'said when somebody is trying to make a fire of wet turf, which gives plenty of smoke and steam but no heat.'
Note: This and others [Part A, 172.1, 182.11, 207 & 324] from this Correspondent resemble those [Part A 83.18, 172.2, 182.12, 185 & 208.4] from another Correspondent from near the same town — Curraghboy, north-west of Athlone — however, all are indexed as they vary

.11 '"That will make a great fire when it reddens," as the fox said when he peed on the heap of stones.'
Limerick City mid-1920s
Q 1973 IFC 1917:12 C m+: 'said when a person would be trying to get a fire to redden'

.12 '"They'll make a good fire," said the fox when he urinated on the heap of stones.'
County Westmeath
Q 1973 IFC 1917:61 C m+. For Correspondent's comment see Part A 13.2

.13 '"That will be a right fire when it light[s]," says the Fox when he pissed on a heap of stones.'
County Wexford
Q 1973 IFC 1917:93 C f+

.14 '"That'll make a good fire when it lights," said the Fox as he peed on the heap of stones.'
County Offaly
IFC 1917:reverse p. 98, on a sheet written in 1986 by SMcR f+, DIF student from the USA, i BE m [d. 1977] basket maker, with the comment: 'ie. saw the steam'

.15 '"That will be a grand fire when it lights up," as the fox said when he pissed on the heap of stones.'
County Tipperary current in 1978
Q 1973(78) IFC 2027:167 C m+: 'this saying is heard in the Thurles area … when somebody is lighting a fire or, to a lesser extent, when somebody is starting a job of some sort'

.16 '"That'll make a fine fire when it lights," as the fox said when he pissed on the stones.'
County Wexford 'and other places'
IFC 1771:11 collected by **JD** with the comment: 'sometimes there is added "and saw the steam rising from them"' [see **.17**]

.17 '"That'll make a fine fire when it lights," as the fox said when he pissed on the stones and saw the steam rising from them.'
County Wexford 'and other places'
IFC 1717:11 for comment see **.16**

.18 '"It will be a good fire when it kindles," as the fox said when he pissed on the stone.'
County Roscommon
Q 1973 IFC 1888:148 C m+. cf **.10**, *qv* for note

.19 '"It'll be a good one when it lights," as the fox said when he pissed on the stone.'
County ?Cavan
Q 2000 EO'B m 70s: 'Probably comes from Co. Cavan. I often heard an elderly Cavan woman, who lived in the village [Duleek, Co. Meath], trying hard to get a fire to light, a wisp of smoke going up the chimney, issuing from black coals, and coming out with the above expression.'
Note: The counties adjoin

.20 '"That'll be a fire when it burns," as the tod said.'
tod=fox
County Donegal between 1880 and 1908
Traynor 1954 under 'tod': 'Phr — saying (H)'

.21 '"It'll be a good fire when it kindles," said the fox.'
County Offaly
Q 1973 IFC 1917:67 C m+

.22 '"That will be a good fire when it lights," as the fox said when he pissed on the fire.'
County Armagh
Michael J. Murphy *Sayings and Stories from Slieve Gullion* .... 1990 Dundalk, p. 118 in section titled 'Urination'

cf 'Of a bad fire in a house it would be said that "it was like the fox when he shit on the ice that it would be a good fire when it lights up."' Co. Armagh Q 1973 IFC 1888:66. For Correspondent's comments see Part A 180.5

DOW 434–35; Kelly p. 115 No. 63 'Nothing but a ridicule upon a bad fire.'; Ramsay p. 62

cf the folktale *TIF* 81* *The Fox's Fire* [5 versions].
firm/Devil *cf Swe

A 84.1 '"Firm and ugly," as the devil said when he sewed his breeches with gads.'
Patrick Weston Joyce 1910, 1991 rpr., of 1979 ed., Ch. 5 'The Devil and his "Territory"' p. 60: '"*Firm and ugly,* as the devil said when he sewed his breeches with gads." Here is how it happened. The devil was one day pursuing the soul of a sinner across country, and in leaping over a rough thorn hedge, he tore his breeches badly, so that his tail stuck out; on which he gave up the chase. As it was not decent to appear in public in that condition, he sat down and stitched up the rent with next to hand

94

materials — viz. slender tough osier withes or *gads* as we call them in
Ireland. When the job was finished he spread out the garment before him
on his knees, and looking admiringly at his handiwork, uttered the above
saying — "Firm and ugly!'"

*cf Swe '"Det var styggt med starkt," sa fan, när han band mor sin med
vidjelänkar.' ['"It was ugly but strong," said the devil when he fettered
his mother with sally withes.'] Ström p. 46.

first/man
**A 85.1 '"I'm first at last, I was always behind before," as the
man long ago said.'**
County Roscommon
Q 1973 IFC 1888:144 C m+: 'used when a person has a job done early.'
For Correspondent's additional comment see Part A 5.1

cf the biblical 'He who was last shall be first.'

fit/serpent
**A 86.1 '"That's not a good fit," as the serpent said when he
swallowed a buck goat, horns and all.'**
Patrick Weston Joyce 1910, 1991 rpt. Ch. 8 'Proverbs' p. 115. In the
opening part of this chapter Joyce says: 'Those that I give here in
collected form were taken from the living lips of the people during the
last thirty or forty years.' Cited in *Addenda* 54.

flay/flaithiúil man
**A 87.1 '"Skin a flay and burn the stairs to roast him!" as the
flaithiúil man said.'**
flay=flea; flaithiúil, Ir=generous
County Cork
Q 1973 IFC 1917:32 + : 'this is used sarcastically when a mean offer is
made'

cf 'He's that mean he'd skin a flea for its hide.' Co. Down Q 1973 IFC
1888:41

cf 'He would skin a flea for the hide and tallow": said of an avaricious
person' Patterson under 'flea'

cf the motif *MI* J 2102.1 *Expensive means of being rid of insects.*

flock/shepherd   Am Eng

A 88.1 '"As one shepherd said to the other, "Let's get the flock out of here."'
P.T.Q. 1965, Belfast n.p.

DOW 448.

Florence/lesbian
A 89.1 '"As one Italian lesbian said to the other, "I think I'll go back to Florence."'
P.T.Q. 1971 Belfast, p. 25

cf the joke 'Did you hear about the Italian lesbian who went back to Florence?' *P.T.Q.* 1973 Belfast, p. 28.

flour/serving boy
A 90.1 '"More flour to your pratie cake ma'am," said the serving boy.'
pratie=potato
County Westmeath
Q 1973 IFC 1917:62 C m+: 'I don't know when exactly this is used though it is quite familiar.' For Correspondent's additional comments see Part A 13.2

follow/night
A 91.1 '"You follow me where're I go," as the night said to the morning.'
The Dublin Journal of Temperance, Science and Literature, 1, No. 19 (3/9/1842), p. 304 in a list of five titled 'Jonathanisms' [this and Part A 139, 141, 260 & 284].

fool/ass   Part B 8 also Ger, Sp
A 92.1 '"You're a long-lugged fool," as the ass said to his brother.'
long-lugged=long-eared
Ulster
Byers Papers Box T4 'S & P' ts T-4-6 p. 58; NB possibly from Morris's translation ie. Morris 1918 No. 130 [Part B 8.1]

see also Part A 20, 30 & 44.

front/man

A 93.1 '"It's all in front of me," as the man with the wheelbarrow said.'
Q 2000 'The John Bennett Show' BBC Radio Ulster, handwritten, probably by John Bennett, 60s, on the printout of an email response to the appeal for wellerisms broadcast on 6/3/2002

.2 '"I have it all in front," as the man said with the wheelbarrow.'
Q 2000 'The John Bennett Show' BBC Radio Ulster, broadcast 6/3/2002 by John Bennett in appeal for wellerisms

cf on hearing a similar version from the Electronic Database printout, Ulster Dialect Archive, UFTM, **IC** said: [That means] 'You're lucky, "Ye have it in front of ye like the man and the wheel barrow" — starting school, job,' collected by FCW in April 1992.

frost/blacksmith

A 94.1 '"Frost and rain and frost again," says the blacksmith.'
County Cavan
IFCS 994:101 after an article on weatherlore

cf '"Frost and rain and frost again," is the blacksmith's toast' Co. Cavan IFCS 1010:80 in a list, mainly of proverbs

cf 'Frost and rain and frost again' Co. Cavan IFCS 998:259, in a list titled 'Weatherlore': 'this is a blacksmith's description of the winter storms. It means that a little white watery frost is always followed by a big slash of rain and, that being done, frost comes again to dry up the ground again.'

fuck/countess   E Eng

A 95.1 '"F–k me," said the Countess and he pulled her on like a well-worn seaboot.'
Derry ?City
Q 1973 IFC 1888:25 + preceded by the comment: 'I'm not sure whether the following [see also Part A 215] qualify — they are rather crude but you can make up your own mind about them' and followed by, 'There were several things which the actress said to the bishop but for the moment they escape me'

?Partridge

Note: this may be linked to Grose's def. of 'dutchess.'

full/tailor
A 96.1 '"That is the thing in full," said the tailor when he put three sleeves on the one coat.'
County Sligo
Q 1973 IFC 1888:114 C m+

cf 'The tailor must cut three sleeves to every woman's gown.' Smith & Wilson pp. 797–98.

full/tick
A 97.1 '"You're not the only one that's full," said the tick to the drunkard.'
full=drunk
County Monaghan
Q 1973 IFC 1888:73 C m+, a customs and excise official: 'This expression, although not common, I heard in the Bragan Mountain area, a relict of the poteen [= illicit homemade alcohol]-drinking days now generally used when two hard-drinking, sore-headed boozers meet "the morning after." The term was used even though the resulting effects were the result of one of the duo having purchased his "poison" and the other having got his load in the Mountain Dew [= illicit homemade alcohol] country, hence the term "tick" being applied to the former.'

funny thing see *amphitheatre*

G

get up see *ass*

getting on/bus conductor
A 98.1 '"How are you getting on?" said the bus conductor to the man with no legs.'
County Antrim
Q 1973? IFC 1888:27.

glad/old maid
A 99.1 '"Glad to be asked," as the old maid said.'
old maid=unmarried woman

Lover *Handy Andy: A Tale of Irish Life*. Earliest edition of novel 1842 but it was previously serialised in *Bentley's Miscellany* both London. n.d. 'Cheap Illustrated Edition' Charing Cross, p. 38: Murtough Murphy, attorney, had just survived a duel and is inviting his friends, who include Bill Doyle, to celebrate "'Hillo [= hello], hillo, Bill!" interrupted Murphy, "you are too hard on the adjectives; besides you'll spoil your appetite if you ruffle your temper, and that would fret me, for I intend you to dine with me to-day."

"Faith, an' I'll do that same, Murtough, my boy, and glad to be asked, as the old maid said."

"I'll tell you all what it is," said Murphy; "boys, you must all dine with me to-day, and drink long life to me since I'm not killed."' Also in Mair p. 40, but probably a citation from Lover.

glory/kettle
A 100.1 "'Glory be to God!" says the kettle to the pot, "you have legs and I have not."'
County Kerry
Q 1973 IFC 1917:17 C m+.

go/Evans of the *Broke*
A 101.1 "'We won't go into that now," as Evans of the *Broke* wittily remarked to his fellow passengers as they stood regarding the sea from the deck of the *Bolivar*.'
Evans of the Broke=Edward Ratcliffe Garth Russel Evans [1880–1957] first Baron Mountevans, admiral b. London, who, when a commander and captain of the Broke, earned his sobriquet from ramming with his vessel a German destroyer in 1917 in Dover harbour. A second exploit, which also captured the public imagination, was in the early 1920s when he swam with a line to rescue survivors from a grounded vessel.
'Na Gopaleen' as cited in *Further cuttings from 'Cruiskeen Lawn.'*: 'I was up before Judge Shannon the other morning. However, we won't go into that now, as Evans of the Broke wittily remarked to his fellow passengers as they stood regarding the sea from the deck of the Bolivar. We have other matters to att-10-d 2, all manner of important matters. ---' London 1976, section titled 'The District and Other Courts' p. 61, originally published in the 'Cruiskeen Lawn,' a regular column in daily newspaper *The Irish Times*, probably between 1947 and 1957, and possibly in 1957 following obituaries for Evans.

God/Old Biddy Davis

A 102.1 '"God bless us and save us," said old Biddy Davis, "the sticks might be drier tomorrow."'
County Laois 1930s
Q 1973 IFC 1917:78 C f+: 'Biddy Davis a v[ery] old woman who died in the late thirties when I was a child ([used as] — an optimistic hope, when something wasn't going quite right)'

see also Part A 103.

God (Dear)/Old Mrs Davis (Oul Mrs Davis)
A 103.1 '"God bless us and save us," says Old Mrs Davis, "I never knew herrins wus fish."'
herrins wus=herrings were
County Louth
Q 2000 i FH who heard it in March 2002 from B., a retired taxi driver in Dublin who heard it when he was growing up on a farm in Faughart. 'It was said if you were surprised.' Received in a phone call 8/3/2002

.2 '"God bless us and save us," says Old Mrs Davis, "I never knew herrins was fish."'
herrins was=herrings were
Q 2000 **JG** who heard it in the mid-1960s in the Teachers' Club, Parnell Square, Dublin, in a monologue. **JG** says it was used 'if taken aback' in place of 'Was that a fact?' Frank Harte/FH in a phone call 22/2/2002 suggests that it may be on a record by Jimmy O'Dea

.3 '"Dear bless us and save us," said oul Mrs Davis, "I never knew herrins wus fish."'
?County Armagh
Q 2000 i f *c.* 45, now living around Belfast, who remembers hearing it used by her grandmother in Glasgow, Scotland, when she was growing up; her grandmother was from the south of Co. Armagh

see also Part A 102.

good turn/countrywoman
A 104.1 '"One good turn deserves another," said a countrywoman as she wound the clock.'
County Roscommon
Q 1973 IFC 1888:146 C f+

Mieder & Tóthné Litovkina pp. 160–61

Note: the proverb 'One good turn deserves another' is currently common in English and also found in Irish.

goodbye/crow
A 105.1 '"Goodbye and good luck," says the crow to the duck.'
County Cavan
Q 1973 IFC 1888:89 C m+
Note: this immediately follows Part A 312.2

cf Behan 1965 p. 71: 'Brending Behing.' 'Good morning Mrs. Brennan.' 'And good luck.' 'As the crow said to the duck.' 'You too, Maria, and your friends in America.' Opening of a piece titled 'Meet a great poet,' originally published between 1954 and 1956 in his column 'Hold your hour and have another' *The Irish Press*, a daily newspaper produced in Dublin

Note: Brady p. 18 notes that 'Says the crow to the duck' is a response by Dublin children when adults say 'Good morrow and good luck!'

grapes (sour)/fox   Am Eng, Dan, Dut, E Ara, E Eng, Fin, Fr,
   Ger, Gr, It, M Ara, Nor, Scots, Swe
A 106.1 '"Sour grapes," says the fox when he couldn't catch the chicken.'
County Louth
IFCS 672:261 in a list, mainly of proverbs. Published in [Carson] Williams 1992 p. 67/2000a p. 7 & p. 66

.2 '"They're sour," said the fox.'
Lover *Handy Andy: A Tale of Irish Life* first published as a novel in 1842 but earlier serialised in *Bentley's Miscellany*, both London. n.d. 'Cheap Illustrated Edition' Charing Cross, p. 38

.3 '"Sour grapes," said the fox.'
County Kerry
Q 1973 IFC 1917:27 C m+: 'was how I used to hear an old man depict someone who spoke disparagingly of something or some person (often a boy or girl in courting) which he or she desperately wanted but could not obtain'

cf 'Dála an mhadarua agus na silíní.' ('The fox's judgement on the cherries.') Rosenstock p. 30/translation and footnote 28 p. 31: 'When he couldn't get his paws on them he declared they were sour.' See also Dinneen under 'silín': 'silíní searbha, "sour grapes"'

DOW 592, 1230–31; Henderson p. 137; Smith & Wilson p. 255

cf the fable Aesop 3; *TIF* 59 *Fox and Grapes* [4 versions] and similar motif *MI* J 871 *Fox and sour grapes*.

grind/clutch
A 107.1 'As the clutch said to the gearbox, "One more grind like that and we'll have to get engaged."'
P.T.Q. 1965 n.p./1970 p. 39 both Belfast.

guts/skeleton
A 108.1 'One skeleton in the cupboard to the other, "If we had any guts we'd get out of here."'
P.T.Q. 1947 Belfast n.p.
cf the joke 'First skeleton "If we had any guts we'd get out of here." Second skeleton, "Yes, but we have no body to help us."' Ransford 1999 London, p. 31.

H

hame/Devil   Scots
A 109.1 '"Hame is hamely," as the devil said when he found himself in the lawcourt.'
hame(ly)=home(ly)
County Sligo
IFCS 155:28 in a list, mainly of proverbs. Published in [Carson] Williams 1992 p. 85/2000a p. 79

cf 'Go to law with the devil and the courthouse in hell' Co. Carlow Q 1973 IFC 1917:33

DOW 607; 'Cheviot' p. 126; Hislop p. 70

cf Mieder & Tóthné Litovkina pp. 207–09

Note: there is another version, possibly in Traynor.

hand/father

102

A 110.1 '"Never lift your hand to a woman while you have a shoe on your foot," said the father to his son on the latter's wedding morning.'
County Donegal
Q 1973 IFC 1888:20 C m+.

hands (Devil)/skull
A 111.1 '"Idle hands tempt the Devil," what a skull said to the man that kicked it in the graveyard.'
County Sligo
Q 1973 IFC 1888:113 C m+

.2 '"The Devil finds work for idle hands," what a skull said to the man that kicked it in the graveyard.'
County Sligo
Q 1973 IFC 1888:113 C m+

Note: 'An idle man tempts the devil' is fairly common in English and is also found in Irish.

hanged/condemned criminal
A 112.1 '"I'll be hanged if I get up early tomorrow," as the condemned criminal said.'
I'll be hanged=I won't
County Leitrim
IFC 1888:106 informant/creator WS m+. For note see Part A 23; others from him are Part A 32, 54, 62, 175, 179, 317 & 319.

hard station/guard
A 113.1 '"It's a hard station," as the guard said when he reached the platform.'
Belfast
Q 2000 i EMcK m 50s senior civil servant b. & r. West Belfast, as he remembers hearing it from his barber 'years ago.'

hard times/monkey
A 114.1 'The monkey said, "Hard times," when he sat on the clock.'
County Mayo
Q 1973 IFC 1888:136 C m+

Note: this and two others [Part A 173.8 & 235.2] are grouped together in a list under 'The monkey said:-' probably indicating a shortcut taken by the Correspondent

hardy man/man
A 115.1 '"Hardy man!" as the man says to the corpse in the ditch.'
County Roscommon 1960s
Q 2000 **JG**, the characteristic approach attributed by those on the Roscommon side of the River Shannon to those from Coolsan on the Westmeath side: 'nothing would faze [= startle] them.'

harm/Jerry
A 116.1 '"What harm?" says Jerry when he burned the house.'
County Kildare
IFCS 774:396 first in a list titled 'Proverbs' with the comment: 'When an old person is being told about some slight accident etc., he says: '" What harm?" says Jerry when he burned the house" [the rest of list is made up of proverbial similes]. Published in [Carson] Williams 1992 p. 3/2000a p. 13.

harm/Old Herbert
A 117.1 '"'Tis their own harm they're doing," like Old Herbert said about the cows in the meadow.'
County Kerry
Q 1973 IFC 1917:18 C (a Herbert) m+: 'Old Herbert was my grandfather! I have heard this as a phrase in West Limerick years ago: "'Tis their harm they are doing like Herbert's cows."'

Note: the counties adjoin.

hash/'Mickey Doran'
A 118.1 "'That will settle your hash,' as 'Mickey Doran' said when he hit his wife with the spade."
settle your hash see note below
County Down
Q 2000 **TC** with his comment: 'I must say I enjoyed reading the proverbs [FCW had sent him a preliminary list of wellerisms], some I had heard before but the vast majority were totally new to me. --- I have difficulty with this type of saying in the context of your research for, while they conform to the format of the quotation proverb, do they necessarily

qualify as such, especially those which flourish for a week or two and then disappear? For instance recently listening to RTE radio I heard a rather long-winded politician catch himself on and say "'I must get to the point,' as the pop star said to the taxi driver." [Part A 236] — obviously a reference to the Point Theatre, Dublin. The type of local saying I have in mind above would run something like "'That will settle your hash,' as Mickey Doran (fictitious name) said when he hit his wife with the spade." Heard in the Mourne area.' Letter 1/8/2000. In a subsequent letter **TC** added 'I have heard the word ['hash'] frequently used in the Mourne area, in every instance in the form of a threat, eg. "I'll settle his/her hash" and intending to mean "I will put an end to his complaining, grumbling or bad mouthing." The example I gave you I only ever heard used on one occasion about a bad-tempered individual who was suspected of having assaulted his wife … The remark was made in company and not very well received, one or two remarking that "it was a shocking thing to say."'

cf the curse 'The Old Boy settle your hash for you and have your guts for garters.' O'Farrell 1995 p. 82 in the section 'Hell and the Devil'

cf 'to settle someone's hash' is familiar in Dublin, p.c. from Bairbre Ní Fhloinn/**BNíF** 15/12/2001. Also used in *Faustus Kelly*, a play by 'Flann O'Brien' first performed in the Abbey Theatre, Dublin, in 1943, 1986 ed. Act III, p. 194, time 1943: '*Reilly* [town council member] *(exploding venomously as he gets ready to depart).* Well, I'm a happy man tonight. I've smashed to smithereens the lousiest twist, the dirtiest ready-up, that was ever tried in this town. I have fixed the hash of that customer gone out, whoever the hell he is.'

cf 'I'll settle Mainwaring's hash' 'Dad's Army.' BBC TV comedy series about the home guard in England written in the 1960s heard on 19/12/2001 by FCW.

haste/pig   Am Eng
A 119.1 '"Excuse haste and a bad pen," as the pig said when it broke out of the stye.'
Ulster
Byers Papers Box T4 'S & P' ts T-4-6 p. 76

DOW 942.

haste/tailor   Am Eng, Scots

A 120.1 '"The more haste the worse speed," as the tailor said to the long thread.'
County Antrim and/or County Down
Patterson 1880 under 'haste': '... saying'

.2 as .1
Ulster
Byers Papers Box T4 'S & P' ts T-4-6 p. 58

.3 '"The mair haste the waur speed," as the tailor said to his lang threed.'
mair=more; waur=worse; lang=long; threed=thread
County Donegal between 1880 and 1908
Traynor 1954 under 'war': '(H)'

.4 '"The more haste the less speed," as the tailor said to the long thread'
Ulster
Byers Papers Box T4 'S & P' ts T-4-6 p. 58

cf 'More haste less speed like the tailor and the long thread.' Co. Cavan IFCS 982:314 after a story about tailor's advice

DOW 562; Ramsay p. 70; 'Cheviot' p. 244; Henderson p. 31; Hislop p. 142; Mair p. 55; Wilson p.193

Notes: the proverb is currently common in English, eg. '"The more haste the less speed" common' collected 1990s by FCW from **IC**.
'"More haste, less speed," as the tailor said to the long thread,' was used as one of the ten, later five, examples on Q 2000. See Appendix 1.

health/Ould Wade
A 121.1 'As Ould Wade used to say, "The health's the wealth of the world."'
County Down *c.* 1933
Q 1973 IFC 1888:45 C m+: 'A tramp or beggar is still very often quoted for a wise observation "As Ould Wade used to say 'The health's ... world,' used whenever a person gives a reassuring reply to your inquiry about his health "How are you keeping?" "Never better, thank God." "That's good — as Ould Wade" etc. Other expressions of opinion or words of wisdom quoted from characters of the past: "As Blind Dan used to say '... you ate' [see Part A 82.1]. All these I heard about forty years

ago but they are not much used here nowadays. I can't think of any such expressions attributed to birds or animals.'

cf 'Health and wealth is above all gold as saith Jesus Syrach.' Smith & Wilson p. 362.

hell/old woman
A 122.1 '"To hell with poverty!" as the old woman said when she threw the cat the canary.'
Belfast 1980s
Q 2000 **TC**. For his comments see Part A 118

cf 'Throw the cat another goldfish' i f 40s, who heard it in the 1980s in an insurance office in Leeds, Yorkshire, England, from a fellow worker m, who used it if someone were being extravagant

Note: see Part A 123.1.

hell/old woman
A 123.1 '"To hell with poverty!" as the old woman said, "We will throw another pea in the soup.'
Belfast 1980s
Q 2000 **TC**. For his comments see Part A 118

cf 'To hell with poverty, put another pea in the soup!' Kerr Peirce 1979 ed. (51) as cited in Kane p. 224

cf 'To hell with poverty we will kill a hen.' Co. Galway IFCS 77:449 in a list, mainly of proverbs, and 'To hell with poverty, put a herring in the pan' collected after a lecture on proverbs by FCW titled 'A herring in the pan ...' from f 50s who heard it when she was growing up on the Cavan/Monaghan border

Note: Part A 122 & 123 were given consecutively in this order in a list of wellerisms by **TC**.

hen/hen
A 124.1 '"It's a bad hen that can't scrape for herself," as the hen said when she left the chickens.'
County Roscommon
Q 1973 IFC 1888:149 C m+

Note: 'It's a bad hen that can't scrape for herself' is a common proverb in English and Irish.

her (she)/Connachtman (Kerryman)
A 125.1 '"That's her!" said the Connachtman to the Bull."'
County Roscommon
Q 1973 IFC 1888:144 C m+: 'another way of saying, "That's it!"' For Correspondent's additional comment see Part A 5.1

.2 as .1
County Cork
Q 1973 IFC 1917:21 C m+, i m+: 'Having worked alongside an old miller from Millstreet, Co. Cork, I picked up the following from him …' [this & Part A 200]

.3 '"That's her!" said the Connachtman to the bull."'
County Tipperary current in 1978
Q 1973(78) IFC 2027:166 C m+: 'still heard in Turtulla [near Thurles] and is quoted when when a particular task has been completed'

.4 '"That's her!" says the Connachtman to the bull."'
County Kerry
Q 1973 IFC 1917:17 C m+

.5 '"That's her!" as the Connachtman said to the bull."'
County Roscommon 1950s
Q 2000 **JG** used, after a discussion on wellerisms, on successfully inserting a lamp plug
.6 '"That's she," said the Connachtman to the Bull.'
County Clare
Q 1973 IFC 1917:50. C m+

.7 'As the Kerryman says to the bull, "There she is now!"'
County Tyrone
IFC 1888:56 collected in 1974 by **SÓC(ii)** from **PÓD** m+. For note see Part A 83.8.

her/she
A 126.1 '"You have her," says she.'
County Wicklow
Q 1973? IFC 2154:279 C m+, i PC f+: 'If you are just finished a job like hanging a picture … or putting a ladder against a wall Bray men are in the habit of saying, "'You have her,' says she."'

here/seagull
A 127.1 '"I was here before you came up," said the seagull to the aeroplane.'
County Westmeath
Q 1973 IFC 1917:61 C m+. For Correspondent's comments see Part A 13.2.

highballs/giraffe
A 128.1 '"The highballs are on me!" said the giraffe.'
County Wicklow
Q 1973? IFC 2154:279 C m+, informant PC f+: 'My father JC(iii), when he came home well-oiled [= intoxicated] and in good form would walk into the kitchen and shout out "'The highballs are on me,' said the giraffe."'

hold up/ceiling
A 129.1 '"Hold me up, I'm plastered!" as the ceiling said to the four walls.'
plastered=drunk
IFC 1888:150 collector **JD**: 'I forget where I heard this.'

hole/rat
A 130.1 '"I will in my hole," said the rat when the cat asked him to wait.'
County Roscommon
Q 1973 IFC 1888:144 C m+: 'used when a person has no intention of doing something they are requested to do.' For Correspondent's additional comment see Part A 5.1

.2 '"I will in my hole," says the rat.'
County Wexford
Q 1973 IFC 1917:92 C f+

cf '"I will in my hole," says Coley' Co. Wexford IFC 1917:64 letter 1973 from **JD**: 'There was one other saying [see Part A 5.8 for the first] that was common in Wexford in my young days and it was used when one wanted to give a more vehement refusal than ordinary. It was "I will ... Coley." I do not know the origin of it or any story about it.'

home see *walk/flea*

honour/black
A 131.1 '"Honour bright," as the black said whin he stole the boots.'
black=bootblack; whin=when
Carleton 'Geography of an Irish Oath,' a short story concerning alcohol abuse in *Traits and Stories of the Irish Peasantry Second Series*, 1833 Dublin, Vol. I, pp. 307–471, p. 325: [Peter, the landlord] '"Now, Condy [a customer wanting credit], whin'ill [= when will] you pay me for this?" [Condy] "Never fret yourself about that; you'll be ped [= paid]. Honour bright, as the black said whin he stole the boots."' I am grateful to John Cronin/JC(ii) and Sophia Hillan for sourcing this wellerism and to Nini Rodgers for defining 'black.' Cited in an extract from Carleton in O'Donoghue 1894 p. 197.

hounds/lap-dog   Part B 91 also Am Eng, Scots
A 132.1 '"We hounds kill the hare," quote the lap-dog.' [*sic*]
County Cavan
IFCS 988:308 in a list, mainly of proverbs. Published in [Carson] Williams 1992 p. 55/2000a p. 59

DOW 624; Kelly p. 222 No. 75 'Spoken to insignificant persons when they attribute to themselves any part of a great achievement'; Ramsay p. 107; Hislop p. 205

Note: 'we' may be a pun on 'wee' meaning 'little,' used in Cavan.

hours/clock
A 133.1 'As one clock said to the other clock, which was going slow, "Shall I kick you on the hours?"'
P.T.Q. 1961 Belfast n.p.

house/man   Part B 187 also *cf Fin
A 134.1 '"An empty house is better nor a bad tenant," as the man said when he got rid of flatulence.'
nor=than
Ulster
Byers Papers Box T4 T-4-6 p. 72

*cf Fin ?Sallinen

Note: the proverb 'An empty house is better than a bad tenant' [usual variant] is common in English and Irish. **IC** has heard it used as an excuse for breaking wind. Collected by FCW April 1992 see also Part A 78.

how/Indian chief
A 135.1 'As the Indian chief said to the mermaid, "How?"'
P.T.Q. 1961 Belfast n.p.

how/tailor
A 136.1 '"How are you?"
"Just so so," said the tailor.'
County Antrim
Q 1973? IFC 1888:27 +.

I

idea/man
**A 137.1 '"It seemed like a good idea at the time," as the man
said when he took off all his clothes and jumped in the bed of
nettles.'**
Belfast area *c.* 1980
Q 2000 **TC**: 'I believe I may also have heard this ['idea/man'] used in an
American film although "cactus bush" replaced "bed of nettles" and the
other [Part A 80] which may also have originated in a film.'
ill/man
A 138.1 '"Ill got, ill gone," as a man said to his pension.'
County Cavan
IFCS 997:126 in a list, mainly of proverbs, with the comment: 'If a man
got a legacy from a relative and in a few years he had all spent his
neighbours would say Ill got, ill gone as a man said to his pension.'

cf 'Ill got, ill gone, like the old woman's bonnet' Co. Cavan IFCS
1011:231 in a list, mainly of proverbs, followed by the comment 'This
old lady was travelling in a train when she discovered a bonnet which
had been left there. She put it on, and stuck her head out of the window,
when the wind blew the bonnet away'

Note: the proverb 'Evil got, evil gone' is common in English and Irish.

impulse/soda-water

A 139.1 '"The impulse of the moment," as the soda-water said to the cork when the string was off.'
The Dublin Journal of Temperance, Science and Literature, 1, No. 19 (3/9/1842), p. 304 first in a list of five titled 'Jonathanisms' [this and Part A 91, 141, 260 & 284].

in/fox
A 140.1 '"It's in and out," said the fox when he urinated in the snow.'
County Cavan
Q 1973 IFC 1888:97 C m+, member of the Order of Jesuits, writes: 'I have very little by way of wise or pithy sayings attributed to birds and animals. I have heard locally ---' [for the other wellerisms from him see Part A 233.1 & 277.6]

cf 'Man describing a crooked sideline on a football pitch "it's like a dog pissing in snow,"' Co. Cavan Q 1973 IFC 1888:90

Note: the proverbial comparison is fairly common and was also noted in the late 1980s by AJH from a Co. Antrim lorry driver p.c.

inquiry/lady's maid
A 141.1 '"I'll make every inquiry," as the lady's maid remarked when she peeped into the letter of her young mistress.'
The Dublin Journal of Temperance, Science and Literature, 1, No. 19 (3/9/1842), p. 304 in a list of five titled 'Jonathanisms' [this and Part A 91, 139, 141 & 284].

instrument/man   Part B 106
A 142.1 '"There's many a sort of instrument," said the man who had the wooden trump.'
trump=Jew's harp
County Armagh
Anon. *National Proverbs: Ireland.* 1913 London p. 57.

iron/blacksmith
A 143.1 '"Strike the iron while it is red," said the blacksmith.'
County Clare
Q 1973 IFC 1917:5 C m+

Mieder & Tóthné Litovkina p. 186 [but no wellerism]

112

Note: the proverb 'Strike while the iron is hot' is currently very common in English.

J

job/Nelson
A 144.1 'As Nelson said at the Battle of Trafalgar, "It's a good job we were there!"'
County Down *c.* 1964
Q 2000 i MMcC m 50s, museum curator, rumoured amongst fellow schoolboys in the 1960s in Bangor Grammar School to be the answer of a pupil considered less able to a history exam question on Nelson's contribution to the Napoleonic Wars.

job/Yank
A 145.1 '"It's a good job that cows can't fly!" as the Yank said when the crow shit on his hat.'
Yank=North American
County Roscommon
Q 1973 IFC 1888:149 C m+

cf a cartoon in *P.T.Q.* Belfast [year not noted] of a farmer with wheelbarrow heavily laden from mucking out the henhouse, saying to his wife, 'It's a good job for me you're not keeping cows!'

K

know/bull
A 146.1 '"I did not know you were there," said the Bull to the Fly when the Fly said, "I must be going."'
County Fermanagh
Q 1973(74) IFC 1888:71 C m+: 'collected from an old parish priest in Derrygonnelly who thought he was not getting his fair share of notice from his curates who were really running the parish'

cf the fable Aesop 1899 ed., 1954 rpt., p. 134 & similar motif *MI* J 953.10 *Gnats apologise for lighting on horn of bull.*

know/man
A 147.1 '"What ye don't know nivir hurts ye," as the man sayd efther he had dhrunk the milk the mouse was dhrounded in.'
nivir=never; efther=after; dhrunk=drunk; dhrounded=drowned
County Tyrone
'Tullyneil' [Robert Lyons Marshall] *At Home in Tyrone: sketches and stories.* 1944 Belfast p. 47 used in a conversation about selling a horse

cf the expression 'I'm afraid there's a mouse in the milk' Q 2000 i JC(i) m, 60s, sheep farmer, Co. Armagh

Mieder & Tóthné Litovkina pp. 226–27 [but no wellerism]

Note: the proverb 'What you don't know never hurts you' is currently common in English.

know/old woman
A 148.1 '"You'll never know anyone until you live with them," says the old woman.' [*sic*]
County Clare
Q 1973 IFC 1917:5 C m+

Note: the proverb 'You'll never know anyone until you live with them' is fairly common in English and Irish.

know/Seán na Scuab
A 149.1 '"Sure I don't know myself, mother!" as Seán na Scuab said.'
Limerick City mid-1920s
Q 1973 IFC 1917:13 C m+: 'among the older people.' Synopsis of story given with wellerism: once Limerick corporation could not agree on a mayor so they decided to appoint the first person who would cross Thomond Bridge on a certain day. This turned out to be a poor man from the Clare Hills who made his living by selling brooms in the city — Seán na Scuab ['Seán of the brooms']. Some time after his installation he was presiding at a court before which his mother, on a charge of begging or vagrancy, was brought. 'When she saw Seán she immediately cried out "Don't you know me, Seán? I'm your mother." He replied as above.'

cf the folktale *TIF* 1383 *Electing a Mayor* [36 versions] & the related motif *MI* J 2012.4 *Fool in new clothes does not know himself.*

knows/woman

114

A 150.1 '"Who knows?" as the woman said when she followed the coach.'
County Cavan
IFCS 994:141 in a list, mainly of proverbs. Published in [Carson] Williams 1992 p. 74/2000a p. 72

Note: **BA** suggested for horse dung, p.c. *c.* 1977.

know-how/man
A 151.1 '"It's all in the know-how," as the man said when he guzzled the goose.'
Seamus Murphy [1907–75], autobiography of a monumental sculptor, *Stone Mad.* 1966 London, 1977 rpt. p. 66: 'Stones up to a ton and a half can be turned in that way. "It's all in the know-how," as the man said when he guzzled the goose.' Ref. via a Co. Mayo Correspondent to Q 1973 1888:139, with the following comment: 'Despite widespread enquiry in this [Shrule] and surrounding districts, and even an enquiry per newsletter to 500 members of an organisation, I cannot find a trace of this figure of speech. I suspect that the figure is too ephermeral to have registered with the community memory. ?Sadly enough Seamus Murphy's book "Stone Mad" contained the only significant Wellerism I have found, this is:- "It's all in ... guzzled the goose"! (Query — how do you guzzle a goose?!.'

L

ladder/spaceman
A 152.1 'Spaceman to 12 foot tall Vesuvian girl, "Take me to your ladder."'
12 foot [feet]=c. 4 metres
P.T.Q. 1967 Belfast n.p.

laid/hen
A 153.1 '"Well laid!" as the hen sayd.'
Ulster
Byers Papers Box T4 'S & P' ts T-4-6 p. 76 with the comment: '"Well laid!' as the hen sayd," is a remark made when a man carrying a heavy sack of potatoes, etc. manages cleverly to deposit it in the exact position where it has to be placed.'

land/Columbus
A 154.1 '"Land!" says Columbus.'

County Kerry
Q 1973 IFC 1917:28: 'was a comment often heard from a man I knew. This implied an ulterior motive by someone who had begun to pay unusual interest in some old person who owned a farm and who was likely to die soon.'

last/shoemaker
A 155.1 '"That'll be the last," as the shoemaker said to his wife.'
Belfast
Q 2000(02) i DM+, mature part-time student UU, who heard it in the 1990s from his father, also DM+, 70s, b. & partly reared in Randalstown, Co. Antrim, now living in Belfast, [usually] 'said when making a "final payment" or a 'reluctant payment such as to a pawnbroker'

cf 'There's nobody as sure as the cobbler's wife' Co. Cavan Q 1973 IFC 1888:81 with the comment: 'This is said because the cobbler's wife is sure of the last (last which the cobbler would have ... on which the shoes are put ...) but, as it is here, the last of good things'

see also Part A 9.

last man/Jack Stone (man)
A 156.1 '"Last man close the gate," said Jack Stone to the Bull.'
County Kilkenny (Castlecomer)
Q 1973(75) IFC 1917:79 C f+. Same Correspondent as **.2**

.2 '"Last man close the gate," said the Man to the Bull.'
County Kilkenny (Gowran)
Q 1973(75) IFC 1917:79 C f+. Same Correspondent as **.1**

cf '"Let the last man bolt the door." This is very common in this area. In other words "Let my successor, whoever he may be, deal with the problem."' Co. Sligo Q 1973 IFC 1888:109

cf the motif *MI* J 1880 *Animals or objects treated as if human—miscellaneous.*

late/Boyce (Boys)   Part B 13
A 157.1 '"You're late," says Boyce.'

116

Lover 'The White Horse of the Peppers, A Legend of the Boyne.' in
Legends and Stories of Ireland [?2nd Series] n.d. New Edition London:
Ward etc. p. 261: "'I was bellowsing away there for better than ten
minutes, and the divil a toe you'd dance, but talking all the time, and then
you come and want to put back the tune. Now, the next time you won't
let good music be wasted; throth it's not so plenty."
"Not such as yours, in throth, Rory," said Aggy, in her own little coaxing
way. —Ah, now Rory!"
"Twon't do, Aggy; you'd think to come over me now with the blarney;
but you're late says Boyce:"* and so saying, off he trudged, leavin the
dancers in dudgeon.
[footnote] *When the Lord Thomas Fitzgerald discovered that treason
was within his castle of Maynooth, the traitor (Parese, I believe) was
ordered for immediate execution in the Bass Court of the fortress; there
he endeavoured to save his life by committing a double treason, and
offered to betray the secret of the English besiegers, but a looker-on
exclaimed, "You're late!" His name was Boyce; and hence the saying
which exists to this day'
Notes: the wellerism is used in the dialogue of the story and then its
origin is explained in a footnote. *The White Horse of the Peppers* was
originally a three act comic drama by Lover, first performed in 1838 in
London.

.2 '"Too late," quoth Boys.'

John J[ames] Marshall *Popular Rhymes and Sayings of Ireland*. 1924
Dungannon, 1931 ed. p. 84: synopsis — during the rebellion of Silken
Thomas in 1534 his castle at Maynooth, Co. Kildare, was besieged by the
Lord Deputy Sir William Skeffington and betrayed by its governor
Christopher Paris [or Parese, Silken Thomas' foster brother].
Skeffington, wishing to reward Paris for this, asked what benefits he had
had under his previous employer. When the Lord Deputy discovered that,
despite many benefits [actually exaggerated by Paris in order to try and
gain more from Skeffington] Paris had still betrayed his master he
decided to reward him as agreed but then immediately execute him. At
this point Paris said that had he known his fate the Lord Deputy would
not have had the castle so easily and the castle's former constable James
Boys, hearing this, 'muttered "too late" in Irish, a saying which became
proverbial for ineffectual repentance, so that this historical incident gave
rise to two sayings "the pardon of Maynooth," an expression for the
headsman's block or gallows, and '"Too late,' quoth Boys." This story
has been told of other fortresses betrayed to enemies as well as
Maynooth.'

late/fool (Jacky Smith, Pat, Billy Thompson)

A 158.1 '"You spoke too late," as the fool said when he swallowed a bad egg, and heard the chicken chirp going down his throat.'

Patrick Weston Joyce 1910, 1991 rpt. Ch. 8 'Proverbs' p. 107. Opening this chapter Joyce says: 'Those that I give here in collected form were taken from the living lips of the people during the last thirty or forty years'

.2 '"Ye're late!" as Jacky Smith sayd when he heard the chirp of the wee bird in the egg he swallowed.'

wee=little
Ulster
Byers Papers Box T4 'S & P' ts T-4-6 p. 71

.3 '"Spoke too late, little bird!" as Pat said when he sucked an egg and the bird began to cheep.'

cheep=chirp
County Donegal
Traynor 1954 under 'cheep'

.4 '"Ye're late!" as Billy Thompson sayd when he heard the croak of the frog as he swallowed it.'

Ulster
Byers Box T4 'S & P' ts T-4-6 p. 71.

late/Paddy Loughran (Paddy)   Am Eng

A 159.1 '"Ye're late," as Paddy Loughran say'd t' the ghost.'

'M'Cart' [Canon Abraham Hume 1814–80] *Poor Rabbin's Ollminick [= Almanac] for the toun o' Bilfawst [= Belfast]... 1863 ...* , a pastiche, n.d. [1862 or 63] Belfast & Dublin, under 'August': 'It wos [= was] about this time that Paddy Loughran seen [= saw] a ghost that hed [= had] come to frighten him, but he only sayd, "ye're late," an' with that, the bye-word riz [= arose] — "Ye're late, as Paddy Loughran sayd t' the ghost."' Cited in Patterson under 'bye-word.' Also in Byers Papers Box T4 T-4-4, on a one page list titled 'Proper Names' comprising *c.* 20 proverbs or sayings containing personal names, with no attribution

.2 '"You're late," as Paddy said t' the ghost.'

118

'M'Cart' *Poor Rabbin's Ollminick [= Almanac]for the toun o' Bilfawst
[= Belfast]... 1863 ...* , a pastiche, n.d. [1862 or 63] Belfast & Dublin, p.
25 in a list titled 'Proverbial Expressions.' Cited in Byers Papers Box T4
'S & P' ts T-4-6 p. 58 with no attribution

DOW 687.

law/client   Am Eng
**A 160.1 "'I'm laying down the law," as the client said when he
floored his counsellor.'**
The Dublin Journal of Temperance, Science and Literature, 1, No. 21
(17/9/1842), p. 334 in a list of three near the bottom of the page [this and
Part A 210 & 223]. Probably reprinted from *Alexander's Weekly
Messenger* 10/7/1839, p. 1/2 or 23/10/1839 p.4/5 as cited in Tidwell

DOW 690.

lean out/Breekers
A 161.1 "'Lean out on it," says the Breekers.'
Breekers=local fishermen
County Kerry
Q 1973 IFC 1917:18 C m+: 'get a move on with the oars. Said about
getting a move on at any job.'

A 162 *does not exist*

Lent/girl
A 163.1 ""'Tis Lent," as the girl said to the soldier.'
Dublin City late 1930s
Q 1973 IFC 1917:15 C m+: 'to which the rejoinder was "But won't you
be getting it back?"'

Note: this immediately follows 'Christmas/girl' Part A 40. See it also for
additional comment. There is something similar in Partridge p. 126.

less/wren   Sc Gae
**A 164.1 "'It's the less of that," as the wren said when she took
a drink out of the river.'**
County Kilkenny 1955 or earlier
Q 1973(75) IFC 1917:78 C f+: 'used by a workman on a farm in Cliften
twenty or more years ago'
?Macdonald

see also the converse Part A 180 & Part B 22.

liberty/King John
A 165.1 'King John, signing the *Magna Carta*, "You're taking a bit of a liberty this time aren't you?"'
P.T.Q. 1970 Belfast p. 55

Note: King John of England [b. 1167, d. 1216] was persuaded to seal the *Magna Carta* on 15/6/1215.

lick/tinker
A 166.1 '"Lick alike," as the tinker said to the wife.'
County Carlow
Q 1973 IFC 1917:73 C m+

cf 'An Seabhac' 1926 No. 2024/1984 No. 2545 '<u>Lick alike</u> — Tadhg agus a mháthair' ['Lick alike — Tadhg and his mother'] and the expression recorded in Co. Armagh 'we can lick thumbs' meaning 'your position or situation is similar to my own' Michael J. Murphy/**MJM** 1990 p. 65 and Byers Papers as cited in the Electronic Database, Ulster Dialect Archive, UFTM: 'lick thumbs and touch elbows' with Byers' def. 'we are both alike' and comment: 'said when one person tries to make out he or she is more innocent than another who is blamed for something.'
lid/cook
A 167.1 'As the cook said, "There's a lid for every pot."'
County Galway 1990s
Q 2000(02) i DM m+, part-time mature student UU, who heard it in the 1990s in the Craft Village, Spiddal, from a local woman in her 40s talking about marriage.'

life/liftboy
A 168.1 '"Life is full of ups and downs," said the liftboy to the passenger.'
County Antrim
Q 1973? IFC 1888:27 +

Note: the proverb 'Life is full of, *or* has its, ups and downs' is currently common in English.

life/self-made man

A 169.1 '"I started life without a shirt to my back," said the self-made man.'
P.T.Q. 1929 Belfast p. 6 with the comment: 'Nothing unusual in that.'

light/hag   Part B 122
A 170.1 '"More light," said the hag when the house was on fire.'
County Cavan
IFCS 1000:124 in a list, mainly of proverbs. Published in [Carson] Williams 1992 p. 5/2000a p. 16
Note: 'Mehr Licht' was part of Johann Wolfgang von Goethe's [1749–1832] dying words. Knowles 'Last Words' No. 15 ?p. 456.

like, liking see *taste/farmer*

lines/Auld Lyons
A 171.1 '"Hard lines," said auld Lyons when young Lyons was born.'
County Tipperary current in 1978
Q 1973(78) IFC 2027:167 C m+ same Correspondent as 'auld done/Dunne' p. 166 [Part A 63.4]: 'still common in Turtulla [near Thurles] and is quoted when a very minor misfortune happens to somebody ... such as striking one's thumb with a hammer etc; also used when one is faced with an unpleasant task'

Note: a version of 'lines/monkey' [Part A 173.4] was also given by the same Correspondent.

lines/cow (dog)
A 172.1 '"Hard lines," says the cow when she ate the railway.'
County Roscommon
Q 1973 IFC 1888:147 C m+. cf .2. For pertinent note see Part A 83.10

.2 '"Hard lines," said the dog when he ate the railway line.'
County Roscommon
Q 1973 IFC 1888:148 C m+. cf .1. For pertinent note see Part A 83.10.

lines/monkey (rabbit)
A 173.1 '"Hard lines!" said the monkey when he sat on the railway track.'
County Galway
Q 1973 IFC 1888:154 C m+

.2 as .1
County Westmeath
IFC 1917:61 C m+. For Correspondent's comments see Part A 13.2
[Repeated IFC 1917:reverse p. 98, on a sheet written in 1986 by SMcR
f+, DIF student from the USA, with the comment 'from brother']

.3 '"Hard lines!" says the monkey as he sat on the railway track.'
County ?Cork not after 1965
Q 1973 IFC 1917:7 + collected from a woman who heard it from her
father who died aged 76 *c*. 1965: 'this wellerism Mr B [name given] used
when something went wrong at home, such as the loss of an animal'

.4 '"Hard lines!" as the monkey said when he sat on the railway track.'
County Tipperary current in 1978
Q 1973(78) IFC 2027:167 C m+ '… also [like others in his list] popular
in Turtulla [near Thurles] and is quoted when one is presented with an
unpleasant task or when a very minor misfortune falls on a person.'
Note: 'lines/Lyons' [Part A 171] was also from the same Correspondent

.5 '"Hard lines!" said the monkey as it sat upon the rails.'
County Donegal
Q 1973 IFC 1888:13 C f: 'This is the only wellerism I can think of about
monkeys but I've heard this expression in the Fanad peninsula'
.6 '"Hard lines!" said the monkey when he sat on the railway.'
County Roscommon
Q 1973 IFC 1888:145 C m+. For Correspondent's comment see Part A
5.1

.7 '"Hard lines!" as the monkey said when he sat on the railway line.'
Dublin City late 1930s
Q 1973 IFC 1917:14 C m+. For Correspondent's comment see Part A 40

.8 'The monkey said, "Hard lines!" when he sat on the railway.'
County Mayo
Q 1973 IFC 1888:136 C m+
Note: this and two others [Part A 114.1 & 235.2] are grouped together in
a list under 'The monkey said:-' probably indicating a shortcut taken by
the Correspondent

.9 '"Hard lines!" said the monkey as he sat on the tram's track.'
IFC 1917:99 on a sheet written *c.* 1973 by ÁB f+ [E & Ir], DIF student in 1973

.10 'As the rabbit said when it sat on the railway track, "Hard lines!"'
County Tyrone
IFC 1888:56 collected in 1974 by SÓC(ii) from PÓD m+. For note see Part A 83.8.

lines/monkey
A 174.1 'As the monkey said when it got its tail cut off, "Hard lines!"'
County Tyrone
IFC 1888:56 collected in 1974 by SÓC(ii) from PÓD m+. For note see Part A 83.8

see also Part A 181, 182 & 203.

lines/passenger
A 175.1 '"Hard lines," as the passenger said when he fell out of the railway carriage window.'
County Leitrim
IFC 1888:104 informant/creator WS m+. For note see Part A 23; others from him are Part A 32, 54, 62, 112, 179, 317 & 319

cf 'For the man who fell off the train, "That's hard lines."' 'The John Bennett Show' BBC Radio Ulster, printout of email response from KM m, possibly South Down, to the appeal for wellerisms broadcast on 6/3/2002

cf the riddle 'What did the man say when he fell off the railway bridge? Hard lines,' Opie 1959 London *et al* p. 82.

little/cook
A 176.1 '"Every little helps," as the cook said when he threw the kitten into the soup.'
County Tipperary current in 1978
Q 1973(78) IFC 2027:168 C m+: 'I heard this in Turtulla [near Thurles] and [it] is used when somebody makes a small contribution to a

collection or, for example, if a load of sand etc. were being filled and if a child or some person threw in a small amount …'

Notes: the proverb 'Every little helps' is currently common in English both in oral tradition, eg. the reply of a woman customer, 50s, to shop assistant on getting discount, overheard in Reid's Shoes, Sandy Row, Belfast 4/5/2002, and in print, eg. on a *Belfast Telegraph* advertisement for their Clubcard Helpline July, 2002.

little/man
A 177.1 "'If you've little to eat you'll have a fine view,'" said the man when he tethered his horse on the top of a rock.'
County Donegal
Traynor 1954 under 'eat: In proverbs and sayings'

.2 "'You've little to eat but you've got a lovely view," is what the man said to the goat on the mountain.'
County Tyrone
Collected 1990s by FCW from **IC**.

little/monkey   Am Eng, Ind Eng
A 178.1 "'A little goes a long way," as the monkey said when he piddled over the cliff.'
piddled, a euphemism for urinated used especially when talking to or about children
County Kilkenny current in 1975
Q 1973(75) IFC 1917:79 C f+, i m+: 'told me by a local clergyman who hailed originally from [the] Castlecomer area, but who wishes to be anonymous! He said they were v[ery] common sayings in that area' [see the two other wellerisms, which also have a monkey as speaker, Part A 180.4 & 292, from the same informant]

.2 "'A little goes a long way," said the monkey as he pissed over the cliff.'
IFC 1917:98 on a sheet written in 1986 by SMcR f+, DIF student from the USA

DOW 739

Mieder & Tóthné Litovkina p. 14.

little/post office official

A 179.1 '"A little goes a long way," as the post office official said when he licked the stamp for Australia.'
County Leitrim
IFC 1888:104 informant/creator WS m+. For note see Part A 23; others from him are Part A 32, 54, 62, 112, 175, 317 & 319

Mieder & Tóthné Litovkina p. 14.

little (drop, everything)/woman (jinny-wren, monkey, old woman)
Part B 22, cf Part B 44 & 136 also Am Eng, Dan, Dut, E Eng,
Fin, Fr, Ger, *Ice*, Nor, Scots, Sc Gae, Swe
A 180.1 '"Every little helps!" as the woman said when she passed water in the sea.' [*sic*]
County Clare 1960s
Q 2000 **JG** who was told it in the 1960s in Dublin by the principal, f 50s, of a Dublin Christian Brothers secondary school 'This is one …' She had heard it in Clare.
Note: when **JG** told FCW he said 'pissed' and when asked whether the headmistress, whom he had described as 'prim and proper,' had said this he said 'Oh, no! "Passed water"'

.2 '"Every little helps!" as the woman said when she made her piss in the river.'
County Roscommon
IFC 1888:150 collected by **JD** from JK m [d. 1980] small farmer and quarry worker

.3 '"Every little helps," as the jinny-wren said when she pissed in the ocean.'
County Armagh
jinny=Jenny familiar form of *Jane* or *Janet*
Michael J. Murphy/**MJM** *Sayings and Stories from Slieve Gullion, …* 1990 Dundalk p. 118, in section titled 'Urination'

.4 '"Every little helps," as the monkey said when he piddled in the ocean.'
County Kilkenny current in 1975
Q 1973(75) IFC 1917:79 C f+, i m+: 'told me by a local clergyman who hailed originally from [the] Castlecomer area, but who wishes to be anonymous! He said they were v[ery] common sayings in that area' [see the two other wellerisms, which also have a monkey as speaker, Part A 178.1 & 292, from the same informant]

.5 '"Every wee drop counts!" said the old woman when she piddled in the sea.'
wee=little [and, as a noun, a euphemism for urine]
County Armagh current in 1974
Q 1973(74) IFC 1888:66 C m+ 60s, sheep farmer: '... used in daily conversation in this area, some of them earthy, no doubt. ... one has to be part and parcel of the scene at work and play to hear or to utter these same phrases. I would like to point out that a parish priest, for example, might minister for thirty years and, unless by accident, ... never hear any of the following. The same applies to any stranger in the district; to hear the full roll [= ?range] of the graphic speech one has to be accepted. --- Some earthy ones I have heard run something like this --- [.5 and Part A 234 are the only wellerisms he gives] I would like to add that, earthy or otherwise, ... [these] run through everyday conversation in and around Slieve Gullion in South Armagh where I live.' The same man also contributed to Q 2000, on that occasion one — see Part A 259.54

.6 '"Everything counts," as the woman said when she pissed in the ocean.'
County Roscommon
Q 1973 IFC 1888:148 C m+

DOW 730, 746–47; Smith & Wilson pp. 231–32; Kelly p. 8 No. 74; Ramsay p. 8; Nicolson p. 281 No. 2
*Ice ref. from Draft for seminar held 1976, p. 4 in Almqvist *Irish Wellerisms* 1973– File

Mieder & Tothné Litovkina pp. 80–81

see also note at A 176 & the converse wellerism Part A 164.

long/monkey
A 181.1 '"That's the long and the short of it," as the monkey said when the train ran over his tail.'
North-East Ulster
Q 2000(02) i DM+, part-time mature student UU, from his father, also DM+, 70s, b. & partly reared in Randalstown, Co. Antrim, now living in Belfast

see also Part A 174, 182 & 203.

long/monkey (fox, fellow, man, lad)   Part B 81 also Am Eng

A 182.1 '"It won't be long now," said the monkey when he got the piece off his tail.'
County Cavan
Q 1973 IFC 1888:87 C m+

.2 '"It won't be long now," said the monkey when he got his tail cut off.'
IFC 1917:99 on a sheet written *c.* 1973 by ÁB f+ [E & Ir], DIF student in 1973

.3 'As the monkey said when it got its tail cut off, "It won't be long now."'
County Tyrone
IFC 1888:56 collected in 1974 by SÓC(ii) from PÓD m+. For note see Part A 83.8

.4 '"'T won't be long now," as the monkey said when he got his tail cut.'
County Cork
Q 2000 i f 60s who heard it in West Cork in her childhood there; she commented that trains were not familiar there. Collected 2002 in Rostrevor, Co. Down

.5 '"It'll not be long now," that's what the monkey said when he got his tail cut off.'
County Monaghan 1950s
Q 2000 IC who heard it as a child from his uncle LC [b. *c.* 1910] shopkeeper in Emyvale. It was his response when the children asked how long it would be until they went on a promised outing such as to Emyvale Lake

.6 '"It won't be long now," as the monkey said when the train ran over his tail.'
Belfast current
Q 2000 TC who comments 'frequently.' For his further comments see Part A 118

.7 '"It won't be long now," said the monkey when the train ran over his tail.'
Q 2000 'The John Creedon Show' RTÉ Radio 1, email dated 17/1/2002 from the programme's researcher listing all the 5 broadcast responses and 4 others to the appeal which was broadcast on 16/1/2002. See Appendix 2

.8 '"It won't be long now," said the fox when he got his tail cut off.'
County Donegal
Q 1973 IFC 1888:11 C m

.9 '"It won't be long now," as the fox said when his tail got caught in a trap.'
County Mayo
Q 1973 IFC 1888:135 C m+

.10 '"It won't be long now," said the fox when he lost his tail.'
County Roscommon
Q 1973 IFC 1888:144 C m+: 'used when something is expected to happen soon.' For Correspondent's additional comment see Part A 5.1

.11 '"It won't be long soon," as the fox said when his tail got caught in a trap.'
County Roscommon
Q 1973 IFC 1888:147 C m+. cf **.12**, for pertinent note see Part A 83.10

.12 '"It won't be long soon," as the fox said when he got his tail caught in the trap.'
County Roscommon
Q 1973 IFC 1888:148 C m+. cf **.11**. For pertinent note see Part A 83.10

.13 '"It won't be long now," as the fellow said when he cut the dog's tail.'
County Galway
Q 1973 IFC 1888:154 C m+

.14 '"It won't be long now," as the man said when he cut the dog's tail.'
1976
Overheard in DIF — first part from **LC**, second part added by PP m and noted on card filed in Almqvist *Irish Wellerisms* 1973– File.

.15 & .16 '"It won't be long now," as the fellow (lad) said when he cut the tail off the cat.'
County Tipperary current in 1978
Q 1973(78) IFC 2027:168 C m+: 'I again [as others in his returned list] heard this in Turtulla [near Thurles] and [it] is quoted when a person is waiting for something or looking forward to something'

DOW 758, 760 & 762

cf the riddle 'What did the monkey say when he was cutting off his tail? It won't be long now.' Opie 1959 London *et al* p. 82

Note: '"That'll be the end of it," as the monkey said when the train ran over his tail,' was used as one of the ten, later five, examples on Q 2000. See Appendix 1

see also Part A 174, 181 & 203.

look/man

A 183.1 '"One look before is better than two behind," as the man said when he fell into the well.'
County Wexford
IFCS 885:19 +. Published in [Carson] Williams 1992 p. 62/2000a p. 64

cf *'Dúirt an madadh rua gurbh fhearr amharc maith amháin romhat ná beirt ' do dhéidh'* ['The fox says that one look in front is better than two behind'] Lúcás under *'roimhe* 3. (of caution)' collected from MBeanMhicL b. 1918

Note: an example in English of the proverb 'One look before is better than two behind' is to be found in Co. Cavan IFCS.

Lord/Tom Malone

A 184.1 '"May the Lord direct me!" says Tom Malone when he pulled the tail out a th' ass.'
a th'=of the
County Kilkenny current when the questionnaire was returned
Q 1973 IFC 1917:83 C f+: 'all these sayings and phrases are common in the language of the people in Co. Kilkenny. I find it hard to get wellerisms. When asked people get confused and cannot remember, although I know they are used in conversation'

.2 '"May the Lord direct me!" says Tom Malone when he pulled the tail outa th' ass.'
County Kilkenny
outa th'=out of the
Q 1973 IFC 1917:86 written down by a Roman Catholic canon: 'used to indicate perplexity in making a decision.'

lose/man

A 185.1 '"That we may never lose but her," as the man said when his mother-in-law died.'
County Roscommon
Q 1973 IFC 1888:149 C m+. For note see Part A 83.10.

lot see *rum lot*

love/man

A 186.1 '"Give my love to Nancy, it's my last time round," as the man said when the bull was chasing him round the field.'
County Down
IFC 1917: reverse p. 98, on a sheet written in 1986 by SMcR f+, DIF student from the USA, i Mrs McC.

love/tennis player

A 187.1 '"Back to love," as the tennis player said when her partner lost his service.'
O'Farrell 1980, 1983 rpt. in Ch. 'Health and worse — with love' p. 35: 'But back to *love* as the tennis player said when her partner lost his service.' Used after a digression from the first theme of the chapter — health — to introduce the second — love.

lover/Scotsman

A 188.1 '"Stand behind your lover," said the Scotsman to his unfaithful wife, "I'm going to shoot you both."'
P.T.Q. 1958 Belfast n.p.

cf the motif *MI* X 600 *Humor concerning races or nations.*

luck/Kerryman

A 189.1 '"Good luck fotever," as the Kerryman said.'
fotever=whatever, nevertheless
Limerick City early 1940s
Q 1973 IFC 1917:13 C m+: 'Heard in a pub … It is illustrative of the difficulty some Kerry people have in pronouncing the letter "w".' I am grateful to Dáithí Ó hÓgáin for discussing this wellerism

cf the toast 'Good luck whatever!' O'Farrell 1993, 1995 rpt. p. 65, in the list titled 'Toasts and Hearty Wishes' with a note on p. 120: 'from my own manuscript sources, compiled over a long number of years.'

luck/tinker
A 190.1 '"It might be all for luck," as the tinker said when he missed mass.'
County Mayo
Q 1973 IFC 1888:135 C m+: 'to miss mass was the greatest misfortune'
see also Part A 60.

luk see *see/blind man*

M

mairg/old woman   *cf Ger
A 191.1 '"It's mairg to be dirty," said the old woman when she washed her cap in the potato-water.'
it's mairg <Ir *is mairg= it is a pity*
County Cavan
IFCS 966:94 in a list, mainly of proverbs

*cf Ger '"Reinlichke is 't halw' Läben," säd de oll Fruu, wascht ehr Nachtmütz in de Dranktunn ut.' ['"Cleanliness is half life," said the old woman, washing out her nightcap in the pig swill trough.'] Neumann Q 635, and there are parallels to this in several other languages.

man/ass (bull) see *everyone/ass (bull)*

man/beatnik
A 192.1 'Then there was the beatnik who looked over the flat-chested girl and said, "Like man."'
P.T.Q. 1967 Belfast n.p.

man/cobbler see *trade/cobbler*
man/man see *hardy man* & *last man*

man/Mrs O'Connor
A 193.1 '"Don't mind the man who does not know whether it is his pants or his breakfast he will go for first," as Mrs O'Connor used to say.'
County Kerry

Q 1973 IFC 1917:27 C m+: 'On healthy appetite.' Mrs O'Connor was a local 'big' land owner ie. owner of extensive land.

man/old man

A 194.1 '"He will be a man before his mother," as the old man said when his daughter had the small male child.'
County Roscommon
Q 1973 IFC 1888:148 C m+

cf '"You'll be a man before your mother," said to comfort a little boy in trouble' Patterson under 'man.'

marry/Saint Paul

A 195.1 '"Better marry than burn," as Saint Paul said.'
County Wexford
IFCS 901:318 in a list, mainly of proverbs. Published in [Carson] Williams 1992 p. 119/2000a p. 103

Note: from I Corinthians 7:8–9.

match/Mick Sheedy (Mick Sheehy)

A 196.1 '"You wouldn't do that to your match," as Mick Sheedy said to the fox.'
match=equal [opponent]
County Limerick
Patrick Weston Joyce 1910, 1991 rpt. Ch. 8 titled 'Proverbs' p. 117: 'Mick Sheedy the gamekeeper had a hut in the woods where he often took shelter and rested and smoked. One day when he had arrived at the doorway he saw a fox sitting at the little fire warming himself. Mick instantly spread himself out in the doorway to prevent escape. And so they continued to look at each other. At last Reynard, perceiving that some master-stroke was necessary, took up in his mouth one of a fine pair of shoes that were lying in a corner, brought it over, and deliberately placed it on top of the fire. We know the rest! (Limerick).' Opening this chapter Joyce says: 'Those that I give here in collected form were taken from the living lips of the people during the last thirty or forty years.' Cited in *Addenda* 91

.2 '"You wouldn't hit your match," as Mick Sheehy said to the fox.'
O'Farrell 1980, 1983 rpt, in Ch. titled 'Fights and Threats' p. 60: 'Here. Hit somebody your own size. You wouldn't hit your match, as Mick Sheehy said to the fox.'

cf 'Would you fight your match?' Lover *Legends and Stories of Ireland* [?2nd Series] n.d. New Ed. London: Ward etc., p. 122; same question also used by Lover in same volume, p. 359

cf the folktale *TIF* 67** *The Fox Caught by the Butcher* [96 versions]

Note: Sheedy is a common personal name in east Galway which borders Limerick while Sheehy is a common personal name in Munster, the province containing Limerick, see MacLysaght

see also Part A 224 & Part B 102, which are different wellerisms with the same tale.

mate see *fill*

me/monkey (fox)
A 197.1 '"Dear me," as the monkey said when he wrote the letter to himself.'
County Roscommon
Q 2000 **JG**, who learnt it as a child from his maternal grandmother ES, née G, b. 1879, Knockcrokery, Co. Roscommon, d., same place, *c*. 1964, who would use it if, for instance, she got polish on her hand, the smell of which would interfere with her snuff-taking habit. Around 1900 she spent a few years in the USA but returned to marry the Knockcrokery post office owner

.2 '"Dear me" says the fox.'
County Clare
Q 1973 IFC 1917:7 +: 'this she [the Correspondent's mother+] said when we, the children, had really exasperated her.'

melting/candle
A 197a.1 '"I'm melting," as the candle remarked when ...'
James Joyce *Ulysses*, a novel, 1922 Paris, 1986 ed., Part I, Episode 1, line 333, p. 10: 'Buck Mulligan tossed the fry on to the dish beside him. Then he carried the dish and a large teapot over to the table, set them down heavily and sighed with relief.

—I'm melting, he said, as the candle remarked when ... But, hush! Not a word more on that subject! Kinch, wake up! Bread, butter, honey. Haines, come in. The grub [= food] is ready.'

mickle/Scotchman

A 198.1 'As the Scotchman says, "Many a mickle makes a muckle."'

Behan *The Hostage*, a play, originally in Irish <u>An Giall</u> and performed in June 1958 in Dublin, first performed in English in Oct. same year in London, Act I an old, run down house in Dublin, time 1958, 1978 ed. p. 134:

'*Monsewer* There will be the two guards and the prisoner.
Pat The prisoner?
Monsewer Yes. Yes, we only have one at the moment, but it's a good beginning.
Pat Yes, indeed, as the Scotchman says, 'Many a mickle makes a muckle.'
Monsewer And as we Irish say, "It's one after another they built the castle[s]. Iss in yeeg a Kale-ah shah togeock nuh cashlawn."' [Is i ndiaidh a chéile is ea a tógadh na caisleáin.]
mickle <Scots *pickle=little; muckle=a great amount*

Notes: the wellerism does not occur in the Irish language version, but substitutes for the following, <u>An Giall</u> 1981 ed. pp. 30–31 [FCW's translation]:
Pat The prisoner?
Monsewer Yes, the prisoner. Maybe we only have one at the moment, but it's a good beginning. A good beginning, that's half the work. It's one after another castles are built. [play text: 'Tosach maith, sin leath na hoibre. Is i ndiaidh a chéile a tógadh na caisleáin.']
The proverb 'Many a mickle makes a muckle' is currently well-known.

mine/devil

A 199.1 '"That's mine," as the devil said to the dead policeman.'

James Joyce *Ulysses*, a novel, 1922 Paris, 1986 ed., Part II, Episode 12, p. 273 line 1466 in an aside during a discussion on nations in a pub:
'—Show us over the drink, says I. Which is which? That's mine, says Joe, as the devil said to the dead policeman.' Cited in *Addenda* 95.

miracles/cobbler

A 200.1 '"Miracles will never cease!" said the cobbler as he stuck the candle to the wall.'
County Cork
Q 1973 IFC 1917:22 C m+, i m+: 'from an old miller'

Note: the proverb 'Miracles will never cease!' is currently common in English.

miss/man
A 201.1 '"That you may never miss but hit," as the man said to his barley.'
miss=fail to germinate
County Donegal
Byers Papers Box T4 'S & P' ts T-4-6 p. 63.

moderates/captain
A 201a.1 '"Call me when it moderates," as the captain said.'
County Antrim
Q 2000 collected 13/10/2002 from RM, 70s, retired engineer, who used it when resting during a cruise. When asked about its origins he said, 'Oh, that's an old one that my wife and I often use as a joke' [when they are sailing their yacht and one of them is going to lie down].

money/oul' woman   Am Eng, Dut, E Eng, Fri, Scots, Swe
A 202.1 '"There's many a thing made for the money," as the oul' woman said when she saw the monkey.'
County Donegal
Byers Papers Box T4 'S & P' ts T-4-6 p. 59

DOW 944 & 1348; 'Cheviot' p. 250.

more/monkey
A 203.1 '"There's more to it than that," as the monkey said looking at his stitched tail that was chopped off and settled again.'
Belfast 1970s
O'Farrell 1980, 1983 rpt. in Ch. titled 'Fights and Threats' p. 57: 'Fighting words heard today do not date back to the nineteenth century, some of them come from the tragic people of a troubled city who still allow themselves a humorous phrase or two. If you fall don't take time to get up but run on. … Were they fighting over the dog? Oh, there's more

to it than that, as the monkey said looking at his stitched tail that was chopped off and settled again'

see also Part A 174, 181 & 182.

mountain/girl
A 204.1 '"If the mountain won't come to M'ammed then the M'ammed must go to the mountain," as the girl said to the soldier.'
Behan *The Quare Fellow*, a play, first performed Dublin 1954, 1978 ed. p. 115, Act III Scene 1, the prison yard, time 1954:
'Hangman --- Don't see any signs of Regan.
Jenkinson (Assistant Hangman) He's probably had to go on duty. You've left it too late.
Hangman Well, if the mountain won't come to M'ammed then the M'ammed must go to the mountain
Warder Regan (from the darkness) As the girl said to the soldier.
Hangman As the girl said to the soldier. Oh, its you, Regan. Will you have a drink?'
M'ammed=Mohammed

Note: the proverb is currently well-known in English

see also Part A 4.

mouth/trout
A 205.1 '"A shut mouth catches no flies," said the trout to the spider.
"Watch it, bullet eyes, all that flutters is not flies."'
County Cavan
Q 1973 IFC 1888:7 C m+

Note: the proverb 'A shut mouth catches no flies' is common in English and known in Irish. 'All that flutters is not flies,' parodies 'All that glitters is not gold' which, again, is a common proverb in English.

much/skeleton
A 206.1 '"You can't get much out of me," says the skeleton to the worm.'
County Kerry
Q 1973 IFC 1917: 17 C m+.

muck/Breege 'V'

A 207.1 '"Where there is muck there is luck," says Breege 'V'.'

County Roscommon
Q 1973 IFC 1888:147 C m+: 'She was a woman who kept a very dirty house and had dirty habits. One would need to be very careful when using that saying in these parts as she has a lot of descendants who get very offended when the saying is used'

Notes: 'V' replaces the last name which was given by the Correspondent. It may be either an actual personal name or, more likely, a nickname which may be related to a word meaning 'dirty.' In substituting 'V,' rhyme, and possibly alliteration, have been lost. I am grateful to Dónall P. Ó Baoill for discussing this wellerism. For additional note see Part A 83.10.
The proverb 'Where there's muck there's luck' is currently very common in English

see also Part A 208 & 209.

muck/man

A 208.1–.3 '"Where there's muck there's brass," as the man said when he found the farthing in the midden/dung heap/manure heap.' [sic]
brass=wealth; farthing=smallest denomination of coinage which, although legal tender until 1960, did not really circulate after the mid-1940s
County Roscommon 1950s & 60s
Q 2000 **JG** on email
Note: This is a rare instance in Ireland of 'Where there's muck there's brass,' this variant of the proverb being associated with Northern England, particularly Yorkshire

.4 '"Where there['s] muck there['s] luck," as the man said when he got the halfcrown in the dung heap.'
halfcrown=a silver coin, latterly the highest denomination, in circulation until decimalisation in 1971; there were eight halfcrowns to the £1
County Roscommon
Q 1973 IFC 1888:149 C m+. For note see Part A 83.10

see also Part A 207 & 209.

muck/wealthy owner

A 209.1 '"Where there's muck there's luck," said the wealthy owner of the dirty, untidy shop down the country.'
down the country=in the country
Counties Cavan & Leitrim
Q 1973 IFC 1888:92 C m+

see also Part A 207 & 208.

music/man   *cf Am Eng
A 210.1 '"Music and drawing taught here," as the man said when he was pulling a wheel-barrow through the streets without any oil on its axles.' [*sic*]
The Dublin Journal of Temperance, Science and Literature, 1, No. 21 (17/9/1842), p. 334 in a list of three near the bottom of the page [this and Part A 160 & 223]

*cf Am Eng '"I give lessons in music and drawing," as the donkey said when he began to bray and drag a cart after him.' *DOW* 854.

N

nature/guard
A 210a.1 '"Do you ever stop to consider the nature of time?" as the sarcastic Guard said to the publican caught pulling a pint at 10.40 p.m.'
Guard=member of the Garda Síochána, the police service
'Myles na gCopaleen' [Brian O'Nolan] 'Cruiskeen Lawn,' a regular column in the daily newspaper, *The Irish Times*, 28/7/1943 as cited in Jackson 1999 p. 106: 'Do you ever stop to consider the nature of time (as the sarcastic Guard said to the publican caught pulling a pint at 10.40 p.m). Look at it this way. Suppose a man's life is 60 years and a horse's 20. The horse is aging three times as fast as the man ... '

Note: 'Cruiskeen Lawn' was begun in 1940 in Irish. The wellerism was the opening sentence of one of the first columns in English.

near/man
A 211.1 '"So near and yet so far," says the man when the bird lit on his gun.'
County Louth

IFCS 672:262 in a list, mainly of proverbs. Published in [Carson] Williams 1992 p. 55/2000a p. 58

Note: 'So near and yet so far' is currently common.

neart see *strength/wren*

necessity/cook
A 212.1 '"Necessity is the mother of invention," as the cook said when she used her night cap to strain the jelly.'
County Tyrone
Clougherney Presbyterian Church Quotation Calendar 1945, a booklet with a daily quote, many being proverbs, from 1/1/1945–31/3/1946, TC f Beragh, quotation for 8/2/1946

Mieder & Tóthné Litovkina pp. 149–50

Note: the proverb 'Necessity is the mother of invention' is common in English and Irish.

news/man
A 213.1 '"No news is good news," as the man said who was about to be hanged.' [*sic*]
Dublin City
Almqvist *Irish Wellerisms* 1973– File p. 13 No. 56 with Almqvist's comment: 'oral communication 1976'; 'news' is glossed 'noose'

DOW 871

Mieder & Tóthné Litovkina p. 155

Note: the proverb 'No news is good news' is currently common in English and Irish.

nice/cat
A 214.1 '"That is nice!" said the cat when she spilt the milk.'
County Longford
Q 1973 IFC 2027:162 C f+: [said] 'when you are caught doing something or "When the cat is out the mice can play"'

cf 'That's nice!' said ironically when the opposite happened collected 21/4/2002 by FCW from AW f b. 1957, b. & r. south Belfast, and a sister-in-law of FCW.

night/countess
A 215.1 '"The (k)night's long in coming," said the Countess gently stirring her tea with her left hand.'
Derry ?City
Q 1973 IFC 1888:25 +. For Correspondent's comment see Part A 95.

nize see *cry*

no/centipede
A 216.1 '"No!" said the female centipede crossing her legs, "A hundred times no."'
P.T.Q. 1965 Belfast n.p.

noise see *cry*

nothing (nothin')/eels (eels at Toome)
A 217 ?.1 '"'Tis nothing when you are used to it," as the eels said when they were being skinned alive.'
Lean 1904, 1969 fac. Vol. IV, p. 19: Swift 1738 … *Polite Conversation* …. While only '"'Tis nothing when you're used to it," is in Swift's … *Polite Conversation* …, the wellerism may be elsewhere in Swift. Lean is, in turn, cited in Smith & Wilson and *DOW* 887

.2 '"It's nothin' when ye're used to it," as the eels at Toome said when they were being skinned alive.'
Ulster
nothin'=nothing; Toome=a place at the head of the Lower Bann river where eel-catching has been commercialised since mediaeval times
Byers Papers Box T4 'S & P' ts T-4-6 p. 65. Published in Carson Williams 2001a p. 14

cf 'he is like the eels, he's got used to it,' with Byers' comment: 'a reference to the skinning of eels' Byers Papers as cited in the Electronic Database, Ulster Dialect Archive, UFTM.

nothing/woman see *anything*

O

off/monkey   Am Eng, E Eng
A 218.1 "'They're off!" as the monkey said when he sat on the circular saw.'
Dublin City late 1930s
Q 1973 IFC 1917:15 C m+. For Correspondent's comment see Part A 40

.2 "'They're off!" as the monkey said when he sat on the razor blade.'
Q 2000(4/3/02) i **BA** who heard it in the last few days in Dublin from CT m *c*. 55, a university administrator. A bishop had pronounced on the forthcoming abortion referendum to be held in the Republic of Ireland on 6/3/02. **BA** said that there were lots of things that the actress said to the bishop and also that the monkey said and quoted 'It won't be long now! …' CT said that there was worse and quoted his

DOW 903

cf the riddle 'What did the monkey say when he backed into the lawnmower? Ans. They're off.' Cray p. 116 No. 18, collected 1959–60 in the USA from a 21 year old.

oiled/car
A 219.1 "'Said one car to another, "Let's get oiled!"'
oiled=drunk
P.T.Q. 1958 Belfast n.p.

one/tailor
A 220.1 "'One at a time," says the tailor.'
County Clare
Q 1973 IFC 1917:5 C m+

cf the following which refers to sewing stitches 'One at a time and that well done leads to excellence.'

orders/bride
? A 221.1 "'Ye're early with your orders," as the bride said at the church door.'
Lean 1903, 1969 fac. Vol. II, Pt. 2, p. 752: '(Irish) Hislop' [*sic*]; cited in *DOW* 913 as Hislop 1870

Note: not apparent in Hislop [1862 or 70 eds.], or the other usual Scottish collections.

out/Breekers see *lean out/Breekers*

out/Ellen
A 222.1 '"Out again with your laughing," says Ellen.'
County Roscommon
Q 1973 IFC 1888:145 C m+: 'used when something slips out of place.'
For Correspondent's additional comment see Part A 5.1.

P

paint/city girls   Am Eng
A 223.1 '"Take care of the paint," as the city girls say when a fellow goes to kiss them.'
The Dublin Journal of Temperance, Science and Literature, 1, No. 21 (17/9/1842), p. 334 first in a list of three near the bottom of the page [this and Part A 160 & 210]. Probably reprinted from *Alexander's Weekly Messenger* 4/9/1839, p. 4/5 as cited in Tidwell

DOW 919.

pair/Divil (Devil)   cf Part B 27 also *cf E Eng, †cf Scots,
   ‡cf Sc Gae
A 224.1 '"There's a pair o' ye now," as the divil said to his knee-buckles.'
o'=of
Lover 'Paddy the Sport' in *Legends and Stories of Ireland* [?2nd Series] New Ed. n.d. London: Ward etc., p.145, context, in a section about Paddy the Sport which contains a version of *TIF* 67** *The Fox Caught by the Butcher*: '"There, now," says he, "you may keep the other [brogue on the

fire] company," says he; "and there's a pair ... knee-buckles."' Also in Mair, p. 70, but probably a citation from Lover

.2 '"You're a right pair," as the Devil said when he looked at his feet.'

Dublin City, North, current

Q 2000 i AO'C f 40s, who heard it in 2002 from a woman of 50, brought up in Cabra, who heard it from her mother b. *c*. 1920 in Cabra. It was used when someone wished to remark disparagingly on something someone was wearing, or on someone

*cf E Eng '"There's a pair on 'em," as the goose said of his legs.' *Addenda* 104

†cf Scots '"Are they no a bonny pair?" as the deil said to his hoofs.' 'Cheviot' p. 41, see also p. 366 for similar variant

‡cf Sc Gae '"Is càraid sin," mar a thuirt an fheannag ri 'casan. ("That's a pair," as the crow said to her feet.') Nicolson p. 222 No. 5 where there is also a Scots version: '"They're a bonny pair," as the craw said o' his legs.' This, in turn, is cited in Cheviot p. 365

Note: perhaps to do with the belief that a devil can become visible and assume a semi-human shape, the lower legs ending in goatlike hooves

see also Part A 196 & Part B 102 which are different wellerisms with the same tale.

parlour/spider   Am Eng, E Eng, NZ Eng

A 225.1 '"Step into my parlour," said the spider to the fly.'

County Antrim 1950s & 60s

FCW personal observation and use. Common within the immediate family at that time and always said for comic effect when someone entered a room or other place

.2 as .1

Belfast *c*. 1980s

Q 2000 collected 20/8/2002 in Enniskillen from KR 40s [former fireman] who recalls hearing it on TV and radio. It was used by Ian Richard Kyle Paisley [1926–] founder and leader of the Democratic Unionist Party in an interview. Paisley had criticised the Republic of Ireland and the controversial Charles J. Haughey [1925–], then Taoiseach, had responded by inviting Paisley to 'Come and see us. We have nothing to hide.' When the interviewer said, 'Mr Paisley, what's the problem? He's

giving you an invitation' Paisley replied, "'Come into my parlour' said the spider to the fly" but, Mr Haughey, we're too darn fly' [= astute]
Note: Haughey was Taoiseach from 1979–81, again in 1982 & also from 1987–92

.3 "'Come into my parlour," said the spider to the fly.'
Q 2000 Used in conversation 24/4/2002 by GMcI, f b. 1970 Cork city, and reared there, academic: 'They [the job interviewers, once a candidate has been agreed] phone you up and say, "Come into our department" — "'Come into my parlour,' said the spider to the fly."'

DOW 225

Notes: while the above New Zealand ref. is to Partridge, p. 36, FCW also collected this in Jan. 2002 from PAP f 30s QUB postgraduate student from Hamilton, NZ, with the comment: 'everybody would know that. Not such a good connotation. If you got a shady invitation. Not super bad. A wee bit sinister,' and also, in August 2002, from KS, m 33, bank official from Gisbourne, NZ. Partridge suggests that it comes from an 1880s song, which may have been when it became more widely-known, however Tidwell (1950), p. 258 notes it as having been published in 1837.
peace/King James
A 226.1 "'Peace be with them!" as King James said to his hounds.'
Leinster 'heard by the writer [Kennedy p. 182] in the province of Leinster.'
Kennedy *The Book of Modern Irish Anecdotes ...* [1872] London, 1891 ed., in a list titled 'Irish Proverbs' p. 186 with note 'I?' ie. King James I [1567–1625], but more likely James II [1685–89]

cf "'Peace gie wi' ye," as King James said to his hounds,' Lean Vol. II, Pt. 2 p. 748 [no source], which could be either another Irish version or a version from elsewhere.

pen/convict
A 227.1 "'This pen leaks," as the convict said when the rain came through the roof.'
P.T.Q. 1938 n.p./1958 n.p. both Belfast.

pet/woman
A 228.1 "'Better be a rich man's pet than a poor man's slave," as the woman said when her daughter married the old man.'

County Roscommon
Q 1973 IFC 1888:149 C m+

Note: the proverb 'Better be a rich man's pet than a poor man's slave' is reasonably common in English.

philately/Chinese stamp-collector
A 229.1 'As one Chinese stamp-collector said to the other, "Philately will get you nowhere."'
P.T.Q. 1958 Belfast n.p.

Notes: the proverb 'Flattery will get you nowhere' is currently very common in English. Even in the late 1950s there were few residents of Chinese origin in Ireland; the first restaurant — *The Peacock*, Fountain Street, Belfast — did not open until 1963. I would like to thank Dean Lee of the Chinese Welfare Association for help with this reference.

pirdies/old woman
A 230.1.'As the old woman said, "There's nothing ates the pirdies like the harns."'
ate=eat; pirdies=potatoes; harns=herrings
County Down 1920s
Q 1973 IFC 1888:45 C m+, a primary school principal: 'then we had expressions attributed to "the old woman" and usually employed in connection with food and meals: "As the old woman ... like the harns."'
For additional comment see Part A 259.29

Note: was she eating them herself?

place/cow
A 231.1 'As the old cow said from the roof of the byre, "The place would [do] if there was plentness in it."'
County Donegal
Q 1973 IFC 1888:7 C m+ [E & Ir]: 'The above was the reply of a woman who was complimented on her well-furnished home'; 'plentness' is glossed: 'a local term for "ample"' [?ample room]

cf the folktale *TIF* 1210 *The Cow is Taken to the Roof to Graze* [209 versions] and the motif of the same name *MI* J 1904.1.

plane/pilot

A 232.1 '"Now let us consider the thing on another plane," as the pilot said to the rear gunner.'

'O'Brien' 1968 *The Best of Myles*, a selection from 'Cruiskeen Lawn' a regular column, at first in Irish, in the daily newspaper *The Irish Times*, 1939–66 p. 333. The majority of the pieces were written in the first five years ie. during the Second World War. This wellerism is used in 'O'Brien's' response to a newspaper entry about what to do if the office stair carpet disappears.

pleasure/fox   Part B 183 also Am Eng, Ind Eng

A 233.1 '"No pleasure without pain," said the fox when he tried to have sex relations with the grainneóg.'

County Cavan

Q 1973 IFC 1888:97 C m+, Order of Jesus. For his comments see Part A 140.1

DOW 960

Notes: the proverb 'No pleasure without pain' is currently common in English and is also known in riddle form in Irish — see Part B 183.

plenty/thief

A 234.1 '"Where there is plenty take plenty and where there is little take all," said the thief when he took the penny from the tramp.'

County Armagh current in 1974

Q 1973(74) IFC 1888:65 C m+ 60s, sheep farmer. For Correspondent's comments see Part A 180.5, although this particular wellerism is listed before his comment 'Some earthy ones …' The same man also contributed to Q 2000, on that occasion one — see Part A 259.54.

point/monkey (farmer)   *cf Am Eng

A 235.1 '"That's the point!" said the monkey when he sat on a tack.'

County Cork

Q 1973 IFC 1917:32 + [E & Ir]

.2 'The monkey said, "That's the point!" He sat on a tack.'

County Mayo

Q 1973 IFC 1888:136 C m+

Note: this and two others [Part A 114 & 173.8] are grouped together in a list under 'The monkey said:-' probably indicating a shortcut taken by the Correspondent

.3 '"That's the point," said the farmer when he sat on the nail.'
County Galway
Q 1973 IFC 1888:155 C m+

.4 '"Isn't that the point?" said the monkey when he sat on the thorn.'
County Roscommon
Q 1973 IFC 1888:144 C m+. For Correspondent's additional comment see Part A 5.1

cf 'My father had a favourite one "Confucius, he say 'He who sits on tack does not see point' email from DÓC, a nephew of SÓC(i), 18/2/2002

*cf Am Eng '"This is brief and to the point, as the man remarked when he got up off a tack.' *DOW* 133.

point/pop-star
A 236.1 '"I must get to the point," as the pop-star said to the taxi driver.'
Current
Q 2000 **TC** with his comment: 'I have difficulty with this type of saying [wellerisms] in the context of your research for, while they conform to the format of the quotation proverb, do they necessarily qualify as such, especially those which flourish for a week or two and then disappear? For instance recently listening to RTE radio I heard a rather long-winded politician catch himself on and say '"I must get to the point,' as the pop star said to the taxi driver." — obviously a reference to the Point Theatre, Dublin [established 1996]. The type of local saying I have in mind [like] the above would run something like '"That will settle your hash,' as Mickey Doran (fictitious name) said when he hit his wife with the spade." [Part A 118] Heard in the Mourne area.'

poison/publican
A 237.1 '"Every man to his own poison," as the publican said when he drank the strychnine.'
County Down 1970s
Q 2000 **TC**. For his comments see Part A 118

Note: 'What's [*or* 'Name] your poison?' is currently a common way of asking what someone would like to drink. cf O'Brien *The Dalkey Archive* 1964, 1986 ed, p. 119: "'I had a few pints of it [Dutch lager] meself [= myself] in Dublin a few years ago. You'd smell the Clydesdale [horse] off of it." Mick drank politely, and smiled. The natural garrulity of publicans could be a real help in his quest. "Ah well," he said, "every man to his own poison, I suppose."'

<u>pola</u>/white bear

A 238.1 'White bear to black bear, "<u>Ama pola.</u>"'
P.T.Q. 1947 Belfast n.p.

poor man/old lady

A 239.1 '"He's a poor man who can neither whistle or cheer," as the old lady said to the man who was unable to call the men from the far land.'
far land=?fields farthest from farmhouse
County Fermanagh
Q 1973(74) IFC 1888:71 C m+.

porter/tinker

A 240.1 '"There's no such thing as bad porter — some of it is just better than other," as the tinker said.'
County Mayo
Q 1973 IFC 1888:135 C m+

cf the Australian 'All palates are different, but "all beer's good only some's better than others."' O'Grady under 'beer.'

power/Old Power (Ould Power)

A 241.1 '"More power!" said old Power when young Power was born.'
County Mayo
Q 1973 IFC 1888:122 C m+: 'I cannot recall any Wellerisms from this place, even though I was born & reared here. The only one I can remember is your example 'I see ...' [Part A 259.51, for his variant]. Another one was "'More power … born "' --- used to praise someone for an outstanding action'

.2 as .1
County Roscommon current in the 1950s & 60s

Q 2000 **JG** who heard it constantly when he was growing up although there were none of that name locally. It was used when scoring goals or clinching deals, such as the sale of a pig, and, in fact, linked to all sorts of things. **JG** on the same occasion in Sept. 2001 also contributed a version of 'done/Dunne' [Part A 63.2]. Context, collected a in phone call 24/10/2002. See also **.4**

.3 as .1
County Kilkenny current 1973
Q 1973 IFC 1917:76 C f+: 'used here often when the word "power" is mentioned'

.4 as .1
County Offaly current
Q 2000 In the call mentioned in **.2 JG** told FCW that he works with a man named 'Power' [BP] from and living in Co. Offaly, who had told him that he had been pestered as a child by other children using the wellerism as a 'chant' in his presence and that, in turn, the same is happening in Co. Offaly to his young son [SP]

.5 '"More power," said Old Power when young Power was born.'
County Roscommon
Q 1973 IFC 1888:69 C m+, i PH m+, same informant as for 'done/Dunne' [Part A 63.5], which immediately follows power/Old Power

.6 '"More power," said ould Power when young Power was born.'
County Meath late 1930s
Q 2000 EO'B m 70s, retired primary school teacher: 'My feeling at the time I heard it — that is back in the 1938–39 era [as a child at national school] — was that it was just a reworking of the "Well done ..." saying, and with a somewhat similar meaning.' In an earlier letter EO'B had contributed 'done/ould Dunne' [Part A 63.5] *qv* for which FCW had asked about meaning and suggested that the other similar one he was trying to recall might be 'power/Power'

.7 '"More power!" says old Power when young Power was born.'
County Kerry
Q 1973 IFC 1917:19 C m+

.8 '"More power!" said old Power when Baby Power was born.'
County Cavan
Q 1973 IFC 1888:86 C m+, same Correspondent as 'done/old Dunne' [Part A 63.1] p. 87

cf the common wish 'More power to your elbow!'

Note: Powers is a well-known brand of whiskey manufactured in Dublin city until the last century, now in Co. Cork.

Q

questions/fiddler
A 242.1 'Says the fiddler to the flies, "Ax no questions, an' you'll (ye'll) be towl (towl') no lies."'
Ulster
ax=ask; towl[']=told
Byers Papers Box T2, T-2-3 Glossary A-Clerk, Fall 1921, under 'AKS' *or* 'AX=verb=to ask,' purple ts.
Bracketed version Byers Box T2 T-2-4 Glossary A-Byre under 'AKS' *or* 'AX=verb=to ask' black ts, which is a revised version of the purple. The bracketed version is probably the one cited in the Electronic Database, Ulster Dialect Archive, UFTM

Notes: 'Ask no questions and I'll tell you no lies,' was current in 1995 when collected by FCW from **IC**, also common earlier in English and found in Irish. cf the put off to children used by **MC** and related to FCW by **IC** in July 1995: 'Ask no questions and you'll hear no lies and I'll show you how the donkey dies.'

R

red chimney/old man
A 243.1 '"A red chimney is the sign of a hot house," said the old man who objected to his daughter marrying a red haired man.'
County Fermanagh
Q 1973(74) IFC 1888:71 C m+.

right/she (he)
A 244.1 '"Right," she said and he never wrote.'
County Cavan
Q 1973 IFC 1888:86 C m+

.2 '"Right," says he, but he never wrote.'
County Cork
Q 1973 IFC 1917:39 C f.

rinner (runner)/Devil (Deil) E Eng, Scots
A 245.1 '"Ye look like a rinner," quoth the devil to the lobster.'
rinner=runner
Anon. *National Proverbs: Ireland.* 1913 London p. 70

.2 '"You're a runner," as the deil said to the crab.'
Ulster
Byers Papers Box T4 'S & P' ts T-4-6 p. 59

DOW 1007 & 1077; Kelly p. 248 No. 260 'Spoken to those who are very unlikely to do what they pretend to do'; Ramsay p. 121; 'Cheviot' p. 409.
rise/patient
A 246.1 '"You are taking a rise out of me," as the patient said to the blister.'
The Dublin Journal of Temperance, Science and Literature, 1, No. 20 (10/9/1842), p. 319, in isolation at the foot of a page.

rolling stone/sitting duck
A 247.1 '"A rolling stone gathers no moss," said the sitting duck.'
County Cavan
Q 1973 IFC 1888:87 C m+

cf the conjoined proverbs 'A rolling stone gathers no moss, an'[d] a clockin'[g] hen never grows fat.' Byers Papers as cited in the Electronic Database, Ulster Dialect Archive, UFTM, and 'A rolling stone gathers no moss and a sitting hen never grows fat.' Smith & Wilson p. 682

Mieder & Tóthné Litovkina pp. 22–23 [but no wellerism]

Note: the proverb 'A rolling stone gathers no moss' is currently very common in English and known in Irish.

room/pauper   Am Eng, E Eng
A 248.1 '"There's plenty of room inside," as the pauper said to the penny loaf.'
The Dublin Journal of Temperance, Science and Literature, 1, No. 8 (18/6/1842), p. 116, in isolation at the foot of a page. Probably reprinted from *Punch*, 2 (1842) as cited in *DOW* 1057.

rooting/seedlings
A 249.1 '"We'll all be rooting for you," as the seedlings said to the nurseryman.'
Dublin City
Q 2000 'The John Creedon Show' RTÉ Radio 1, a response to the radio appeal made on the previous day, by email on 17/1/2002 from DK m, a variant of which was broadcast on 17/1/2002 'Good luck with the show today, John, remember '"We'll all be rooting for you," as the seedling said to the nurseryman"; see Appendix 2.

Rostrevor/man
A 250.1 'As the man said, "That's like Rostrevor, it's beside The 'Point."'
The 'Point=Warrenpoint; it and Rostrevor are neighbouring Co. Down towns
County Tyrone
IFC 1888:56 collected by **SÓC(ii)** in 1974 from PÓD m+. For note see Part A 83.8.

rum lot/Devil   ?E Eng
A 251.1 '"Quite a rum lot," as the devil said when he first saw the Ten Commandments.'
County Donegal
Q 1973 IFC 1888:23 C m+. For Correspondent's comment see Part A 55

DOW 778.

runner see *rinner*

rushes/man
A 252.1 '"I'll throw green rushes under your feet," as the man said to his long-awaited visitor.'
County Cavan
Q 1973(74) IFC 1888:88 +

cf *Lady Smart (to Lord Sparkish)* 'My Lord, methinks the sight of you is good for sore Eyes: If we had known of your coming, we would have strown Rushes for you. How has your Lordship done this long time?' Swift 1738, 1963 ed. p. 57.

S

sack/tinker
A 253.1 '"One sack, one sample," as the tinker said to the man picking nails.'
picking=choosing
Ulster
Byers Papers Box T4 'S & P' ts T-4-6 p. 68 with the comment: 'said by a seller to someone who takes too many samples when buying something.'

Notes: **IC** says the proverb 'One sack, one sample' is 'well-known' in Co. Tyrone, and it has been found generally in English.

saw/cat   Part B 41 also Sp
A 254.1 '"I saw you before," says the cat to the boiling water.'
County Louth
IFCS 678:133 in a list, mainly of proverbs. Published in [Carson] Williams 1992 p. 35/2000a p. 45

.2 '"I saw you before," said the cat to the hot milk.'
County Cavan
IFCS 996:230 in a list, mainly of proverbs

Note: '"I saw you before," as the cat said to the boiling milk,' was used as one of the ten, later five, examples on Q 2000. See Appendix1.

say/old man
A 255.1 '"Just to have it to say," said the old man who ate the bit of the dog.'
County Monaghan

IFCS 941:8–9 + in a list, mainly of proverbs, titled 'Local Sayings' collected by a schoolgirl from her parents. Published in [Carson] Williams 1992 p. 22/2000a p. 30.

scraigh/Divil
A 256.1 "'I'll light on you with a scraigh," as the Divil said to the ould seceder.'
scraigh ?<Irish scréach= 'or skreagh, a shrill cry or shriek, especially of a bird. The phrase "scraigh o' day" is applied to the break of day, cock-crow' Byers def. with the wellerism; seceder=one who seceded from mainstream presbyterianism in 1740, separate congregations were maintained until 1840
Ulster
Byers Papers Box T4 'S & P' ts T-4-6 p. 61. Published in Carson Williams 2001a p. 13.

scrape/barber
A 257.1 "'I'm always in a scrape," as the barber said.'
Ulster
Byers Papers Box T4 'S & P' ts T-4-6 p. 68.

seat belts/pilot
A 258.1 'Pilot to passengers coming in to land at Belfast, "Fasten your seat belts and turn your watches back fifty years."'
P.T.Q. 1971 Belfast p. 17

cf the joke, well-known for the past few decades throughout Ireland, to the same effect with the quotation often ascribed to a named GB politician.

see (there, luk)/blind man (Jansy, Gansey, Blind Hugh)
Part B 40 also Am Eng, *Aus Eng*, Can Eng, Dut, E Eng, †*Est*, Fr, Ger, It, ‡*NZ Eng*, Scots, Sc Gae, Sp & §cf Dan, Δcf Fin, ~cf Nor, xcf Swe
A 259.1-.9 "'I see," says (said) the blind man. "You're a liar," says (said) the dummy.'
dummy=mute

.1-.5 'says'
County Down

154

.1 Q 2000 i JB brother of RÓB, 60s, retired teacher who heard it from his father [1901–74] of Lurgan

.2 Q 2000 i RÓB +, brother of JB, 60s, retired MD who heard used it in primary school in Lurgan with both 'says' & 'said'

.3 Q 2000 i EW f 60s, with the comment that it was a retort used to those who gave clever answers at primary school in Newtownards.

.4 Q 2000 i m 60s Newtownards, who commented that the term 'dummy' is now politically incorrect

.5 Q 2000 i WW m 70s b. & r. Dromore, retired primary school principal

.6–.9 'said'

.6 County Donegal

Q 1973 IFC 1888:16 C f: 'both these phrases were almost always used by two people — first person saying "I see ..." second person retorting with "You're a liar ..." I have been aware of the use of these on somebody's tongue (and frequently my own) since childhood in the Rosses area. I can't pin down any particular instance ... but my impression is that the words were used when someone was sceptical of some statement or didn't "see" the point at issue'

.7 County Donegal

Q 2000 i CMcC f 30s b. & r. Buncrana, editor in Belfast, heard from her mother b. 1919 b. & r. Derry city

.8 County Londonderry

Q 2000 i WC m 60s b. & r. Coleraine, historian in Belfast

.9 North-East Ulster

Q 2000(2) i DM+, part-time mature student UU, from his father, also DM+, 70s, b. & partly reared in Randalstown, Co. Antrim, now living in Belfast

.10 '"I see," says the blind man. "Ye're a liar," says the dummy.'

Ulster

Byers Papers as published in Macafee 1996 under 'dumb' with the explanation: 'jocular reply to someone who says "I see"'

.11 '"I see," said the blind man. "You're a liar," said the beggar.'

County Antrim 1950s

Q 2000 common among primary school children in Ballymoney, FCW personal observation and use

.12-.17 '"I see," said the blind man and (but, when) he couldn't (could not) see at all.'

.12 'and' & 'couldn't'

County Kilkenny

Q 1973 IFC 1917:75 C m: 'The only echo of a wellerism that I can discover in this locality is '"I see,' said the blind man and he couldn't see at all" which was rattled indiscriminately among children as a sort of jingle that had no specific application except to indicate no interest in the conversation'

.13 as .12

County Kilkenny

Q 1973 IFC 1917:82 C f+: 'all these idioms etc are common in the local vocabulary. --- I find it hard to get Wellerisms. When asked, people get confused and cannot remember, although I know they are used in conversation ...'

.14 'but' & 'couldn't'

County Down

Q 2000 i MMcN f 50s b. & r. Co. Down, editor, with the comment that it was: 'always in our family'

.15 as .14

Dublin City North

Q 2000 i **BNíF** b. 1954 b. & r. Clontarf

.16 'when' & 'could not'

County Sligo

Q 1973 IFC 1888:128 C f

.17 as .16

County Roscommon

Q 1973 IFC 1888:142 C m

.18 '"I see," says the blind man.
"He cannot see at all."'

County Longford current when the questionnaire was returned

Q 1973 IFC 2027:162 C f+: 'often when you would tell a person something he would say '"I see,' says the blind man." "He cannot see at all," the other person would say. Another answer to it is, '"You're a liar,' says the Dummy, well he could not speak at all. 'I get up and kick you out,' says the cripple. He could not walk at all."' [**.31**]

.19–.24 '"I see," said the blind man.'

County Cavan current when the Questionnaire was returned
Q 1973 IFC 1888:95 C m+: 'common locally'

.20 as .19
County Cork current when the Questionnaire was returned
Q 1973 IFC 1917:40 C m+: 'well-known and frequently used'

.21 as .19
County Wexford
Q 1973 IFC 1917:81 C m, originally from Wexford, now in Kerry: 'I have often heard or read this and with it there were two other sentences but I cannot now recall them. I think (but I am not at all certain) they referred to a lame man and a dummy (one who is dumb). I have never heard of sayings (Wellerisms) attributed to the characters mentioned in the questionnaire — these Wellerisms are quite a new idea to me'

.22 as .19
County Tipperary
Q 1973(78) IFC 2027:166 C m+: 'I only heard this saying [**.46**] once but the shorter version "'I see,' said the blind man, " is more common.' For Correspondent's further comment see **.46**

.23 as .19
Belfast South *c.* 1970
Q 2000 i CW [FCW's daughter] b. 1980 b. & r. South Belfast

.24 as .19
Belfast 1960s
Q 2000 i LG f 50s mature, part-time student b. & r. Belfast, now living in Armagh city collected QUA

.25-.27 "'I see," says the blind man.'
James Joyce *Ulysses*, a novel, 1922 Paris, 1986 ed., Part II, Episode 15, p. 459, line 3716. Leopold Bloom is having his fortune told by palmistry by Zoe 'a woman of the night':
'BLOOM (points to his hand) That weal there is an accident. Fell and cut it twentytwo years ago. I was sixteen.
ZOE I see, says the blind man. Tell us news.
STEPHEN See? Moves to one great goal. I am twentytwo. Sixteen years ago he was twentytwo too.'

.26 as .25
County Wexford *c.* late 1920s

ugh.

Q 1973 IFC 1917:64 letter from **JD** who also contributed **.50** *qv* for further comment

.27 as .25
County Offaly current when Questionnaire was returned
Q 1973 IFC 1917:67 C m+: 'All the usual ones are used "'I see,' says the blind man," etc.'

.28 "'I see, I see," says the blind man.
"You are a liar," says the dummy.
"I'll rise to you," says the cripple.'
County Donegal *c.* 1925
Q 1973 IFC 1888:17 C m+: 'heard parish of Glenfin about 1925'

.29 "'I see," said the blind man.
"You're a liar," said the dummy.
"I'll kick your ...," said the cripple.'
County Down 1920s
Q 1973 IFC 1888:45 C m+, a primary school principal: 'I don't think wellerisms ... were a feature in this district at any time nevertheless we had, at least up to fifty years ago, a goodly selection of witty turns of speech not unlike those employed by the famous Sam Weller, for example, expressions such as this, used for pure amusement "'I see ... said the cripple."' For the other wellerism from this Correspondent see Part A 230

.30 "'I see," said the blind man,
"You're a liar," says the dummy,
"Give him a kick in the arse," says the cripple.'
County Fermanagh 1970s
Glassie *Passing the Time, Folklore and History of an Ulster Community* 1982 Dublin p. 276: 'Clever chat becomes "crack" through the logical, free play of wit. Crack snaps with humorous figures of speech. The convention of attributing proverbs generally bids and particularly eases Wellerisms into talk. At last comprehending: "I see, said the blind man, ... says the cripple." Starting a fire: "As the fox said when he pissed on the snow, That'll make a fire if it lights."' [Part A 83.7]

.31 "'I see," says the blind man.
"You're a liar," says the Dummy, well he could not speak at all.
"I get up and kick you out," says the cripple. He could not walk at all.'

158

County Longford current when the questionnaire was returned
Q 1973 IFC 2027:162 C f+: 'often when you would tell a person
something he would say "'I see,' says the blind man." "He cannot see at
all," [.18] the other person would say. Another answer to it is, "'You're a
liar,' says the Dummy, well he could not speak at all. 'I get up and kick
you out,' says the cripple. He could not walk at all."'

**.32 "'I see you," says the blind man.
"Deed ye don't," says the dummy.
"I'll kick ye out," says the cripple.'**
County Tyrone
Q 2000 **IC** who heard his mother **MC** use it

**.33 "'I see," said the blind man,
"You're a fool," said the dummy,
"I'll kick you," said the man with no legs.'**
Belfast East
Kerr Peirce *Keep the kettle boiling. Rhymes from a Belfast Childhood.*
1983 Dublin p. 66 in final section 7 'Wee songs and poems,' b. Irwin
Avenue 1931, attended Strandtown Primary School

**.34 "'I see," said the blind man,
"Hear, hear," said the man with no ears,
"I'll give you a toe on the behind," said the man with no legs.'**
County Down late 1940s
Q 2000 i GWB m Newtownards: 'I heard and used the above (and
variants) in public elementary school in Newtownards in the late 1940's.'
Note: This questionnaire may have been returned by the man who spoke
to FCW after her lecture to the Ards Historical Society saying his version
had to be 'cleaned up'

**.35 "'I see," said the blind man.
You're a liar," said the dumb man and the cripple got up and
walked away.'**
County Londonderry 1960s
Q 2000(02) i PMcC, mature part-time student UU, who heard it in the
1960s from his father, PMcC b. 1909, b. & r. near Maghera

**.36-.38 "'I see," said the blind man, "a hole in the wall."
"You're a liar," said the dummy, "you can't see at all."'**
Limerick City *c.* mid-1920s
Q 1973 IFC 1917:12 C m+: 'I heard the above ... mainly from school
children'

.37 as .36
County Galway
Q 1973 IFC 1888:155 C m+

.38 as .37 with **'you are'** in place of **'you're'**
County Cork
Q 1973 IFC 1911:72 C f+ [E & Ir], a nun

.39 "'I see," said the blind man, "a hole in the wall."
"You're a liar," says the dummy, "you can't see at all."'
County Offaly
Q 1973 IFC 1917:66 C f+: 'common saying'

.40 & .41 "'I see," said (says) the blind man, "there's a hole in the wall."
"You're a liar," said (says) the dummy, "(for) you can't see at all."'
County Roscommon with 'said' & 'for'
Q 1973 IFC 1888:144 C m+. For Correspondent's comment see Part A 5.1

.41 as .40 with **'says'**
County Roscommon
Q 1973 IFC 1917:55 C f+: 'this strikes me as more of a children's rhyme than a wellerism, but it could be said after some "wise" man would have solemnly declared "he saw"'

.42 "'I see," said the blind man, "a hole in the wall."
"You're a liar," said the dumb man, "you can't see at all."'
County Roscommon
Q 1973 IFC 1888:147 C m+

.43 "'I see," said the blind man, "a hole in the wall."
"Shut up!" said the dummy, "You can't see at all."'
County Roscommon 1950s & 60s
Q 2000 i **JG**, used among primary school children in Roscommon town

.44 "'I see," said the Blind man, "a hole in the wall."
"You Fool," said the Dummy, "there is no hole there at all."'
County Kerry
Q 1973 IFC 1917:20 C m+: 'Taking your examples, "'I see,' said the Blind Man," I find, "'I see,' said Gansey when he saw nothing" [**.61**]

(Tralee 1900) — that was common (not any more). Stackmountain (Tullig), North Kerry has a parody on it viz, "I see ... at all'" [.56]

.45 "'I see," says the blind man, "a hole in the wall."
"You are wrong," says the dummy, "you can't see at all.'"
County Kerry
Q 1973 IFC 1917:26 C m, i SS m, followed by the rhyme: 'One fine day in the middle of the night two dead man got up to fight. Two blind men were looking on. Two cripples for the police they ran. Two dummies told them "Hurry on." Back to back they faced each other—.'

.46 "'I see," said the blind man, "a hole in the wall."
"You can't," says the dumb man, "you can't see at all.'"
County Tipperary c. 1968
Q 1973(78) IFC 2027:166 C m+: 'This saying was heard in Turtulla [near Thurles] about ten years ago.' Used when a person understands what someone has explained. 'I only heard this saying once but the shorter version "'I see,' said the blind man, " [.22] is more common'

.47 "'I see," said the blind man, "a hole in the wall."
"You're a liar," said the dummy, who could not talk at all.'"
County Galway
Q 1973 IFC 1888:152 C m+, titled 'Local jingles' and followed by: 'One fine day in the middle of the night two blind men got up to fight, two cripples ran for the guards, two dummies cried "Halt!"'

.48 "'I see," said the blind man, "a hole in the wall."
"You're a liar," said the dummy, "sure you can't see at all.'"
County Wicklow
Q 1973? IFC 2154:279 C m+, i PC f+: 'My granny MÓN would always say to little children, "'I see,' said the blind man ...see at all'"

.49 "'I see," said the blind man, "through a hole in the wall."
"You can't," said the dummy, " 'cos you can't see at all.'"
'cos=because
County Meath
Q 2000 i EO'B m 70s, retired primary school teacher: 'nothing more than a nonsense rime'

.50 "'I see," says the blind man, "through a stone wall."
"Ye're a liar," says the dummy, "ye can't see at all.'"
County Wexford c. late 1920s

IFC 1917:64 letter from **JD**: 'As children we used to chant "'I see,' … at all." Of course, the first part was also used being simply "'I see,' says the blind man"' [**.25**]

.51 "'I see," said the blind man, "and through a stone wall."
"Deed you don't," said the dummy, "you can't see at all."'
County Laois
Q 1973 IFC 1917:78 C f+

.52 "'I see," said the blind man, "through a limestone wall."
"You are a liar," said the dummy, "you cannot see at all."'
County Mayo
Q 1973 IFC 1888:122 C m+: 'I cannot recall any wellerisms from this place even though I was born and reared here. The only one I can remember is your example "'I see … at all" --- used when the normal answer to a question would be "I see" — that is "I understand"'

.53 "'I see," said the blind man as he looked across the wall.
"You're a liar," said the Dummy, "you can't see at all."'
Counties Cavan & Leitrim
Q 1973 IFC 1888:92 C m+

.54 "'I can see," said the blind man, "I can see through a wall."
"You are a liar," said the Dummy, "you can't see at all."'
County Armagh
Q 2000 i JC(i) m 60s, sheep farmer and well-known storyteller, who heard it from his mother. The same man had also contributed to Q 1973, on that occasion two — Part A 180.5 & 234

.55 "'I see," says the blind man.
"I hear," says the deaf.
"You're a liar," says the dumb.
"Shut up or I'll kick you," says the cripple.'
County Tyrone
Q 2000(02) i MD mature, part-time student UU, who heard it as a child in the 1950s and 60s from her mother, b. and living in Drumshanbo, Cookstown, and who also heard her mother telling it to her [MD's] own children in the 1970s and 80s. Her [MD's] mother heard it from her parents when she was a child

.56 "'I see," says Jansy and he saw nothing at all.'
County Kerry

Q 1973 IFC 1917:17 C m+: 'Jansy was an old blind boatman on the Killarney Lakes. The above quotation was in general use in the Killarney area some years ago but I think is forgotten by the younger people.'
Note: see **.56** which may be the same name

.57 "'I see,' said Gansey when he saw nothing.'
County Kerry 1900
Q 1973 IFC 1917:20 C m+: 'Taking your examples, "'I see,' said the Blind Man," I find "'I see,' said Gansey when he saw nothing" (Tralee 1900) — that was common (not any more). Stackmountain (Tullig), North Kerry has a parody on it viz, "I see ... at all"' [**.43**]
Note: see **.55** which may be the same name

.58 "'Would I could see it," quoth blind Hugh.'
Swift ... *Polite Conversation* ... 1738 London, 1963 ed. p. 77; spoken by Miss Notable. Cited in *DOW* 1105
For comments on Swift's version see Taylor 1959, especially p. 291

.59 "'I see," says the blind man when he was directed on his way.'
County Louth
IFCS 672:264 in a list, mainly of proverbs. Published in [Carson] Williams 1992 p. 73/2000a p. 71

.60 "'Are you there?" said the blind man and he couldn't see at all.' [*sic*]
County Sligo
Q 1973 IFC 1888:111 C f+: '... from the neighbours ...'

.61 "'Luk now!" said the blind man.'
County Londonderry
Q 2000 i TM m 30s b. & r. Limavady, technician in a Belfast university college

DOW 1103, 1105, 1119, 1130, 1147–48, & 1161 cf 1104 & others; 'Cheviot' p. 417; Nicolson p. 137 No. 2; cf Smith & Wilson p. 456
*Aus Eng Q 2000(02) CL m *c.* 25, collector Paul Tempan, as **.1**
†*Est* "'Ennäe," ütles pime vastu laternaposti joostes.' ("'We'll see," said the blind man running into a lamp post.') EKM ERA, II 170, 66 (129), 1937, and *c.* 30 other examples, the majority of which begin 'Ennäe'
‡*NZ Eng* Q 2000(02) m b. 1982 Auckland, heard from his father, collector Paul Tempan, as **.1**
§cf Dan from Sallinen

Δcf Fin "'Niin näkkyy," sanoi sokkee.' ["'It looks like it," said the blind man.'] Sallinen p. 108 (524), No. 64, see also No. 65

~cf Nor from Sallinen

xcf Swe "'Låt mej se," sa den blinde.' ["'Let me see," said the blind man.'] Holm p. 282

Notes: "'I see," said the blind man' was used as one of the four examples on Q 1973 and "'I see," says the blind man. "You're a liar," says the beggar' as one of ten, later five, on Q 2000, see Appendix 1. For a discussion of this wellerism see Taylor 1959

see also Part A 15.

see/tippler

A 260.1 "'I shall never see thee more," as the tippler said when he handed a sixpence to the publican.'
The Dublin Journal of Temperance, Science and Literature, 1, No. 19 (3/9/1842), p. 304 in a list of five titled 'Jonathanisms' [this and Part A 91, 139, 141 & 284].

Sent Sweeten's Day/sweep chimley

A 261.1 "'Ivver since Sent Sweeten's Day heavy wet." That wos what the sweep chimley said when he hid inside iv a shower bath an' thried to climb up the rope.'
ivver=ever; Sent Sweeten's Day=Saint Swithin's Day, 14th July; wos=was; sweep chimley=chimney sweep; iv=of; an'=and
'M'Cart' [Canon Abraham Hume 1814–80] *Poor Rabbin's Ollminick [= Almanac] for the toun o' Bilfawst [= Belfast]... 1861 ...* , a pastiche, n.d. [1860 or 61] Belfast & Dublin, under July. In Byers Papers Box T4 'S & P' ts T-4-6 pp. 61–62 with no attribution

Note: the belief is common in English and Irish. Sayings like 'Swithin's Day 15th July, if thou doest rain, forty days it will remain; Swithin's Day, if thou be fair, forty days it will rain no more' Co. Monaghan IFCS 939:40 & 41, are quite common in English. Saint Swithin, Bishop of Winchester, England, d. 862.

shag/duchess   E Eng

A 262.1 "'Shag me," said the duchess, more in hope than in anger.'

O'Farrell 1993, 1995 rpt. p. 113, first in the list under the final section titled 'Coarse, Profane and Mixed' with a note on p. 120: 'from my own manuscript sources, compiled over a long number of years'

Partridge p. 65.

she see *her/Connachtman (Kerryman)*
shelter see *cowl'*

shots/poacher
A 263.1 'As the poacher said, "The shots you see when you have no gun."'
Q 2000 **TC**. For his comments see Part A 118

cf 'Many a shot is seen when you haven't got a gun' collected 2/2/2001 by FCW from her aunt MJRC, who heard it from her husband SHC [1908–83] b. & r. Co. Monaghan; who said it at the sight of a girl in very high heels.

silence/man   Am Eng
A 264.1 '"Silence gives consent," as the man said when he kissed the dumb woman.'
County Donegal between 1880 and 1908
Traynor 1954 under 'silence': 'In phr. Silence … woman (H)'

DOW 1192

Mieder & Tóthné Litovkina pp. 181–83 & Tóthné Litovkina 1999 p. 151

Note: the proverb 'Silence gives consent' is currently found in English.

silly/fiddler
A 265.1 '"That is silly," said the fiddler when he rosined [?his] bow.'
County Longford current in 1973
Q 1973 IFC 2027:162 C f+: 'This or other remarks are often said to people when they would like something that another would not like or think silly … "Everyone to their own taste" or '"That is silly … [?his] bow."'

slice/fellow

A 266.1 '"There's nothing like the slice off the cut loaf," as the fellow said when he ran off with the neighbour's wife.'
County Kilkenny
Q 1973 IFC 1917:77 C f+

cf the proverb 'A slice off a cut loaf is never missed.' Co. Donegal Q 1973 IFC 1888:10.

smart/donkey
A 266a.1 '"They say you're smart," as the donkey said to the ass.'
Belfast South
Unsolicited example from FCW's younger son FC-W [b. 1989]: 'I've thought of a wellerism …' 4/1/2002. Included to demonstrate how easily the form can be copied.

something/monkey
A 267.1 '"There's something in that," like what the monkey said when he put his nose in the piss pot.'
County Monaghan current in 1973
Q 1973 IFC 1888:76 C m+: 'used in the Clones area when a person was at least partly agreeing with a statement made by another person. I thought it a bit indelicate to include on the official list …'
sort see *instrument*
sour see *grapes*

spalls/Ranzo
A 268.1 '"Mortar spalls and porter — and what I said last to come first," as Ranzo said.'
County Kerry
Q 1973 IFC 1917:27 C m+. Ranzo was a local mason. I am grateful to Bairbre Ní Fhloinn/**BNíF** for suggesting that 'Ranzo' may be short for 'Lorenzo.' With the expansion in church building in the 19th century many Italian craftsmen came to Ireland.

stand/juggler
A 269.1 '"I can't stand that," as the juggler said when he tried to balance the eel upon the point of his nose.'
Ulster
Byers Papers Box T4 'S & P' ts T-4-6 p. 64.

station see *hard station*

stickup/man
A 270.1 'Man on phone to bank teller, "This is a stickup. Mail me ten thousand pounds."'
P.T.Q. 1965 Belfast n.p.

stomach see *belly*
stone see *rolling stone*

stone dead/Cromwell
A 271.1 '"Stone dead hath no fellow," said Cromwell when he tried to exterminate the Irish.'
Shaw *On the Rocks: a political comedy* 1934 London 'Preface — Extermination' p. 146: 'The extermination of what the exterminators call inferior races is as old as history. "Stone dead hath no fellow," said Cromwell when he tried to exterminate the Irish. "The only good nigger is a dead nigger" say Americans of the Ku-Klux temperament.' Listed in Bryan & Mieder 1994 p. 227, under No. 6

Note: Oliver Cromwell [1600–58] lord lieutenant of Ireland, campaigned in Ireland 1649–50. See Smith 1968 'The Image of Cromwell in Folklore and Tradition' and Ó Súilleabháin 1976 'Oliver Cromwell in Irish Oral Tradition.'

straes (sthroes)/wife (oul' woman)   cf Scots
A 272.1 '"Lang straes are nae worth," as the wife said when she pulled the suggaun out of the brochan.'
lang=long; strae=straw; nae worth=no good or *no use; wife=woman, housewife; suggaun [CUD 'suggan'] <Ir súgán=straw rope; brochan=porridge*
County Donegal between 1880 and 1908
Traynor 1954 under 'straw: Phr. Lang ... brochan (H)'

.2 '"Long sthroes is no motes," as the oul' woman sayd when she pulled the back suggaun out o' the stirabout.'
sthroe=straw; back suggaun=a thick, plaited or woven straw mat for a donkey's back fitted for protection under the panniers or carrying baskets which hung down the animal's sides; stirabout=porridge
'M'Cart' [Canon Abraham Hume 1814–80] *Poor Rabbin's Ollminick [= Almanac] for the toun o' Bilfawst [= Belfast]... 1863 ...* , a pastiche, n.d. [1862 or 63] Belfast & Dublin, under October: 'There's many a quare [=

queer] sayin' in country places. A'll [= I'll] tell ye one. "Long sthroes is no motes, as the oul' woman sayd when she pulled the back suggaun out of the stirabout." Now what d'ye [= do you] think o' [= of] that?' *Idem* Byers Papers as cited in the Electronic Database, Ulster Dialect Archive, UFTM, but Byers is probably citing 'M'Cart'

.3 '"Long sthroes is no motes," as the oul' woman say'd when she pulled the long suggawn out of the stirabout.'
sthroe=straw; suggawn=a straw rope
Ulster
Byers Papers Box T4, T-4-6 p. 66

cf Scots '"Lang straes are nae motes," quo' the wife when she haul'd the cat out o' the kirn.' [= *churn*] 'Cheviot' p. 230 and Murison p. 61

Note: a def. for **.2** in the Electronic Database, Ulster Dialect Archive, UFTM, under 'mote' runs 'meaning that something is no drawback'

see also Part A 273.

sthroes/ould woman
A 273.1 '"Long sthroes is no motes," as the ould woman sayd when she pulled the back suggawn aff the donkey.' [*sic*]
sthroe=straw; back suggawn, see def. for 'back suggaun' at 271.2
Ulster
Byers Papers as cited in the Electronic Database, Ulster Dialect Archive, UFTM

cf the proverbial simile 'as hungry as the man that ate the back suggaun aff [= off] the donkey' Byers Papers as cited in the Electronic Database, Ulster Dialect Archive, UFTM

see also Part A 272.

strange/girl
A 274.1 '"Strange, but not at all disagreeable," as the girl said to the soldier.'
Behan *Borstal Boy*, autobiography, originally published serially Sept. – Oct. 1956 in the Ireland ed. of *The Sunday Dispatch*, and first in complete form in 1958, 1980 ed. p. 364: 'It was strange to be out at night and going up the long road in the windy dark to the New Camp, and the noise of the North Sea constant with the wind and the trees, but not at all disagreeable, as the girl said to the soldier.'

168

strength/tailor   *cf Dan, †cf Fin, ‡cf Nor, §cf Swe
A 275.1 '"Strength!" said the tailor as he lifted the bag of chaff.'
County Fermanagh
Q 1973(74) IFC 1888:71 C m+, i MM m

*cf Dan from Sallinen
†cf Fin '"Sankavoimia," sano Kuivala, ko kissaa hännäst nosti.' ['"That's real strength," said Kuivala as he lifted up the cat by the tail.'] Sallinen p. 394, No. 15
‡cf Nor from Sallinen
§cf Swe from Sallinen

see also Part A 276 & 277.

strength/woman   *cf Dan, †cf Fin, ‡cf Nor, §cf Swe
A 276.1 '"Strength!" said the woman when she broke the twine.'
County Roscommon 1960s
Q 2000 **JG**

*cf Dan from Sallinen
†cf Fin '"Voima se on, joka tytäjää," sano suutari, kun silakalta niskat katkaasi.' ['"That's strength you hear," said the cobbler as he twisted the herring's neck.'] Sallinen p. 394, No. 15
‡cf Nor from Sallinen
§cf Swe from Sallinen

see also Part A 275 & 277.

strength (_neart_)/wren (scutty wren, robin, rann, wreneen)   Part B 143
A 277.1 '"Strength!" said the wren when she pulled the snail out of the dirt.'
County Leitrim
IFCS 212:14 in a list, mainly of proverbs

.2 '"Strength!" said the scutty wren when she pulled the maggot out of the hole.'
County Louth

IFCS 675:200j in a list, mainly of proverbs. Published in [Carson] Williams 1992 p. 69/2000a p. 69 [*sic*]

.3 '"Strength!" says the scutty wren when he pulled the worm out of the dunghill.'
County Monaghan
IFCS 932:22 in a list, mainly of proverbs

.4 '"Strength!" says the wren when he pulled the worm out of the ground.'
County Tipperary
Q 1973 IFC 1917:42 C m+

.5 '"Strength!" said the wren when she pulled the worm out of the ground.'
County Westmeath
Q 1973 IFC 1917:62 C m+. For Correspondent's comments see Part A 13.2

.6 '"Strength!" said the robin when he pulled up the worm out of the ground.'
County Cavan
Q 1973 IFC 1888:97 C m+, Order of Jesus. For his comments see Part A 140.1

.7 '"Strength!" says the rann as he pulled the worm from the gutter.'
rann=wren
County Clare
Q 1973 IFC 1917:7–8 +: 'this she [Correspondent's mother+] used when she was very pleased about something'

.8–.9 '"Strength!" said the wren(een) when he pulled up the worm.'
County Galway
Q 1973 IFC 1888:155 C m+; 'said when a feat of strength is performed e.g. when a man lifts a heavy weight

.10 '"Strength!" said the Wren when he broke the worm.'
County Roscommon
Q 1973 IFC 1888:144 C m+: 'used when somebody breaks something like a rope or the handle of tool etc.' For Correspondent's additional comment see Part A 5.1

.11 '"There's no strength like a strong arm," said the robin when he killed the worm.'
County Antrim
Q 1973? IFC 1888:28 +

.12 '"Strength!" said the robin when he killed the worm.'
County Antrim
Q 1973? IFC 1888:28 +

.13 '"Strength is no load," said the Robin when he pulled the worm out of the ground.'
County Kilkenny
Q 1973 IFC 1917:79 C f+

.14 'When the wren flung a beetle against the wall, *"Is mór an nidhe an neart!"'*
Is mór an nidhe an neart!=strength's a great thing!
County Cork
Q 1973 IFC 1917:33 C m

.15 '"Main strength!" says the robin.'
main=?mainly
County ?Cork
Q 1973 IFC 1917:7 + collected from a woman who heard it from her father Mr B+ who died aged 76 *c.* 1965 and who used it 'when doing something which demanded very little effort'
see also Part A 275 & 276.

such/farmer
A 278.1 '"There's no such thing," as the farmer said when he saw the giraffe.'
Limerick City mid-1930s
Q 1973 IFC 1917:12 C m+: 'mainly said by secondary school pupils'

cf '--- a rustic, seeing a giraffe for the first time, exclaimed "There ain't no sech [= is not any such] animal!"' Partridge p. 217.

sugar/Auntie Mary
A 279.1 '"Sugar to your liking," says Auntie Mary with the bowl on the dresser.'
County Cork
IFC 1911:72 C f+ [E & Ir], a nun

cf 'Sugar to your taste. Attributed to a visitor' Co. Cavan Q 1973 IFC 1888:85

Note: ie. the sugar was not to hand.

suit/tailor
A 280.1 '"My suit is hopeless," as the tailor said to the young girl whom he was courting.'
County Antrim
Q 1973? IFC 1888:27.

swimming/man
A 281.1 '"It wants to be swimming dead and alive," as the man said when taking the long drink of water after he had eaten the fish.'
County Kerry
Q 1973 IFC 1917:28 C m+

cf the related medical proverb [Taylor 1962 fac., 1985 rpt., p. 125] which has been noted once only in English in the indexed part of the Schools' Collection.

T

tail/monkey   Am Eng
A 282.1 'As the monkey said, "Thereby hangs a tail."'
Q 2000 **TC**. For his comments see Part A 118

DOW 547.

take/crow
A 283.1 '"Take it or leave it," as the crow said when he flew over.'
County Offaly
Q 1973 IFC 1917:67 C m+.

tale/young lady
A 284.1 '"I feel deeply affected by your tale," as the weeping young lady said to the honey-bee.'

The Dublin Journal of Temperance, Science and Literature, 1, No. 19 (3/9/1842), p. 304 in a list of five titled 'Jonathanisms' [this and Part A 91, 139, 141 & 260].

taste/critic
A 285.1 '"All his taste," said the critic, "is in his mouth."'
County Monaghan
Q 1973 IFC 1888:74 C m+: 'a term [ie. wellerism] generally in use when a person's work lacks imagination.'

taste/dog **Est*
A 286.1 '"Every man to his own taste," as the little dog said when [withheld].'
County Down 1999
Q 2000 **TC**. For his comments see Part A 118

*Est '"Maitse asi," ütles kass ja [withheld]' ('"It's a matter of taste," said a cat and') EKM ERA, RKM II 428, 182 (1), 1989 and two similar

Mieder & Tóthné Litovkina pp. 81–82 & p. 206

see also Part A 287.

taste (fancy, like, liking)/farmer (woman, old woman, Morris, husband, man, Nancy, old one, good woman)
> Am Eng, Dut, E Eng, **Est*, Ger, Scots, Sc Gae & †cf Fin,
> ‡cf Nor

A 287.1 & .2 '"Everyone to his taste," said the farmer (woman) when he (she) kissed the cow.'
County Roscommon
Q 1973 IFC 1917:55 C f+: 'usually said when another party has done something extraordinary or unusual eg. Married someone unsuitable, gone to live in an outlandish place etc.'

.3 '"Everyone to his taste," as the old woman said when she kissed the cow.'
County Cork
Q 2000 i JC(ii) m+ [E & Ir] b. Cork *c.* 1930, retired professor of literature, who heard it from his elderly aunt in Kanturk

.4 '"Everyone to his taste," as Morris said when he kissed the cow.'

James Joyce *Ulysses*, a novel, 1922 Paris, 1986 ed., Part II, Episode 13, p. 311, lines 1224–25. Leopold Bloom's evening musings on Sandymount Strand: 'Three cheers for Israel. Three cheers for the sister-in-law he hawked about, three fangs in her mouth. Same style of beauty. Particularly nice old party for a cup of tea. The sister of the wife of the wild man of Borneo has just come to town. Imagine that in the early morning at close range. Everyone to his taste as Morris said when he kissed the cow.' Cited in *DOW* 1328
Notes: Later, Part II, Episode 15, Joyce uses this version of the proverb: 'Chacun son gout.' Morris is a common second name in Co. Galway; 'Morris' also used in parts as a first name

.5 '"Everyone to her taste," as the woman said when she kissed the cow.'
County Kilkenny
Q 1973 IFC 1917:76 C f+

.6 '"Everyone to his own taste," as the man said when he kissed the cow.'
County Galway
IFCS 77:450 in a list, mainly of proverbs

.7 '"Everyone to his own taste," as the woman said when he kissed her cow.'
County Galway
IFCS 768:159 + in a list, mainly of proverbs, written down by a schoolgirl

.8 '"Everyone to his own taste," said the old woman said when she kissed the cow.'
County Kerry
Q 1973 IFC 1917:18 C m+

.9 '"Every man to his taste," as the man said when he kissed his pig.'
Ulster
M'Kean 'Ulster Proverbs.' *The Irish Naturalists' Journal*, 3 (Mar. 1930) p. 43 in a short article

.10 '"Everyone to their own taste," as the woman said when she kissed the cow.'
Dublin City, North 1960s

Q 2000 i **AB** f b. 1958 b. & r. Dublin; heard in Dublin as a child. Collected in DIF

.11 '"There's no accounting for taste," as the farmer said when he saw the man kissing the cow.'
Limerick mid-1930s
Q 1973 IFC 1917:13 C m+: [used] 'among secondary school pupils'

.12 '"Everyone to their own," as the man said when he kissed the cow.'
Dublin City 1960s–70s
Q 2000 i f 40s mature part-time student in QUA, b. & r. Dublin; heard in Dublin

.13 '"Every man to his fancy but I to my Nancy," as the man said when he kissed his own cow."
County Dublin
IFCS 788:32 in a list, mainly of proverbs, with the comment after it: '[used] when discussing a person's taste in husbands or wives or clothes etc.'

.14 '"Every man to his fancy, and me to my own Nancy," said the old woman when she kissed her cow.'
County Monaghan
IFCS 941:8 + in a list, mainly of proverbs, titled 'Local Sayings' collected by a schoolgirl from her parents. Published in [Carson] Williams 1992 p. 29/2000a p. 37

.15 '"Everyone to his fancy and I to my Nancy," as the man said when he kissed his cow.'
County Westmeath
Photocopy from IFC ms in Almqvist *Irish Wellerisms* 1973– File Q 1973 C f

.16 '"Everyone to their own fancy," as the man said when he kissed his cow.'
County Wexford
IFCS 885:16 + in a list, mainly of proverbs, with the comment 'When a pair are getting married and one of them ugly the old people say: '"Everyone to their … cow."'

.17 '"Everyone to their fancy," as the old one said when she kissed the ass.'

Behan *Borstal Boy*, autobiography, originally published serially Sept.–Oct. 1956 in the Ireland ed. of the *Sunday Dispatch*, and first in complete form in 1958, 1980 ed., p. 46, Mrs Gildea: 'Nice place too [the Isle of Man], and a nice class of people, be [= by] all accounts. Talk Irish and all, some of them. More nor [= than] I could do. Though the cats don't have any tails ... God knows they must be the queer-looking beasts. Still, '"Everyone to their fancy," as the old one said when she kissed the ass.'

.18 '"Everyone to his fancy and meet my Nancy," as the farmer said as he kissed the cow.'
County Londonderry
Q 1973 IFC 1888:25 +: 'a local variation on the one you quote' [on Q 1973, see Note below]

.19 '"Every man to his fancy," said Nancy as she kicked the cow.'
County Mayo
IFC 1888:121 C m, in a letter dated 1975

.20 '"Everyone to his fancy," said Nancy as she kissed the cat.'
County Offaly
Q 1973 IFC 1917:66 C f+, i RR m

.21 '"Every one as they like," as the good Woman said when she kiss'd her Cow.'
Swift ... *Polite Conversation* ... 1731 London, 1963 ed. p. 55; spoken by the Colonel

.22 '"Everyone to his liking," as the old woman said when she kissed her cow.'
County Leitrim
IFCS 215:48 in a list, mainly of proverbs

.23 '"Everyone to his fancy and I to my Nancy," as the man said.'
County Cavan
Q 1973 IFC 1888:95 C m+

cf 'Everyone to their fancy and me to my Nancy' Co. Sligo, IFCS 178:383 in a list, mainly of proverbs

cf 'Everybody to his fancy and me to my duck' Co. Sligo Q 1973 IFC 1888:112

cf **IC** '"Everyone to his taste" common,' collected some years ago by FCW

DOW 196, 400–04, 716, 719, 780, 893–95, 909, 1328–35, 1338, 1340–41; *Addenda* 101 & 126; Smith & Wilson pp. 228–29; Ramsay p. 27; Nicolson p. 308 No. 3a

**Est* '"Maitse asi," ütles tädi ja andis lehmale suud.' ('"It's a matter of taste," said aunt and kissed the cow.') EKM ERA, RKM, Normann I, 294, 1960, one of the six in the archive

†cf Fin '"Oikeus valita," sano ukko, kun lehmää suuteli.' ['"The right to object," as the old man said when he kissed the cow.'] Sallinen p. 394, No. 26

‡cf Nor from Sallinen

Mieder & Tóthné Litovkina pp. 81–82, pp. 130–31 [but no wellerism] & p. 206

cf the motif *MI* J 1880 *Animals or objects treated as if human—miscellaneous*

Note: '"Everyone to his taste," said the farmer when he kissed the cow' was used as one of the four examples on Q 1973 and '"Everyone to their fancy," said the old woman when she kissed her cow' was used as one of the original ten on Q 2000

see also Part A 77 & 286.

taste/husband
A 287a.1 '"Everyone to his taste," said the husband of the very plain woman, "for you know love is blind and lovers cannot see."'
Counties Cavan & Leitrim
Q 1973 IFC 1888:92 C m+.

taste/tinker
A 288.1 '"Everyone to his own taste," said the tinker as he watched the ass eating thistles.'
County Roscommon
Q 1973 IFC 1888:146 C f+

cf the proverb 'A thistle is a salad fit for an ass's mouth.' Bohn p. 111

cf the fable L'Estrange *The ass eating thistles* Fable XCIX, p. 198, illustration p. 199.

tea/Mrs Grogan

A 289.1 '"When I makes tea, I makes tea," as old mother Grogan said, "and when I makes water I makes water."'
James Joyce *Ulysses*, a novel, 1922 Paris, 1986 ed., Part I, Episode 1, p. 11, lines 357–58: 'Haines sat down to pour out the tea.
—I'm giving you two lumps each, he said. But, I say, Mulligan, you do make strong tea, don't you?
Buck Mulligan, hewing thick slices from the loaf, said in an old woman's wheedling voice:
—When I makes tea, I makes tea, as old mother Grogan said. And when I makes water I makes water.
—By Jove, it is tea, Haines said.
Buck Mulligan went on hewing and wheedling:
—*So do I Mrs Cahill*, says she. *Begob, ma'am*, says Mrs Cahill, *God send you don't make them in the one pot.*'
He lunged towards his messmates in turn a thick slice of bread, impaled on his knife.
—That's folk, he said very earnestly, for your book Haines. Five lines of text and ten pages of notes about the folks and the fishgods of Dundrum.'
[North Dublin]
cf article title '"When I makes Tea, I makes Tea ...": Innovation in Food — the Case of Tea in Ireland.' Lysaght 1987 *Ulster Folklife*, 33, pp. 42–71.

tell/duck

A 290.1 '" No one can tell what he is able to do till he tries," as the duck said when she swallowed a kitten.
Patrick Weston Joyce 1910, 1991 rpt. Ch. 8 'Proverbs' p. 106. Opening this chapter Joyce says: 'Those that I give here in collected form were taken from the living lips of the people during the last thirty or forty years.' Cited in *Addenda* 127.

there see *see/blind man*
thing see *full/tailor*
time/flea see *walk/flea*

time/lad (fellow)
A 291.1 & .2 '"Time flies," as the lad (fellow) said when he threw the clock out the window.'
County Tipperary current in 1978
Q 1973(78) IFC 2027:168 C m+: 'This is to be heard in Turtulla [near Thurles] and is quoted when the passage of time is a topic of conversation'

Mieder & Tóthné Litovkina p. 212

Notes: Part A 328.5 & .6 are in the same Correspondent's list.
'Time flies and man dies' Co. Sligo IFCS 170:260 in a list, mainly of proverbs, is the only instance of the proverb itself in the indexed Schools' Manuscripts, however, 'Time flies' is currently very common in English and is often extended to 'Time flies when you're having fun,' eg. the extended variant heard from the aerobics teacher AW f 30s b. & r. [?East] Belfast, during her aerobics class in South Belfast, Oct. 2002

see also Part A 294.

time/monkey
A 292.1 '"First time I had my a– on tick," said the monkey when he sat on the alarm clock.'
County Kilkenny current in 1975
Q 1973(75) IFC 1917:79 +, i m+: 'told me by a local clergyman who hailed originally from [the] Castlecomer area, but who wishes to be anonymous! He said they were v[ery] common sayings in that area' [see the two other wellerisms, which also have a monkey as speaker, Part A 178.1 & 180.4, from the same informant].

time/snail   *cf Nor
A 293.1 '"Time and patience," as the snail said when it reached America.'
County Mayo
IFC 1888:126 collected by SÓC(ii) in 1975 from MC m

*cf Nor ?Christiansen.

time/woman (drunk man, carpenter)   Am Eng
A 294.1 '"Time flies," as the woman said when she threw the clock at her husband.'
Dublin City late 1930s

Q 1973 IFC 1917:14 C m+. For Correspondent's comment see Part A 40

.2 '"Time flies," as the drunk man said when his wife threw the kitchen clock at him.'
Q 2000 i RÓB+ 60s, retired MD, as he recalls hearing it from some time back: 'may not be *verbatim*' email 14/3/2002

.3 '"Time flies," as the carpenter said when he threw the clock at his wife.'
Irish play performed in Belfast Grand Opera House as FCW recalls hearing it in the late 1970s

DOW 1390

Mieder & Tóthné Litovkina p. 212

Note: see information at Part A 291

see also Part A 291.

times see *hard times*

tit/Napoleon
A 295.1 '"I feel a right tit," as Napoleon said when he surveyed the carnage of Waterloo.'
Belfast *c.* 1990
Q 2000 **TC** first in his list of wellerisms with his comment: 'normally said with the left hand held horizontally inside the jacket.' For his further comments see part A 118

cf well-known joke party piece — 'Will I do my impression of Napoleon?' — instead of the expected speech the enquirer then stands up and tucks his hand into his jacket. eg. senior Belfast academic 1990s.

toil/Billy Ban (widower)   Am Eng, E Eng, Scots
A 296.1 '"Never make a toil of a pleasure," as Billy Ban said when he dug his wife's grave only three feet deep.'
Billy Ban [<Ir Bán]=White- or Fair-haired Billy; three feet, or a metre, would be precisely half the normal depth
MacManus [*c.* 1868–1960] *Heavy Hangs the Golden Bough*, a collection of Donegal folktales and legends retold with a saying, usually a proverb, after every one headed 'The Old Word,' ie. a literal translation of the

Irish word for proverb 'seanfhocal.' 1950 New York, p. 71. The book contains one other wellerism, also misogynist, Part A 45

.2 '"Don't be making a toil of a pleasure," as the widower was alleged to have said to the mourners bearing his wife's coffin.'
County Down
UFTM Notebook 1959 C AJHS f.

DOW 1399; 'Cheviot' p. 183; Hislop p. 126, with the following from Kelly: 'A man going under his wife's head to the grave was bid go faster, because the way was long and the day short; answered, "I will not make a toil of a pleasure."'

Note: the proverb 'Don't make a toil of pleasure' is known but not common in English.

tongue/cook
A 297.1 '"That's my long tongue," as the cook said.'
Pepper Early 1970s Used for the main heading of 'John Pepper's Column,' a regular column about [mainly Belfast] idioms in the daily newspaper, *The Belfast Telegraph* before Wed. 12/9/ *c.* 1973; cutting in IFC 1888:40: the title is based on the story of a new bride, through ignorance, asking the butcher for too much meat

cf 'Don't worry said the judge as he sentenced girl to hang' [*sic*] *Evening Press*, a Dublin-based daily newspaper, 11/4/1975, p. 8, cutting in IFC 1917:95, as another example of the wellerism structure as a newspaper heading. [The judge wished to convey that she would be reprieved.]

tools/tailor
A 298.1 '"Down tools!" said the tailor as he dropped the needle.'
Seamus Murphy [1907–75] 1966 London, 1977 rpt. *Stone Mad*, autobiography of a monumental sculptor, p. 196: '"When I worked in the Stradbally [Co. Waterford] quarries we had a fella [= fellow] who could do what he liked with a scavelling hammer --- 'twas about eighteen pounds weight [*c.* 8 kg.] and after using it for about an hour you could hardly lift your head or straighten your back. But this boyo would just revel in it. An' when he'd have the trimming done he'd drop it and say 'Down tools! Said the tailor as he dropped the needle!' Isn't that wan [= one] of the most disparaging remarks you ever heard about another craft?"'

torn/hen
A 299.1 '"That's torn it!" as the hen said when she laid the square egg.'
County Down
Q 2000 **TC**

cf the riddle 'What did the hen say when it laid a square egg? Ouch!'
P.T.Q. 1947 Belfast n.p. and 'What did the hen say when she laid an egg? Ouch!' Gallant 1993 New York p. 21.

trade/cobbler
A 300.1 '"Every man to his trade," as the cobbler said when he killed his wife with the last.'
County Kilkenny
Q 1973(75) IFC 1917:79 C f+

cf 'The last what the cobbler struck the wife with, Farmers' proverb [used when] cutting last sod of turf or sheaf of corn' Co. Cavan Q 1973 IFC 1888:85.

trifle/monkey
A 301.1 '"That's only a trifle!" said the monkey as he pissed on the sponge cake.'
trifle=a dessert, consisting in part of cake soaked in sherry
IFC 1917:98 on a sheet written in 1986 by SMcR f+, DIF student from the USA.

troubles/man   Part B 121
A 302.1 '"Troubles niver come singly," as the man said when his wife died on him an' the hen laid away.'
niver=never; an'=and; laid away=laid an egg outside the hen house
County Armagh
Paterson *Armagh Miscellanea* 1920s– ts Vol. XII in article titled 'Marriage Customs' pp. 104–13, p. 113, with the comment: 'the last trouble was the worst of all.' Published as '"Troubles never come singly," as the man said when his wife died an' the hen laid away an' the last trouble was the worst of all' in Paterson *Country Cracks.* 1939, 1945

ed., Dundalk, in final part which is a list titled 'Familiar Country Sayings' p. 113. Paterson says that the stories were collected during field work from 1927–30 from informants whose ages ranged from 70–93, Foreword pp. 14–15

cf 'One trouble never comes alone, John is idle and the hen laid out.' *laid out=laid an egg outside the hen house.* Co. Dublin IFCS 786:235 in a list, mainly of proverbs, with the comment: 'A woman in Lusk once said "One trouble never comes alone, John is idle and the hen laid out."'

cf 'Dick died and the hen laid out.' Co. Carlow IFCS 907:418 in a list, mainly of proverbs

cf 'Cute as a fox. The cutest of hens lays out ([used] when a reputedly wise person does a foolish thing)' Co. Wexford IFCS 901:310

cf locally composed song in which the proverb 'one trouble never comes without two' is used in response by a man getting a doctor's bill just after his wife had died for the doctor's visit to his wife the day before she died Co. Monaghan IFCS 939:227

Notes: women cared for the hens. 'laid out' can also mean laid out for display between death and burial — if Dick were dead he would be 'laid out.' This pun does not operate in Irish.
The proverb 'Troubles never come singly' is currently common in English and Irish.
tumblin'/showman
A 303.1 '"The aisiest way of tumblin' is the best," as the showman say'd.'
aisiest=easiest
Ulster
Byers Papers Box T4 'S & P' ts T-4-6 p. 62.

turn/countrywoman see *good turn*

turn/Divil (Devil)   Am Eng, E Eng
A 304.1 '"Turn about is fair play," as the divil said to the smoke-jack.'
smoke-jack=mechanical device operated by hot air fixed in a chimney for turning a roasting spit, def. based on COED 2883
Lover 'A Legend of Clonmacnoise. The King and the Bishop.' in *Stories and Legends of Ireland.* Dublin; London; Edinburgh, 1831 [possibly slightly earlier in a Dublin magazine] p. 84: 'I said I'd be even with you,'

says he, 'and so I will; and if you spoil my divarshin [= diversion = amusement], I'll spoil yours and turn about is fair play, as the divil said to the smoke-jack.'

.2 '"Turn-about is fair-play," as the devil said to the smoke-jack.'

Anon. *National Proverbs: Ireland.* 1913 p. 35

DOW 1429

Notes: also in Mair *A Hand-book of Proverbs* ... n.d. [late 19th century] London, p. 74, but probably a citation from Lover, & in O'Griofa *Irish Folk Wisdom* 1993 New York, p. 119 which, in turn, is probably from Mair or from Anon. *National Proverbs: Ireland.*

two see *company*

U

up see *again*

W

wait/train
A 305.1 '"You're in for a long wait," said the train to the bridge.'
Q 2000 'The John Creedon Show' RTÉ Radio 1, a response [to the radio appeal made on the previous day] in a letter from PJ m, a variant of which was then broadcast on 17/1/2002. It seems that there were several from this Correspondent; see A 67 and Appendix 2.

walk/duck   Part B 154 also Nor
A 306.1 '"Walk, walk!" said the duck.
"No," said the duck house raider, "I'll carry you."'
County Westmeath
Q 1973 IFC 1917:62. For Correspondent's comments see Part A 13.2

cf the fable Aesop 126

cf Eccles XIII:17.

walk/flea
A 307.1 'Said one flea to another, "It's about time we went home — shall we walk or take a dog?"'
P.T.Q. 1958 Belfast n.p.

.2 'Two fleas came out of the cinema, one of them said, "Shall we walk or take a dog?"'
P.T.Q. 1970 Belfast p. 30

cf the riddle 'What did one flea say to the other flea? Shall we walk or shall we take a dog?' Hegarty *Amazing Animal Jokes.* 1987 London n.p.

Note: local cinemas are known as 'flea pits.'

walking/Pat   Part B 135
A 308.1 '"Anything is better than walking," as Pat said when he went ariding on the pig.'
County Roscommon
Q 1973 IFC 1888:148 C m+

cf the proverb to the converse 'First class walking is better than third class riding.' Co. Monaghan IFCS 945:250.
want/botch carpenter
A 309.1 '"What do you want," said the botch carpenter, "a big, ugly mortice or a neat six inch nail?"'
County Monaghan
Q 1973 IFC 1888:73 C m+: 'This saying is commonly used in the Clones area and was first spoken by a famous character … who is now a much better carpenter. [He] made this comment when one of his first jobs, a cabinet, was severely criticised by his employer. The phrase is used not only in carpentry circles, but in many others to justify shoddy work etc. when the exponent is not very expert.'

waste/farmer
A 310.1 'Farmer, "Wilful waste makes woeful want." Milkman, "Wilful water makes woeful milk."'
County Cavan
Q 1973 IFC 1888:86 C m+

Mieder & Tóthné Litovkina p. 224 [but no wellerism]

Note: The proverb 'Wilful waste makes woeful want' is currently very common in English and is also found in Irish.

way/fly   Am Eng
A 311.1 'As the fly said as it was walking over the mirror, "That's another way of looking at it."'
County Tyrone
IFC 1888:56 collected in 1974 by **SÓC(ii)** from PÓD m+

DOW 766 & 774

Note: see Part A 83.8.

way/Punch see *divil*

welcome/Pára Ban (Porra Bawn, Párach Bhoe)
A 312.1 '"You are welcome out," as Pára Ban said to the gosling.'
Pára=diminutive form of Pádraig [Patrick]; Ban <Ir *Bán=White-* or *Fair-haired*
County Leitrim
IFCS 205:112 in a list, mainly of proverbs, with the following explanation after this particular item: 'There lived a man in this district and his name was Pára Ban. He set a goose on eggs. One of the goslings was slow in coming out and, when it came out he said "welcome out."'
Published in [Carson] Williams 1992 p. 38/2000a p. 48

.2 '"You're welcome out!" says Porra Bawn to the gosling.'
Porra <Ir *Pára=diminutive form of Pádraig [Patrick]; Bawn* <Ir *Bán=White-* or *Fair-haired*
County Cavan
Q 1973 IFC 1888:89 C m+
Note: this is immediately followed by Part A 105

.3 '"Welcome out!" as Párach Bhoe said to the gosling.'
Párach=diminutive form of Pádraig [Patrick]; Bhoe <Ir *Bhui=Yellow-* or *Fair-haired*
County Cavan
IFCS 994:191 in a list, mainly of proverbs

cf the motif *MI* J 1880 *Animals or objects treated as if human—miscellaneous*

186

Note: as 'Pára' is a common name, it is often necessary to identify people by a sobriquet. The colour of the man's hair may have resembled gosling down.

well see *again/girl*

whate/pigeon
A 313.1 '"It's the rale whate," as the pigeon said on November Day.'
rale=real, genuine; whate=wheat; November Day, 1ˢᵗ November, beginning of winter
County Carlow
Q 1973 IFC 1917:73 C m+.

whip/cricket
A 314.1 '"Whip it," said the cricket when he was nine days old.'
County Cavan
Q 1973 IFC 1888: 86 C m+

Note: possibly a pun on 'whippet.'

will/crow
A 315.1 '"Where there's a will there's away," said the crow when he flew away.'
County Wicklow
Q 1973 IFC 2154:279 C m+, i PC f+: 'A popular wellerism in our school, St Cronan's, Vevey Rd., Bray, was, '"Where there's ... flew away.'""

Mieder & Tóthné Litovkina pp. 231–32

Note: the proverb 'Where there's a will there's a way' is currently common in English.

Willie/master
A 316.1 'As the master said to the servant, "Wha ca's 'Willie'? I was aye ca'ed 'Maisther.'"'
wha ca's=who calls; aye ca'ed maisther=always called master
County Donegal
Q 1973 IFC 1888:15.

wind/old gentleman
A 317.1 '"Gone with the wind," as the old gentleman said watching his tall hat float peacefully down the Shannon.'
[River]
IFC 1888:105 informant/creator WS m+. For note see Part A 23; others from him are Part A 32, 54, 62, 112, 175, 179 & 319.

woman/fool
A 318.1 '"We'd be very happy if we had a woman apiece," as the fool said to his mother.'
apiece=each
County Fermanagh
Q 1973(74) IFC 1888:69 C m+: 'common in Bellanaleck.'

work/sweep
A 319.1 '"That's a dirty piece of work," as the sweep said to the housemaid.'
County Leitrim
IFC 1888:103 informant/creator WS m+. For note see Part A 23; Part A 32, 54, 62, 112, 175, 179 & 317.

work/taxi driver
A 320.1 '"It's not just the work I enjoy," said the taxi driver, "it's the people I run into."'
P.T.Q. 1961 Belfast n.p.

work/tinker
A 321.1 '"A wud rether hev yer work nor yer music," as the tinker said t' the jackass.'
wud=would; rether=rather; hev=have; yer=your; nor=than; t'=to
'M'Cart' [Canon Abraham Hume 1814–80] *Poor Rabbin's Ollminick [=Almanac] for the toun o' Bilfawst [= Belfast]...1863 ...* , a pastiche, n.d. [1862 or 63] Belfast & Dublin, in a list titled 'Proverbial Expressions' p. 25. Also in Byers Papers Box T4 T-4-6 p. 61 with no ascription.

work/undher millstone
A 322.1 '"Close work," as the undher millstone said to the upper, when there was no corn.'
undher=under

188

Lover *Treasure Trove: The First of a Series of Accounts of Irish Heirs: Being a Romantic Irish Tale of the Last Century*, a novel, 1844 London p. 19: '… the shout of pursuit was heard at the entrance of the "close," [= yard] and the portal was barely shut and barred when the heavy tramp of men was heard rushing past …The party within made no move till the tramp of the pursuers died away in the distance, then Phaidrig, with a low chuckle, spoke. "Close work," said he, "as the undher millstone said to the upper, when there was no corn."
"'Twould have been grinding work, sure enough, had we been taken," said the stranger.'

works/man

A 323.1 '"Marvellous are the works of man," as the man said stepping over the baby.'

The Tailor and Ansty, a biography of Tadhg Buckley, 'The Tailor' [b. Co. Kerry 1863 d. Co. Cork 1945] and his wife Anastasia by Eric Cross, 1942, 1972 ed., p. 111. 'The Tailor' is trying to describe an invention which he read about in the paper to Eric Cross, while Ansty is at the same time talking about a beggar man calling for work: '"I remembered last night, after you had gone, a piece I had out of the paper, and all the morning I was looking for it, but, the divil mend it, I can't find it anywhere … But I remember the most of it. It was a bit about a German doctor in America, who was in a hole thirty-five feet deep in the ground, and he was weighing the earth. ---"
[Ansty] "Did you see the great shtal [= stallion] of a beggar that walked up the road today?"
"That wasn't all he was doing, however ---"
"—My shtal walked into me and said how he was looking for work, and I told him to go to Mick Lucey—"
"—he was also making a kind of a clock --- and it keeps the daylight so that it would be day inside the house when it would be night outside --- that's a powerful patent, I can tell you—"
"—and I told him he—"
"—Marvellous are the works of man, as the man said, stepping over the baby—"
"—could scratch my bottom—"
Everyone, actors and audience, is exhausted after this. There is a moment's breathing space.
"Stepping over the baby! Wisha! How well you were there to see him! Get up and see where the cow is. Johnny Con's cows are easht [= east], and she'll be fighting with them."'

worse/man

A 324.1 '"It could be worse," as the man said when he lost his mother-in-law.'
County Roscommon
Q 1973 IFC 1888:147 C m+. For note see Part A 83.10.

X

x/Mr Algebra
A 324a.1 '"Let x equal my right name and address," as Mr Algebra remarks *passim*.'
right=proper
James Joyce *Ulysses*, a novel, 1922 Paris, 1986 ed. Part III Episode 16, p. 537, lines 1636–37: '... to the accompaniment of large potations of potheen [= illegal homemade alcohol] and the usual blarney [= smooth talk] about himself for as to who he in reality was let X equal my right name and address, as Mr Algebra remarks *passim*.'

Y

[?youth]/farmer
? A 325.1 [?Youth must have its fling], **'said the farmer as he threw the bonhams from the rail.'**
bonham=young pig
Q 1973 IFC 1917:21 C m+: 'The wittiest W[ellerism]s I read about concerned "... said the Farmer as he threw the Bonhams from The Rail. Some years later I read a parody of it viz: "... said the Farmer as he threw the child out the Window when it was crying" [Part A 327.7] (I forget the first part of it).' The Correspondent's address is Co. Kerry.

youth/old woman
A 326.1 '"Ye have the youth, a chroí," says the old woman.'
a chroí Ir (voc.)= *heart, a term of endearment*
County Kerry
Q 1973 IFC 1917:19 C m+.

youth/old woman   Ger, Swe, *cf Am Eng
A 327.1 '"Youth must have its fling," said the old woman when she jumped over the besom.'
besom=a broom, formerly one made of heather

190

County Cavan
IFCS 1011:238 in a list, mainly of proverbs

*cf Am Eng '"Young girls are crazy," as the old woman said when she jumped over the straw.' *DOW* 257

Notes: 'to jump over the besom' or [as in the American, German and Swedish examples] 'over the straw' symbolised entering the new married state. The expression is current in Ireland, eg., see title on the back page 'The Double Edge' of Section 2, 'Sport' of the Dublin-based newspaper, the *Sunday Independent,* 23/12/2001'Ken Doherty jumps the cue — and the broom': 'Ken Doherty has gone to pot. And to get married too. The former World Snooker champion is on cue to jump the broom this week in Australia ...' Jason O'Callaghan. p. 26. I thank Paul Tempan for this reference.
The proverb 'Youth must have its fling' is currently common in English but does not seem to have been noted in Irish.

youth/ woman (old woman, lad, fellow, farmer)
A 328.1 '"Youth must have its fling," as the woman said when she threw the baby out the window.'
County Roscommon *c.* 1962
Q 2000 **JG** who heard it used by VMcM, driver of a travelling shop from Knockcrockery; he used it about neighbours doing something more suited to younger people

.2 '"Youth must have its fling," said the woman when she threw the child out the window.'
County Galway
Q 1973 IFC 1888:155 C m+

.3 '"Youth must have its fling," said the old woman as she threw her child through the window.'
County Clare
Q 1973 IFC 1917:5 C m+

.4 '"Youth must have its fling," as the woman said when she threw the child through the window.'
County Kilkenny
Q 1973 IFC 1917:76 C f+

.5 & .6 '"Youth must have its fling," as the lad (fellow) said when he threw the child out the window.'

County Tipperary current in 1978
Q 1973(78) IFC 2027:167 C m+: 'still heard in the Turtulla [near Thurles] area and is quoted when older people talk about the younger generation.' Note: Part A 291 is in the same Correspondent's list

? .7 [?Youth must have its fling], **'said the farmer as he threw the child out the window when it was crying.'**
Q 1973 IFC 1917:21 C m+: 'The wittiest W[ellerism]s I read about concerned "... said the Farmer as he threw the Bonhams from The Rail [Part A 325]. Some years later I read a parody of it viz: "... said the Farmer as he threw the child out the Window when it was crying" (I forget the first part of it).' The Correspondent's address is Co. Kerry

Note: see notes at Part A 327, last two lines.

youth/woman
A 329.1 '"Youth must have its fling," as the woman said when she threw the clock at her husband.'
Dublin City late 1930s
Q 1973 IFC 1917:14 C m+. For Correspondent's comment see Part A 40

Note: see notes at Part A 327, last two lines.

PART B: WELLERISMS IN IRISH

A

abhaile/gabhar

B 1.1 "'Abhaile má fhéadaim!" a ndubhairt an gabhar.'
['"Home, if I'm able," said the goat.']
Munster
'An Seabhac' 1926 No. 832/1984 No. 997 with the following: ['A billy goat, lightheartedly and proudly, went 'ag lorg mná' ['looking for a wife'] as he said himself, in the season when goats normally do this. A short time afterwards, he returned to the same place, tired and exhausted from fighting with other billy goats over the nanny goats. He was asked where he was going "Home, if I'm able," he said']

see also Part B 139.

aga/gadaí

B 2.1 "'Béarfadsa an t-aga liom," aduairt an gadaí.'
['"?I'll seize my opportunity," said the thief.']
County Cork
Ó Cróinín 1980 in a list titled 'Seanfhocail agus Canúinní' ['Proverbs and Sayings'], p. 342 No. 21 collected by **SÓC(i)** between 1943 and 1944 from AÓL m.

aimsir/bean an iascaire (bean)

B 3.1 "'Aimsir mhaith chughainn!" arsa bean an iascaire nuair fuair sí a fear báidhte.'
['"May we have good weather soon!" said the fisherman's wife when she found her husband drowned.']
Irisleabhar na Gaedhilge, 13, No. 151 (April 1903), p. 273, in a short, untitled list, mainly of proverbs

.2 "'Aimsir mhaith chughainn!" mar adubhairt an bhean nuair a fuair sí a fear báithte.'
['"May we have good weather soon!" as the woman said when she found her husband drowned.']
Munster
'An Seabhac' 1926 No. 799/1984 No. 961

aire/Súil Gheam

B 4.1 '"Tá go leor ar ar n-aire," mar adubhairt Súil Gheam.'
['"We have enough to look after," as Súil Gheam [*lit.* 'Jewel Eye']
said.']
Connacht
'An Beirneach' [Liam Ó Beirn *c.* 1869–1949] 1926 Dublin *An Troid
agus an t-Uaigneas*, a novel, 10 as cited in Ó Máille 1948 No. 257.

airgead/fear na feoirlinge (f. na feóirline)
**B 5.1 '"Airgead!" a ndubhairt fear na feoirlinge nuair a bhain
sé an glór as an lic.'**
['"Money!" said the man with [only] a farthing when he made the rock
ring out.']
Munster
'An Seabhac' 1926 No. 815/1984 No. 980

**.2 '"Airgead, am baist'!" a ndúirt fear na feóirline nuair a
bhuin sé glór as an lic.'**
['"Money, I declare!" said the man with [only] a farthing when he made
the rock ring out.']
County Kerry
Almqvist *Collection of proverbs* ... ts, collected by **BA** from **MÓG**
between 1966 and 1974.

am/Seán Phaid
**B 6.1 '"An dial gurb é am dhuit é," mar a ndúirt Seán Phaid le
Beití fudó.'**
['"By the devil, it's your time," as Seán Phaid said to Beití long ago.']
County Kerry
Almqvist *Collection of proverbs* ... ts, collected by **BA** from **MÓG**
between 1966 and 1974: 'Seán Phaid, a Blasket [Island]-man, said this
when when his wife went into labour in the middle of a stormy night and
he was reluctant to get up and bring in the midwife from the mainland'

**.2 '"An daigh gurbh é am dóibh é," mar dubhairt Seán Phaid
le Beití fadó.'**
['"Faith, but what a time time they picked," as Seán Phaid said to Beití
long ago.']
County Kerry
Ó Gaoithín/**MÓG** *Is trua nach fanann an óige*, autobiographical, 1953
Dublin p. 24; ref. via Almqvist *Collection of proverbs* ... ts. The
following context is from Enright's translation [O'Guiheen 1982] of Ó

Gaoithín 1953. **MÓG** and his father are out fishing and conscious that bad weather is brewing when they see the islanders on shore running: '"I suppose it's some stranger that has come to the village." "It is, Dad," said I, "a currach [= open boat] has come into the quay now and 'tis full of strangers." "Faith, but what a time they picked, as Seán Phaid said to Betty long ago. I wonder what brought them up here?" my father said.' Ch. 7 'The Mackerel Season' p. 26, where 'Betty' is glossed as 'Betty Rice, the local landowner.' Flower 1944, 1978 ed., pp. 98–99, relates that Betty Rice lived near Dingle town but owned one of the uninhabited Blasket Islands — Teeraght [<Tiaracht]. Every year, when the young puffins on it were well-grown she used to send over a boat to catch them for food, however, the islanders, believing that there could be no ownership of wild birds, used to go over to Teeraght for the same reason before Betty Rice's men. One year they were spotted returning from their expedition and subsequently taken to court where Daniel O'Connell [1775–1847] is said to have spoken so eloquently on their behalf that they got off with a warning and Betty Rice never again sent for the puffins.

am/taidhbhse

B 7.1 '"Sé d'am é," mar adubhairt an taidhbhse le Liam.'
['"It's time for you," as the ghost said to Liam.']
County Mayo current in the early 1960s
Stockman 1974 No. 315 under 'Occasional Sayings' with the following: 'Liam was an old man who used to look for his cows after darkness. On one occasion he claimed that he saw a ghost who greeted him with the above words. The phrase is still used e.g. when a person comes to help with work after the work has been done'

see also Part B 186.

amadán/asal   Part A 92 also cf Part A 8, 20 & 44

B 8.1 '"A amadáin na gcluasa fada," ars' an t-asal le n-a dhearbhrathair.'
['"Oh, you long-eared fool!" said the ass to his brother.']
County Donegal
Morris 1918 No. 130

.2 '"A amadáin na g-cluas fada," ars an t-asal le na dearbhráithair.'
County Donegal
IFCS 1072:88 +

.3 & .4 '"Amadán na gcluas fada," adubhairt an t-asal le n-a dhearbhráthair.'
['"Long-eared fool!" said the ass to his brother.']
County Galway
both Ó Máille 1948 No. 1286

.5 as .3 & .4
County Galway
Ó Lubhlaí 1976 Desktop pub. p. 229 in section titled 'Dea-chaint' ['Witty speech' *or* 'Smart talk'] preceded by the comment: 'Beirt ag dispeagadh a chéile agus déarfadh duine a bheadh ag eisteacht leo: '"Amadán na gcluas fada!' a dúirt an tasal lena dheartháir" nó "'Tá beirt agaibh ann,' mar a dúirt an gabhar lena adharca,"' ['Said by a person hearing a pair belittling one another: '"Long-eared fool …' or "'That makes two of you,' as the goat said to his horns"' [Part B 27.2]]

see also Part B 27.

amadán/fear bocht
B 9.1 '"Ní tusa an t-umadán ach is mise an t-umadán a dh'fhág agut iad," ers' an fear bocht fudó leis an mbithúnach, nuair a ghoid sé a dhá mholtachán uaig.'
['"You're not the fool, but I'm the fool to have left them with you," said the poor man long ago to the rogue when he stole his two wethers from him.']
County Kerry
Almqvist *Collection of proverbs* … ts, collected by **BA** from **MÓG** between 1966 and 1974.

amárach/iasc *cf Scots
B 10.1'"Tar i mbárach," adeir an t-iasc.'
['"Come tomorrow," said the fish.']
County Galway
Gearrbhaile, 1938–39 as cited in Ó Máille 1952 No. 4720

.2 as .1
Connacht
Ar Aghaidh, July 1942 as cited in Ó Máille 1952 No. 4720

.3 as .1
County Galway
Ó Máille 1952 No. 4720

.4 '"Taraidh amárach," ars' an t-iasc.'
County Mayo current in the early 1960s
Stockman 1974 No. 428 with the comment: 'This is said to a fisherman who is not having much luck with his fishing.' Note: **.4**, plural form of verb.

*cf Scots 'The sea bids, "Come again."' Fyvie Mayo p. 45.

anam/táilliúir
B 11.1 '"Is luachmhar an t-anam," mar adubhairt an táilliúir agus é ag rith ó'n nganndal.'
['"Life is precious,"as the tailor said when he ran away from the gander.']
County Cork
Irisleabhar na Gaedhilge, 6, No. 4 (OS 64) (1 July 1895), in a list titled 'Proverbs and Sayings — (Continued). From North Cork (D. J. Galvin+, Glashakinleen, N[ational] S[chool], Newmarket),' pp. 60–61, No. 13, p. 61. Galvin's list begins in 6, No. 4 (OS 64), p. 60 and is in four parts with three wellerisms in all [this and Part B 46.1 & 186.1]

.2 '"Is luachmhar an t-anam," mar dubhairt an táilliúir 's é a' rith ón ngandal.'
Connacht
Irisleabhar na Gaedhilge, 14, No. 179 (Aug. 1905) in a list titled 'Seanfhocail II do bhailigh Tomás Ó hEidhin' ['Proverbs II collected by TÓhE'+], Nos. 132–302, pp. 844–45, No. 285, p. 848. This long list of 653 items won first prize at the Oireachtus [= festival promoting the Irish language etc.] of 1902, Competition 18. It was published in 7 parts, the first section being in Vol. 14, No. 178 (July 1905) pp. 827–31. The list consists mostly of proverbs but contains four wellerisms [this and Part B 41.5, 56 & 140.1]. Cited in Ó Máille 1952 No. 3616

.3 '"Is luachmhar an t-anam," mar adubhairt an táilliúir agus é ag rith ó'n nganndal.'
O'Rahilly 1922 under No. 112 [which is simply the proverb] on which he comments: '… also with a humorous addition thus: …'

.4 '"Is luachmhar an rud an t-anam!" mar adubhairt an táilliúir agus é ag rith ó'n nganndal!'
['"The soul is a valuable thing," as the tailor running from the gander said.']
Munster
'An Seabhac' 1926 No. 812/1984 No. 977

198

.5 '"Is luachmhar an t-anam," mar aduairt an táilliúir agus é ag rith ón ngandal.'
County Cork
IFC 43:239 in a list, mainly of proverbs, written *c.* 1933

.6 '"Is milis an rud an t-anam," mar a dúirt an táilliúir agus é ag rith ón ngandal.'
['"The soul is a sweet thing," as the tailor running from the gander said.']
Munster
'An Seabhac' 1984 No. 977

Note: the proverb 'Is luachmhar an t-anam' is common in Irish.

ann/fear
B 12.1 '"Táim ann, as!" mar adubhairt an fear leis an treabhadh.'
['"I'm all in and out," as the man said of the ploughing.']
Munster
'An Seabhac' 1926 No. 823/1984 No. 988 with the comment: ['The ploughing wasn't going very well, it appears, as the plough was moving up and down. *Or* one foot is in the furrow and the other on the bank.']

antragh/Boice   Part A 157
B 13.1 '"Antragh!" [?adúirt] Boice.'
['"Too late!" quoth Boice.']
Holinshed *Holinshed's Irish Chronicle The Historie of Irelande from the first inhabitation thereof, vnto the yeare 1509. Collected by Raphaell Holinshed, & continued till the yeare 1547 by Richarde Stanyhurst* [b. Dublin 1547, d. Brussels 1618] 1577 Dublin, 1979 ed., pp. 279–80: 'The Deputie Parese, at this cold salutation [being offered the promised monetary reward but to be afterwards beheaded] of farewell and behanged, turning his simpring to whimpring, sayd: "My Lord, had I wist you would haue dealte [= have dealt] so straitely with me, your Lordship shoulde not haue wonne this fort with as little bloudshed as you dyd." Whereat, M. Boice, a Gentleman of worship, and one that retained to that olde Earle of Kildare, standing in the preasse [= ?throng], saide in Irishe Antragh, which is as much in English as 'too late,' whereof grewe the Irish prouerbe, to thys day in that language vsed, Too late quoth Boice; as we say, beware of had I wist [= realized], or after meat mustard, or you come a day after the faire, or better done than sayde. The Deputie demaunded them that stood by what was that he spake, M. Boyce, willing to expounde his owne wordes, stept forth and answered, "My

Lord, I said nothing but that Parese is seized of a towne neare the water side named Baltra, and I would gladly know how he will dispose of it before he be executed.' The gouernoure, not mistrusting that M. Boice had glozed (for he had understood the true signification of the tearme [= term], it was very like that too late had not bin so sharp to Parese, but too soone had bin as soure to him) willed the money to be told to Parese, and presently caused him to be cut shorter by the head: declaring therby, that although for the time he embraced the benefyte of the treason, yet after he could not digest the treacherie of the Traytor,' with a woodcut of Parese's execution on p. 280. Ref. via Lean, Vol. II, Pt. 2, p. 751, where it is cited as '"Too late," quoth Boise.'

aonar/Mongan
B 14.1 'Mar adubhairt Mongan le Colum Cille, "Tá tú féin i d'aonar, a chleirigh!"'
['As Mongan said to Colm Cille, "You are alone, o cleric!"']
County Donegal
'Máire' *Le Clap-Sholus*, a novel, 1967 Dublin p. 119, line 1

Notes: Mongan ?Mongán, a northern prince who, according to mediaeval tradition, was converted to Christianity by St Colm Cille/Colmcille, Ó hÓgáin 1990, p. 302. Colmcille b. Co. Donegal 6th century, is one of the most important Irish saints. He is the speaker in Part B 23, 89 & 164.

araon/banbh (leanbh)
B 15.1 & .2 '"Iad araon!" arsan banbh (leanbh) maith.'
['"Both of them," said the good piglet (child).']
Munster
'An Seabhac' 1926 No. 819/1984 No. 984 with the comment: ['A strong, healthy piglet (or child) would eat everything given to it, or every kind of food available. *Or*, often said of a child who was asked whether it preferred its father or mother.']

.3 '"Iad araon!" ers' an leanbh, "an t-'rán is an t-obh in aonacht.'
['"Both of them," said the child, "the bread and the egg together."']
County Kerry
Almqvist *Collection of proverbs* ... ts, collected by **BA** from **MÓG** between 1966 and 1974.

200

arís/búistéir   Part A 3
B 16.1 '"Seo chuige arís," mar dúirt an tarbh leis an mbúistéir.'
['"Again to it," as the bull said to the butcher.']
County Kerry
Collected prior to 1973 by **BA** from a man

Note: the above was used as one of the four examples on Q 1973, and collected prior to it by **BA**, p.c. Sept. 2001. See Appendix 1 for the English-language version used on Q 1973.

B

bac/fear a' tighe
B 17.1 '"Ná bac leo siúd, a Pheigí. Beidh fear agad-sa nuair a bhéas na mná eile falamh," mar dubhairt fear a' tighe le n-a mhnaoi nuair a bhí sí ag achrann leis nuair nach n-éireochadh sé moch ar nós fir eile an bhaile.'
['"Don't worry about them, Peigí, you'll have a husband when the other wives are bereft," as the husband said to his wife when she was remonstrating with him that he didn't get up early like the other men in the district.']
County Galway
Ó Máille 1948 No. 1192

cf 'Beidh fear ag do bhean-sa nuair bhéas daoine eile falamh.' ['Your wife will have a husband when others have none.'] Ó Máille *ibid.*

baochas/fear an Oileáin
B 18.1 '"Baochas le Dia," ersa fear an Oileáin fudó, "gur tú atá geártha agus nach í mo bhróigín nú peirce."'
['"Thank goodness," said the [Blasket] Islandman long ago, "that it's you [foot], who's torn and not my new, little welted shoes."']
County Kerry
Almqvist *Collection of proverbs ... ts*, collected by **BA** from **MÓG** between 1966 and 1974

cf '"Moladh agus buíochas le Rí Mór na Glóire mar is tú atá loitithe agam agus nach í mo bhróg," er seisean (an fear a bhí ag dul ón Daingean fadó),' ['"Praise and thanks to the King of Glory that it's you who's damaged and not my shoes," he said [the man going from Dingle [town] long ago'] Ó Gaoithín 1970 *Beatha Pheig Sayers*, a biography of his mother, p. 120, ref. via Almqvist *Collection of Proverbs* ... ts with the comment: 'he said this when he struck his big toe against a stone.' Peig *ibid.* explains that it was the custom for the Islanders, when they reached Gallán na Cill Brice, near Milltown, on their way home from Dingle, to remove their shoes and walk barefooted and, as she herself was doing this on one occasion, it reminded her of the story about the man

Note: also found as a humorous tale see Ó Súilleabháin 1963 *Handbook* summary No. 12 p. 641: 'A man, carrying his first pair of new boots, strikes his foot against a stone. Is glad he hadn't his new boots on!' Ref. via Almqvist *Collection of proverbs* ... ts.

barraídheacht/sean-chat   Am Eng

B 19.1 '"Chan fhuil aon rud níos measa nó an bharraídheacht!" ars' an sean-chat nuair a bháidheadh é ins a' bhainne.'
['"There's nothing worse than a surfeit!" said the old cat when he drowned in the milk.']
County Donegal
Ua Muirgheasa 1907 No. 1451/1976 No. 1693

.2 '"Ní fhuil dadamh níos measa 'ná an bharraidheacht," mar dubhairt an sean-chat nuair a bhítear dá bháthadh i gcuinneoig an bhainne.'
['"Nothing's worse than a surfeit!" as the old cat said when it was drowning in the churn of milk.']
County Donegal
Mac Meanman *Rácáil agus Scuabadh*. 1955 Dublin p. 34, in a section titled 'Natháin agus Abraidhe atá leighte i ndearmad.' ['Neglected Sayings and Expressions.'], pp. 30–35, in which five wellerisms [this and Part B 24, 52, 77 & 141] are listed together, with the comment that they are still to be heard amongst the over fifties

DOW 1351.

beag/athair
B 20.1 '"Níl sí beag deas na mór gránna," arsa an t-athair nuair a tháinig a mhac abhaile le na mná chéile.'
['"She's neither small and nice nor big and ugly," said the father when his son came home with his wife.']
County Donegal
Q 1973 IFC 1888:21 C m+

Note: the saying quoted with 'míofar' in place of 'granna' is quite common.

beag/bean

B 21.1 "'Is beag an rud nach cuidiú é," mar adúirt an bhean a mhún ar an cháil.'
['"It's a small thing that doesn't help," as the woman who urinated on the cabbage said.']
County Donegal
Q 1973 IFC 1888:18 C m+, same Correspondent as Part B 22.3.

beag/dreolán (dreoilín, éan, dreolan)   Part A 180
B 22.1 "'Is beag an rud nach cuidiú é," dúirt an dreolán nuair a rinn sé a mhún san fharraige.'
['"It's a small thing that doesn't help," said the wren when he urinated in the sea.']
County Donegal
Lúcás 1986 under 'beag 7,' collected from ÉMacGB m b. 1940

.2 "'Is beag an rud nach cuidiú é," arsa an dreoilín nuair a rinne sé a mhúin san fharraige.'
IFC 1917:99 on a sheet written *c.* 1973 by ÁB f+ [E & Ir], DIF student in 1973

.3 "'Is beag an rud nach cuidiú é," mar adúirt an t-éan a rinne a mhún san fharraige.'
['"It's a small thing that doesn't help," as the bird that urinated in the sea said.']
County Donegal
Q 1973 IFC 1888:18 C m+, same Correspondent as Part B 21

.4 'Mar dúirt an dreolán nuair a rinne sé a mhún san fharraige, "Is beag a' rud nach cuidiú."'
['As the wren said when he urinated in the sea, "It's a small thing that doesn't help."']
County Donegal
Q 1973 IFC 1888:12 C m+: 'I only know of one wellerism that I have heard very frequently here. It is "Mar a dúirt …"'

.5 "'Is beag an rud nach cuidiughadh é," ars' an dreolan.'
['"It's a small thing that doesn't help," said the wren.']
County Donegal

Morris 1918 No. 155. In a comment with this wellerism Morris adds that it is used in the same way as a proverb, No. 35, in the list, 'The smallest help is a help and the greatest help is a help' which, in turn, is accompanied by this comment: 'said by a person who renders some small assistance by way of apology for not giving more'

cf de Bhaldraithe under 'fly': 'F[amiliar]: to play the fly on the wheel, cúnamh an dreoilín don fharraige ['the wren's help to the sea']; "Nach mise a thóg an ceo?" mar dúirt an chuileog i ndiaidh an chóiste.' ['Haven't I raised the dust?' as the fly after the carriage said.] Part B 71.2

see also Part B 44 & 46 & the converse Part A 164.

beagán/Colum Cille
B 23.1 '"Mar dubhairt Colum Cille, "An té ar leor leis beagán do Dhia, is leor le Dia beagán dó.'
['As Colm Cille said, "The person who thinks that a little is good enough for God, God will think that a little is good enough for him."']
County Donegal
'Maire' *An Teach nár Tógadh,* short stories, 1948 Dublin p. 151, line 6

Note: for information on Colm Cille see Part B 14.

béal/Mac an Bháird
B 24.1 '"Faraor, gur ó béal do mholadh a's gur ó chroidhe do cháineadh," mar dubhairt Mac an Bháird le h-Ó Domhnaill.'
['"It's a pity that your praise comes from your mouth but your criticism from your heart," as Mac an Bháird said to Ó Domhnaill.']
County Donegal
Mac Meanman *Rácáil agus Scuabadh.* 1955 Dublin p. 34, in a section titled 'Natháin agus Abraidhe atá leighte i ndearmad.' ['Neglected Sayings and Expressions.'] pp. 30–35, in which five wellerisms [Part B 19.2, 52, 77 & 141] are listed together, with the comment that they are still to be heard amongst the over fifties. Mac an Bháird and Ó Domhnaill represent clan leaders. One Mac an Bháird head was renowned for finely-honed insults. I thank Ciarán Ó Duibhín for this information. See Part B 111 for another wellerism with Mac an Bháird as speaker.

204

bean (pósfaidh)/fear
B 25.1 '"Fan go fóill go bpóstar bean leat," mar dubhairt an fear leis an ngirrfhiadh.'
['"Wait until a woman marries you," as the man said to the hare.']
County Galway
Ó Máille 1952 No. 3425 with the comment, which is below all his items at this number: ['Said to a person complaining about something which he has only started']

.2 '"Fan go bpósfaidh tú," mar a dúirt an fear leis an ngiorria.'
['"Wait until you're married," as the man said to the hare.']
Mac Con Iomaire 1988 p. 213 with a photographic illustration

cf 'Fan go fóill go bpóstar bean leat' ['Wait until a woman marries you'] and similar Ó Máille *ibid*.

beart/dreancaid
B 26.1 '"'Chuile bheart ar a luas," mar adeir an dreancaid.'
['"Everything at its own pace," as the flea said.']
County Galway
Ó Máille 1948 No. 1661 with the comment: ['perhaps from English …']
ie. from 'Nothing must be done hastily but killing of fleas' Smith & Wilson p. 580 ref. via Ó Máille.

beirt/gabhar   cf Part A 224
B 27.1 '"Tá beirt agaibh ann," mar deir an gabhar le n'adharca.'
['"There's a pair of you," as the goat said to his horns.']
Connacht
An Stoc, Oct. 1925 as cited in Ó Máille 1948 No. 1286

.2 '"Tá beirt agaibh ann," mar a dúirt an gabhar lena adharca.'
County Galway
Ó Lubhlaí 1976 Desktop pub., p. 229 in a section titled 'Dea-chaint' ['Witty speech' *or* 'Smart talk'] preceded by the comment: 'Beirt ag dispeagadh a chéile agus déarfadh duine a bheadh ag eisteacht leo: '"Amadán na gcluas fada!' a dúirt an tasal lena dheartháir." nó '"Tá beirt agaibh ann," mar a dúirt an gabhar lena adharca.' ['Said by a person hearing a pair belittling one another: '"Long-eared fool!' as the ass said

to his brother." [Part B 8] or "'That makes two of you,' as the goat said to his horns.'"].

biadh/An Sotach

B 28.1 "'Suarach an biadh do phutóga falamha bheith ag éisteacht le glór aingle," mar adubhairt an Sotach le n-a mháthair.'
["'Listening to the voices of angels is paltry fare for empty stomachs," as the Sotach said to his mother.']
County Galway
Ar Aghaidh, June 1939 as cited in Ó Máille 1948 No. 828

cf the proverb 'Ní lionann beannacht bolg.' ['Blessings don't fill the stomach.'], and similar variants, which is fairly common, eg. Ó Máille *ibid.*

cf the dialogue poem 'An Seabhac' 1936 'An Sotach 's an Mháthair' ['An Sotach and his Mother']

Note: the name *An Sotach* may be related to *sotal=impudence* see Ó Dónaill.

biríní/púca

B 29.1 "'Fainic na biríní géara!" adeireadh an púca agus é seo ag imtheacht ar a dhruim.'
["'Mind the sharp prickles!" said the pooka to the person on his back.']
púca/pooka=a supernatural, malevolent, solitary horselike creature
Connacht
Ó Máille 1948 No. 1207a with the comment: ['He himself was being torn by the briars'].

blas/bean bhocht

B 30.1 "'Bíonn blas ar an bheagán," arsa an bhean bhocht ag rannadh an beagán a bhí aice ar a clann.'
["'There's flavour on a little," said the poor woman apportioning the little she had to her family.']
County Donegal
Q 1973 IFC 1888:21 C m+

Note: the proverb 'Bíonn blas ar an bheagán' is currently very common in Irish and as 'A little tastes sweet' very common in English.

bó/cearc

B 31.1 '"Is fearr mé ná bó!" arsa an chearc, "beirim ubh sa ló."'

['"I'm better than a cow," said the hen, "I lay an egg every day."']
County Cork
Q 1973 IFC 1911:72 C f+ [E & Ir], a nun.

bréagach see *chífimíd*

bróga/cailleach

B 32.1 '"Nuair bhéas bróga ort, seas orm!" mar dubhairt an chailleach leis an gcat.'

['"When you get shoes stand on me!" as the hag said to the cat.']
County Mayo *c*. end of the 19th century
Ó Máille 1948 No. 1714 with the comment: ['When the circumstances allow you can do the thing you want to']

cf 'Nuair a bheas bróg ort-sa, seas orm-sa [when you are wearing shoes, stand on me]. This is said to a cat or a dog one stands on unintentionally.' Stockman 1974 'Occasional Sayings' No. 210

cf 'Ach go bhfágaidh tú bróga nua, seas orm' ['If you get new shoes stand on me'] Ó Máille *ibid*.

buile/Conán   Scots

B 33.1 '"Bíoch buile er bhuile anis aguin," fé mar dúirt Cunán leis an ndial fudó.'

['"Let's have blow upon blow now," as Conán said to the devil long ago.']
County Kerry
Almqvist *Collection of proverbs* … ts, collected by **BA** from **MÓG** between 1966 and 1974

cf the proverb 'An eye for an eye'

DOW 102

Note: Conán was one of the Fianna, Fionn Mac Cumhail's warrior band. Conán is also the speaker in Part B 84 & 85.

C

cabhail see *duine uasail*

cathú/Mathúin
B 34.1 '"Mo chathú thú!" a ndúirt Mathúin leis an sprid.'
['"Good grief!" said Mathúin to the ghost.']
County Kerry
Flower 1957 'Measgra ón Oileán Tiar' ['Miscellany from the Western
Island' ie. the Great Blasket] in folktale No. 20 'Mála an tSeanduine'
['The Old Person's Bag'], probably collected from Gobnait Ní Chinéide
[active 1920] p. 94. Ref. via Almqvist *Collection of proverbs* ... ts

.2 '"Mo chathú é!" a ndúirt Mathúin leis an sprid.'
County Kerry
Almqvist *Collection of proverbs* ... ts, collected by **BA** from **MÓG**
between 1966 and 1974.

ceann (Dia)/fear
**B 35.1 '"Tá mo cheann saor, ach go saorfai' Dia mo thún,"
ers' an fear do chuaig i bhfolach ósna splanncacha fé thúin na
leapa fudó.'**
['"My head's safe, but God save my backside," said the man who hid
from the lightning under the bed long ago.']
County Kerry
Almqvist *Collection of proverbs* ... ts, collected by **BA** from **MÓG**
between 1966 and 1974, with the comment: 'Known to **SÓD** as ...' —
see **.2**

**.2 '"Go saorfai' Dia mo thúin, tá mo cheann <u>alright</u>," ers' an
fear a chuir a cheann i bpoll na h-iadharta ón dtórnaig.'**
['"God save my backside, my head's alright," said the man who put his
head in the niche to get away from the thunder.']
*poll na h-iadharta=a small recess, usually in the wall near the fire and
well up above floor level where things could be kept safe and dry*
County Kerry
Almqvist *Collection of proverbs* ... ts; see **.1** for source.

ceann/sonas (saidhbhreas)
B 36.1 '"Cuir ina cheann," adubhairt an sonas.'
['"Add to it!" said good fortune.']
Connacht

208

An Stoc, Feb. 1919 as cited in Ó Máille 1952 No. 3904

.2 "'Cuir ina cheann,' adeir an sonas.
"Bain as,' adeir an donas.'
['"Add to it!" said good fortune.
"Take from it!" said bad fortune.']
County Galway
Ó Máille 1952 No. 3904

.3 "'Cuir í mo cheann,' adeir an saidhbhreas.'
['"Add to me!" said wealth.']
County Mayo
Ó Lochlainn 1936 in a list titled 'Sean-fhoclaí Ó Phartraighe an tSléibhe'
['Proverbs from Partry'], p. 58, collected from MUíÉ m d. 1922 aged 92

.4 "'Cuir 'mo cheann,' adubhairt an saidhbhreas.'
['"Add to me!" said wealth.']
County Mayo *c.* 1900
Ó Máille 1952 No. 3904

cf the proverb 'Is fusa sgapadh ná cruinniú,'s sé dubhairt an sonas a
bheith a' cur ina cheann.' ['It's easier to spend than to save, and what
good fortune said was to accumulate.'] Co. Galway, Ó Máille *ibid.*

Note: the proverb 'Is fusa sgapadh ná cruinniú' is currently common in
Irish and also in English.

ceart/Brátun
B 37.1 "'Sé an ceart an ceart a dhéanamh," mar dubhairt
Brátun nuair bhí sé a' roinnt na mbruithneog.'
['"It's right to do right," as Brátun said when he was dividing the baked
potatoes.']
County Galway
Ar Aghaidh, Mar. 1933 as cited in Ó Máille 1948 No. 1176.

céile/gabhar
B 38.1 "'Mar a chéile dhíbh," mar adubhairt an gabhar le n-a
chosa.'
['"You're all the same," as the goat said to his legs.']
Munster
'An Seabhac' 1926 No. 810/1984 No. 975 with the comment: ['This
would be said of two people similarly misbehaving']

.2 '"Mar a chéile daoibh," 'ndubhart an gabhar le n-a chosaibh.'
['"You're all the same," said the goat to his legs.']
County Cork
Irisleabhar na Gaedhilge, 16, No. 15 (OS 194) (Nov. 1906), in a list signed Seaghán Ua Cadhlaigh and titled 'Proverbs XVI ó Chuilinn Uí Chaoimh ("Cullin")' [Cuilleann Uí Chaoimh ('Cullen')], pp. 230–35, No. 204, p. 231. The list is in 3 parts and was begun in Vol. 16, No. 12 (OS 191) (Aug. 1906)

.3 '"Is mar a chéile sibh," a ndúirt an gabhar lena chosa.'
County Kerry
Almqvist *Collection of proverbs* ... ts, collected by **BA** from **MÓG** between 1966 and 1974

.4 '"Is mar a chéile iad," mar a dúirt an gabhar lena chosa.'
['"They're all the same," as the goat said of his legs.']
County Cork
Q 2000 i CÓC m 50s, who heard it from his mother [b. Ballyvourney, d. c. 1970].

ceo see *dusta*

ceoil/sean-bhean
B 39.1 'Mar dubhairt a' tsean-bhean, "bhí barraidheacht ceoil i n-a cuid caointe."'
['As the old woman said, "There was too much musicality in her lamentation."']
County Donegal
'Máire' *Cioth is Dealán*, short stories, 1926 Dublin p. 78, line 14.

ceóil & ceòil see *glèus ceòil*

chífimíd (chím, bréagach)/dall (balbhán)   Part A 40 & 259
B 40.1 '"Má mhairimíd beo chífimíd súd," a ndubhairt an dall.'
['"If we live we'll see that," said the blind person.']
Munster
'An Seabhac' 1926 No. 808/1984 No. 971

**.2 '"Chím," ars an dall.
"Thug tú t'eitheach," ars an balbhán.'**

["I see," said the blind person.
"You lie," said the mute.']
County Mayo
Ó Máille 1948 No. 1286. Cited in [Carson] Williams 1992 p. 73/2000a
p. 70

.3 '"Bréagach tú," arsa an balbhán.'
["You're a liar," said the mute.']
IFC 1917:99 on a sheet written *c.* 1973 by ÁB f+ [E & Ir], DIF student in
1973. NB this [.3] is likely incomplete and part of 'Chím ...' as in **.2** or
similar

Note: the first of the four examples on Q 1973 was *'Chím,' arsan fear
dall.* See Appendix 1 for the English-language version.

chím see *chífimíd*
chon(n)ac see *chonaic*
chónach see *conách/fear* & *conách/Seághan Muimhneach*

chonaic (chon(n)ac, scéal)/cat   Part A 254
**B 41.1 '"Chonaic mé cheana thú!" mar a dúirt an cat leis an
mbainne bruite.'**
["I've seen you before!" as the cat said to the seething milk.']
de Bhaldraithe 1959 under 'burnt': 'A burnt child dreads the fire,
"Chonaic mé cheana ... an mbainne bruite.'

**.2 '"Chonaic mé cheana thú!" mar a dúirt an cat leis an
mbainne te.'**
["I've seen you before!" as the cat said to the hot milk.']
County Mayo
Q 1973 IFC 1888:123 C m+ with the comment: ['Someone who wanted
to avoid something because of his previous experience would say this'].
For Correspondent's further comment see Part B 169. cf a similar variant
in Mac Con Iomaire 1988 p. 214 with a photographic illustration

**.3 '"Chonnac cheana thú!" mar adubhairt an cat leis an
mbainne beirbhithe.'**
Munster
'An Seabhac' 1926 No. 824/1984 No. 989. Cited in [Carson] Williams
1992 p. 35/2000a p. 45

**.4 '"Chonac cheana thú!" mar a dúirt an cat leis an mbainne
te.'**

Munster
'An Seabhac' 1984 No. 989

.5 "'Tá fhios agam cia'n scéal é," arsan cat leis an mbainne bruithte.'

['"I know the news you have," said the cat to the seething milk.']
Connacht
Irisleabhar na Gaedhilge, 15, No. 4 (OS 183) (Dec. 1905) in a list titled 'Seanfhocail IV Tomás Ó hEidhin do bhailig' ['Proverbs IV collected by TÓhE'+] pp. 55–56, No. 590, p. 56/translation p. 56, where a variant is also given — see **.9**. This long list of 653 items won first prize at the Oireachtus [= festival promoting the Irish language etc.] of 1902, Competition 18. It was published in 7 parts, the first section being in Vol. 14, No. 178 (July 1905) pp. 827–31. The list consists mostly of proverbs but contains four wellerisms [this and Part B 11.2, 56 & 140.1]. Cited in Ó Máille 1948 No. 1506. For his comment see **.6**

.6 as .5

County Mayo
Ó Máille 1948 No. 1506 with the comment for all three versions which he lists [**.5**, **.6** & **.10**]: ['A wise person isn't deceived twice']

.7 "'Chonnac cheana tú," mar dubhairt an cat leis an bhainne theith.'

County Kerry
Irisleabhar na Gaedhilge, 5, No. 2 (OS 50) (1 May 1894) in a list titled 'Popular Proverbs, Co. Kerry, Collected and Translated by Mr. William Long [Liam Ó Luing], Ballyferriter, Dingle.' pp. 21–25, No. 14, p. 21/translation p. 24. His list, which continues to Vol. 6, No. 4 (OS 52) (1 July 1894), p. 62, contains 137 items in all but this is the only wellerism

.8 as .7

County Kerry
Almqvist *Collection of proverbs … ts*, collected by **BA** from **MÓG** between 1966 and 1974

.9 "'Chonnac cheana tú," mar dubhairt an cat leis an mbhainne the.'

County Kerry
Seosamh Laoide 'Mac Tíre na Páirce' [Joseph Henry Lloyd 1865–1939, editor, for a time, of *Irisleabhar na Gaedhilge*] *Tonn Tóime Tiomargadh … ó Chiarraighe Luachra*, a collection of folklore, 1915 Dublin. Section XLVIII, in a list titled 'Seanfhocail: dhá chéad a líon,' pp. 105–12,

consisting mainly of proverbs, collected by Liam Ó Lúing [William Long] and others, p. 106 No. 13

.10 '"Do chonnac cheana thú," ar san cat leis an bainne the.'
?Munster
Irisleabhar na Gaedhilge, after 1894, place lost

.11 '"Chonaic mé do leitheid cheana," mar dubhairt an cat leis an mbainne te.'
['"I've seen your sort before," as the cat said to the hot milk.']
County Galway
Ó Máille 1948 No. 1506. For his comment see **.6**.

chonnac see *chonaic*

cíos/seanduine
B 42.1 '"Is orain araon atá an cíos," a ndúirt an seanduine fudó lena mhnaoi.'
['The rent applies to us both,' said the old man long ago to his wife.']
County Kerry
Almqvist *Collection of proverbs* … ts, collected by **BA** from **MÓG** between 1966 and 1974 with the comment: 'On another occasion **M[ÓG]** said "Ith suas do chuid a Mháire, orain araon atá an cíos."' ['Eat up your share, Máire, the rent applies to us both'].

clann/bean an tighe
B 43.1 '"Nár ba fearr a bhéas bhur gclann dá chéile," mar dubhairt bean an tighe leis na madraí nuair bhíodar a' troid.'
['"May your offspring agree no better [than you]," as the housewife said to the dogs when they were fighting.']
County Galway
Ó Máille 1952 No. 4478.

cóir see *maith (cóir)/Cailleach M(h)uigheo (Cailleach Bhéar(r)a, Cailleach Tír Eoghain)* comaoin/dreoilín   cf Part A 180

B 44.1 "'Sin comaoin ort, a fhairrge mhór," mar adubhairt an dreóilín nuair a dhein sé a mhún sa bhfairrge.'

['"That puts you in my debt, sea," as the wren said when he urinated in the sea.']

Munster

'An Seabhac' 1926 No. 841

.2 "'Mo chomaoin ort, a fharaige mhúir," ers' an dreóilín fudó, nuair a dhin sé a bhraoinín uisce ínte.'

['"You're in my debt, sea," said the wren long ago when he added his little drop of water into it.']

County Kerry

Almqvist *Collection of proverbs* ... ts, collected by **BA** from **MÓG** between 1966 and 1974, with the comment: 'on another occasion **M[ÓG]** said: ...' — see **.3**

.3 "'Mo chomaoin ort, a fharaige mhúir," ers' an dreóilín fudó, nuair a mhún sé ínte.'

['"You're in my debt, sea," said the wren long ago when he urinated in it.']

County Kerry

Almqvist *Collection of proverbs* ... ts, collected by **BA** from **MÓG** between 1966 and 1974. For **BA**'s comment see **.2**

4 "'Mo chomaoin ort," arsa an dreoilín agus a mhún a dhéanamh aige sa bhfarraige.'

['"You're in my debt," said the wren when he was urinating in the sea.']

County Cork

Q 1973 IFC 1917:32 C + [E & Ir] with the comment: ['this was heard from an old man who did not understand its significance']

.5 "'Comaoin ort, a fhairraige mhór," mar a dúirt an dreoilín nuair a mhún sé sa bhfarraige.'

['"You're indebted, sea!" as the wren said when he urinated in the sea.']

Munster

'An Seabhac' 1984 No. 1008

.6 Irish lacking

['"That's a compliment to you!" as the wren said when she pissed in the sea.']

Q 1973 IFC 1888:58 C m+. The Correspondent's address is Co. Galway. After listing some proverbial comparisons in English he writes: 'agus ón

214

Ghaeilge:' ['and from Irish:'] and then gives the above [Part B 44.6] and
a further two in English translation [Part B 107.6 & 143.12 & .13]. He
then adds, in Irish, that he knows scores of them in Irish

see also Part B 22 & 136.

cneastacht (macántas)/fear (Páidín)
**B 45.1 '"Níl aon rud mar chneastacht," mar dubhairt an fear
nuair bhí na bróga goidthe fá n-a ghualainn.'**
['"There's nothing like honesty," as the man with the stolen shoes over
his shoulder said.']
South Connacht, probably County Galway, 19th century, not before 1864
Royal Irish Academy mss, in a list, mainly of proverbs, as published in Ó
Máille 1948, No. 1175

**.2 '"Macántas thar an saoghal!" mar dubhairt Páidín dearg
agus an meadar goidte ar an muin aige.'**
['"Honesty before life!" as red-faced Páidín with the stolen churn on his
back said.']
County Galway
Irisleabhar na Gaedhilge, 6, No. 11 (OS 71) (Mar. 1896), No. 1 under
'M,' in a glossary by Eoin Riocaird Ó Murchadha titled 'South Aran
Irish (Continued),' pp. 167–68. Cited in Ó Máille 1948 No. 1175

Mieder & Tóthné Litovkina pp. 102–03.

conách/fear (fear bocht, ceannaidhe mála)
**B 46.1 '"Chonách san ar na daoine go bhfuil na ba aca!" mar
adubhairt an fear nuair d'fheuch sé amach maidin fhuair
shneachta.'**
['"Such luck attend the people with the cows!" as the man said when he
looked out on a cold, snowy morning.']
County Cork
Irisleabhar na Gaedhilge, 6, No. 5 (OS 65) (1 Aug. 1895), in a list titled
'Proverbs — (Continued). From D. J. Galvin+, Glashakinleen, N[ational]
S[chool], Newmarket, Co. Cork,' pp. 78–79, No. 18, p. 78. Galvin's list
begins in Vol. 6, No. 4 (OS 64), p. 60 and is in four parts with three
wellerisms in all [this and Part B 11.1 & 186.1]

**.2 '"A chonách sin ar na daoine go bhfuil na ba aca!" a
ndubhairt an fear bocht maidin sheaca.'**

['"Such luck attend the people with the cows!" said the poor man on a frosty morning.']
Munster
'An Seabhac' 1926 No. 798/1984 No. 960 with the comment: ['The person without cows had no need to get out of bed in the cold but, on the other hand, he had neither milk nor butter']

.3 '"A conách sin ar an muintir a bhfuil ba acu!" ars an ceannaidhe mála maidin sheaca.'
['"Such luck attend the people with cows!" said the peddler on a frosty morning.']
County Galway
Ó Máille 1948 No. 495 with the comment: ['The poor do not have to worry about stock'].

conách/Seághan Muimhneach (Seán Muimhneach)
B 47.1 '"A chonách sin ort," mar dubhairt Seághan Muimhneach le n-a mháthair agus ní raibh sí lá tí(ní) b'fhéarr ó shoin.'
['"Such luck to you!" as Seághan Muimhneach [ie. Seán the Munsterman] said to his mother and she was never any better since then.']
County Mayo
Irisleabhar na Gaedhilge, 4, No. 48 (Feb. 1894), p. 249 in a list in the 'Popular Proverbs' series titled 'V. Proverbs sent by Mr. Lloyd,' [Seosamh Laoide, editor, for a time, of *Irisleabhar na Gaedhilge*] pp. 248–49. Cited in Ó Máille 1948 No. 1

.2 '"A chonách sin ort," mar dubhairt Seán Muimhneach le n-a mháthair 's ní raibh sí lá ní b'fhéarr ó shoin.'
County Mayo
Ó Máille 1948 No. 1.

congnamh/dreoillín
B 48.1 '"Congnamh na bhfear," mar dubhairt an dreoillín le n-a chlainn.'
['"Help from the men," as the wren said to his clutch.']
County Mayo *c.* 1900
Ó Máille 1948 No. 1335 with the comment: ['the wren said it to his clutch when they were pulling bait from the stone']. Ó Máille *ibid.* includes a couplet from Co. Mayo with the part quoted which may have

216

been used by the wrenboys, bands of youths who, on St. Stephen's Day, 26th Dec., captured a wren and paraded it from house to house.

corruigh/bean fhallsa

B 49.1 "'Ná corruigh é!" mar dubhairt an bhean fhallsa leis an bpota bréun.'
['"Don't touch it!" as the lazy woman said of the stinking pot.']
West Connacht
Irisleabhar na Gaedhilge, 5, No. 5 (OS 53) (1 Aug. 1894), No. 11, p.71/translation p. 73, in a list titled 'Popular Proverbs, West Connaught' pp. 71–73. Cited in Ó Máille 1952 No. 2649.

creasgannaí/Cailleach Bhéarra

B 50.1 "'Ná bíodh tús ná deireadh na gcreasgannaí agat," adeir an Chailleach Bhéarra.'
['"Don't have anything to do with stony land," said the Hag of Beara.']
creasgannaí=land full of stones ..., def. Ó Máille 1952 p. 417
Connacht
Ar Aghaidh, July 1942 as cited in Ó Máille 1952 No. 4507 where it and similar expressions are accompanied by Ó Máille's comment: ['The beginning of any piece of work']?is hazardous

Notes: The Cailleach Bhéarra/Hag of Beara is a mythological figure believed to have married many times in her long life and also said to have been an indefatigable tiller and reaper — see Hull 1927. I thank Ruairí Ó Bléine for examining this wellerism and suggesting that 'creasgannaí' may be <Ir *crios/creas=girdle* and that the wellerism may be referring to the tie of marriage which should have no beginning or end. The Cailleach Bhéarra is also the speaker in Part B 83 & 129.

Críostaidhe/sagart

B 51.1 "'Críostaidhe thú?" ars an sagart le fear. "Ní headh," ars an fear, "ach Ultach."'
['"Are you a Christian?" said the priest to the man.'
"No," said the man, "an Ulsterman."']
County Mayo
Ó Máille 1948 No. 1623a with the comment that 'Protestant' is a secondary meaning of 'Ultach' in 'the North'

.2 ?Irish lacking
['"Are you a Christian?" asked the priest of the man.
"I am not," he replied, "I'm a Connachtman."']

Ulster

Champion 1938 p. 48 No. 89 with the comment: 'said only in Ulster. (The traditional dislike of Ulster for Connacht is nearly two thousand years old).' NB as all the material in Champion is in English it is not possible to know whether or not **.2** was originally in Irish or English

cf the joke '… an Englishman who was travelling through the Highlands … came to an inn near a village. Seeing nobody around he knocked on the door, but received no reply. So he opened the door and walked in. He spied a man lying on a bed and asked him, "Are there no Christians in this house?" Whereupon the man replied "No, sir, none. We are all Camerons."' Irving 1969 *The Wit of the Scots* pp. 51–52 [with another version on p. 51]

Note: there are other published and unpublished versions of this common wellerism.

cruacha/sean-duine

B 52.1 '"Níor dhóigh sé seacht gcruacha mónadh léithi go foill!" mar dubhairt an sean-duine a chuala an brídeogach ag moladh na brídeoige.'

['"He hasn't burned seven stacks of turf with her yet," as the old man said on hearing the bridegroom praising the bride.']
County Donegal
Mac Meanman *Rácáil agus Scuabadh.* 1955 Dublin p. 34, in a section titled 'Natháin agus Abraidhe atá leighte i ndearmad.' ['Neglected Sayings and Expressions.'] pp. 30–35, in which five wellerisms [this and Part B 19.2, 24, 77 & 141] are listed together, with the comment that they are still to be heard amongst the over fifties

Note: 'to burn seven turfstacks' ie., to spend seven years, is a common expression for a measure of time.

cuid an tsolais see *solas*

cuis/fear

B 53.1 '"Níl ann ach gur fearr é ná cuis," mar a dúirt fear an drochghadhair.'

['"He's only just better than 'Shoo!'" as the man with the bad dog said.']
Munster
'An Seabhac' 1984 No. 1006, with the comment that 'Cuis!' is said to hens
cf 'cush' '1. A call to cows' Wright.

218

cúis gháire (cuis gháire, ochón)/Peadar

B 54.1 '"Cúis gháire chughainn!" mar adubhairt Peadar nuair a fuair sé an t-asal báithte.'
['"May we soon have cause to laugh!" as Peadar said when he found the ass drowned.']
Munster
'An Seabhac' 1926 No. 800/1984 No. 962 with the comment: ['Even though faced with a reason to cry, he realized that crying was no better than laughing when nothing could be done about it']

.2 '"Cuis gáire chughainn, a bhean," fe mar adubhairt Peadar fadó nuair a fuair sé an t-asal báidhte.'
['"May we soon have cause to laugh, wife!" as Peadar said long ago when he found the ass drowned.']
County Kerry
Ní Chinnéide, Editor, *Machtnamh Seana-mhná*, a biography of Peig Sayers, 1939 Dublin p. 87: '"Mhuise, cuis gáire chughainn, a bhean," fe mar adubhairt Peadar fadó nuair a fuair sé an t-asal báidhte' ['"Indeed, may we soon have cause to laugh, wife!" as Peadar said long ago when he found the ass drowned.'] as cited in Almqvist *Collection of proverbs* … ts

.3 '"Ochón!" ersa Peadar nuair a fuair sé an t-asal báite.'
['"Alas!" said Peadar when he found the ass drowned.']
County Kerry
Almqvist *Collection of proverbs* … ts, collected by **BA** from **MÓG** between 1966 and 1974

Note: see Dinneen under 'cúis' 'c. gháire chughainn, may we have cause to laugh (said when something ridiculous is said or happens).'

cuma/fear
B 55.1'"Is cuma liom," ars a' fear a chiall a' leithphighinn.'
['"I don't care," said the man who lost the halfpenny.']
County Monaghan
Ua Muirgheasa 1907 No. 1436/1976 No. 1677 with the comment: 'A satire on those who make a show of magnanimity over nothing'

.2 & .3 '"Is cuma liom," adeir an fear a chiall an leithphinghin.'
both County Galway
Ó Máille 1952 No. 2825.

D

dada/bean

B 56.1 '"Ní déarfaidh [?sé] dada," mar dubhairt an bhean a chuir an baile thrí na chéile.'

['"He'll say nothing," as the woman who upset the town said.']
Connacht

Irisleabhar na Gaedhilge, 15, No. 1 (OS 180) (Sept. 1905), in a list titled 'Sean-fhocail III do bhailigh Tomás Ó hEidhin' ['Proverbs III collected by TÓhE'+] pp. 5–9, proverb No. 427, p. 8/translation p. 9. This long list of 653 items won first prize at the Oireachtus [= festival promoting the Irish language etc.] of 1902, Competition 18. It was published in 7 parts, the first section being in Vol. 14, No. 178 (July 1905) beginning p. 827. The list consists mostly of proverbs but contains four wellerisms [this and Part B 11.2, 41.5 & 140.1]. Cited in Ó Máille 1952 No. 2902 with 'sé tada' and the comment: ['It was she herself who was causing the uproar'].

daoine/Ponncánach

B 57.1 '"Imthíonn na daoine acht fanann na cnuic," ars an Ponncánach ag teacht abhaile dó indiaidh leath chéad blian i gcéin.'

['"People go but the hills remain," said the Yankee coming back after fifty years abroad.']
Ponncánach=one born of parents who had migrated from Ireland to America, Correspondent's def., with the English equivalent 'Yankee' being from Ó Dónaill
County Donegal
Q 1973 IFC 1888:21–22 C m+

Note: the proverb 'Imthíonn na daoine acht fanann na cnuic' is common in Irish.

déannan see *'nois*

deireadh/cat

B 58.1 '"Maith go leor go dtí an deireadh," mar adubhairt an cat, 's é ag ithe na geireadh.'

['"Good enough until the end," as the cat that was eating the tallow said.']
County Mayo

i Aindriú de Búrca b. 1875 in Gleann Sál. Published in de Búrca 1958 Dublin, in Ch. IX Texts, section 403 '... a short selection [89 in all] of proverbs and other common expressions' [all from the same informant] pp. 82–93, No. 60

.2 '"Tá sé go maith go dtigeann a deireadh," mar a dúirt an cat a bhí ag ithe na geireadh.'
['"It's good until it comes to an end," as the cat that was eating the fat said.']
County Mayo
Q 1973 IFC 1888:123 C m+ with the comment: ['This is said, for example, if a man who was drinking had spent the last of his money'].
For Correspondent's further comment see Part B 169

.3 '"Fan go fóill go dtí ar deireadh," arsa'n cat a bhí ag ithe na geireadh.'
['"Stay on until the end," said the cat that was eating the lard.']
County Mayo
Stockman 1974 No. 616 under 'Proverbs.'

Dia/bean see *Éire*
Dia/fear see *ceann*

Dia/fear an ocrais
B 59.1 '"Slán leat, a Dhia, nú go bhfásfai' na prátaí nú," ersa fear an ocrais fudó.'
['"Goodbye, God, until the new potatoes grow," said the hungry man long ago.']
County Kerry
Almqvist *Collection of proverbs* ... ts, collected by **BA** from **MÓG** between 1966 and 1974.

Dia/fear lag
B 60.1 '"Go bhfóiri' Dia ar a' laige," ars' an fear lag.'
"Nár fhóiridh ná Muire," ars' an fear láidir, "mar ná fuil sí un chuige!"'
['"May God help the weak," said the exhausted man.
"May he not, nor Mary," said the strong man, "for that's not what she's there for"' *or* "for even she's not able to do that."']
County Kerry
IFC 929:62 Collected in 1944 by TÓM m+ from SS, 72, stone mason, fisherman and farmer. Context: in isolation. I thank Ruairí Ó Bléine for

examining this wellerism and suggesting that the man is so weak that he
cannot even bear help.

Dia/sac
B 61.1 '"Dia linn!" ars' an sac nuair a thuit an pionall.'
['"God be with us!" said the sack when the pannel [pack-saddle] fell.']
County Monaghan
Irisleabhar na Gaedhilge, 12, No. 148 (Aug. 1902), in a list compiled by
Énrí Ó Muirgheasa titled 'Farney (Co. Monaghan) Proverbs, Sayings and
Riddles,' pp. 116–22 [92 items], No. 64, p. 117/translation etc., p. 120:
'The pannel was a rustic saddle — a bag filled with hay, or the like —
put under the sack on the horse's back, in the time when there were no
carts, and everything had to be carried on horseback. The walking of the
horse moved the sack off the pannel, and the latter fell to the ground;
then the sack was in imminent danger also. Suppose a person saw his
neighbour evicted he might use this remark.' Cited in Ua [previously Ó]
Muirgheasa 1907 No. 1111/1976 No. 1331, with the more general
remark, 'The proverb is said on seeing some disaster happen to your
neighbour which may happen to you also,' rather than specifying
eviction. Ua Muirgheasa also says there [1907] that the pannel could be
filled with hay or straw

Note: There is a pack-saddle of twisted hay made in 1961 for Armagh
County Museum by James Loughran of Co. Louth, currently on display
in the museum, ACM 197-1961; see Michael J. Murphy 1983, facing p.
87 for a photograph of James Loughran holding a pack-saddle. A second
pack-saddle commissioned about the same time from the same man, and
which is probably the one in the photograph, is currently on display in
the National Museum of Country Life, Turlough Park, Co. Mayo,
F1961:84. For a description of these see Lucas 1961.

diail see *now*

díhal/duine bocht
**B 62.1 '"Gurab é sin do dhíhal," a ndúirt an duine bocht le Dia
fudó, nuair a bhí sé á chíapa 'na bheathaig.'**
['"I hope that's the best you can do," said the poor man to God long ago
when he was tormented by life.']
County Kerry
Almqvist *Collection of proverbs* … ts, collected by **BA** from **MÓG**
between 1966 and 1974.

222

díol/leadaidhe

B 63.1 '"Ní tú an díol truaighe, ach an té atá a' sgaradh leat,"
mar dubhairt an leadaidhe leis an leabaidh.'
['"You're not the miserable object to be pitied, but the one who's parted
from you!" as the loafer said to the bed.']
County Galway
Ó Máille 1952 No. 2658.

díreach/seana-phortán Swe

B 64.1 '"Siúl díreach, a mhic!" mar a dúirt an seana-phortán
leis an bportán óg.'
['"Walk straight, son!" as the old crab said to the young crab.']
County Kerry
Almqvist *Collection of proverbs* ... ts, collected by **BA** from **MÓG**
between 1966 and 1974 and published in Almqvist 1982–83 p. 35. Cited
in Carson Williams 2001a pp. 9–10. cf a similar variant in Mac Con
Iomaire 1988 p. 210, in a short introduction to a set of wellerisms titled
'Quotation Proverbs' which is cited again in the first of the set with a
photographic illustration p. 211

.2 '"Ná siúlófa díreach?" a dúirt an seana-phortán leis an
bportán óg.'
['"Will you not walk straight?" said the old crab to the young crab.']
County Kerry
Almqvist 1982–83 p. 35, collected by **BA** from **SÓD**+ *c*. 1980

cf the proverb 'The young crab has the same walk as the old crab.'
Editors Hippocrene Books *Irish Proverbs* 1999, p. 103. This proverb, in
Irish and English, is more usual in the synonym: 'The kitten walks like
the cat,' for example, Co. Sligo IFCS 184:117

cf the folktale AT 276 *Crab Walks Backward: Learned from his Parents,*
illustrated, for example, in Croxall 1841 *The Fables of Aesop* ... Belfast,
p. 142

Notes: see Almqvist 1982–83 for a discussion of this wellerism in depth.
In it [p. 35] he notes that he heard the same wellerism in the same part of
Kerry 'cúpla uair eile' ['two or three other times'], refers to the fable,
including an Irish-language version from Peig Sayers, mother of **MÓG**,
[pp. 48–49] and gives the Swedish reference Ström 1929, 333.

domhan/fear
B 65.1 '"Ní fheadar an domhan," arsan fear nuair d'imigh a léine.'
['"I just don't know at all," said the man when his shirt went missing.']
County Cork
IFC 43:249 collected in 1921 by CNíL+ who wrote down the list, mainly of proverbs, *c.* 1933.

Domhnach/Pádraig
B 66.1 '"Cuir an Domhnach ar cáirde," mar adubhairt Pádraig.'
['"Postpone Sunday," as Pádraig said.']
Munster
'An Seabhac' 1926 No. 804/1986 No. 967.

dúbailt/cor-éisc
B 67.1 '"Is múr an ní dúbailt," ers' an cor-éisc leis an ngabhar fudó.'
['"Double's a great thing," said the heron to the goat long ago.']
County Kerry
Almqvist *Collection of proverbs* … ts, collected by **BA** from **MÓG** between 1966 and 1974 with the comment: 'The heron noticed that the goat had four legs'

see also Part B 68.

dúbailt/gabhar
B 68.1 '"Is múr an ní dúbailt," ers' an gabhar lena chosa.'
['"Double's a great thing," said the goat of his legs.']
County Kerry
Almqvist *Collection of proverbs* … ts, collected by **BA** from **MÓG** between 1966 and 1974

see also Part B 67.

duine uasail (cabhail, mac)/Tadhg Ó Séaghdha
(Seán Ó Néill, fear)
B 69.1 '"Tá an ceart agat, a dhuine uasail bhréagh ghléigil," arsa Tadhg Ó Séaghdha leis an mBlack.'
['"You're right, you fine, bright sir," said Tadhg Ó Séaghdha to the Black.']
Munster

224

'An Seabhac' 1926 No. 805/1984 No. 968

.2 "'Muise, do chabhail ghléigeal!'" mar dubhairt Seán Ó Néill leis an mblack.'
["'Well, your lilywhite body!'" as Seán Ó Néill said to the black.']
County Galway
Ó Máille 1952 No. 2978 with the comment for both variants [.2 & .3]:
['false or mocking praise']

.3 "Cé chaoi 'bhfuil tú, a mhac bán?" mar dubhairt an fear leis an mblack.'
["'How are you, fair fellow?'" as the man said to the black.']
County Galway
Ó Máille 1952 No. 2978. For his comment see .2.

dul/cailín ruadh bréagach
B 70.1 "'Bhí mé a' dul dá dhéanamh," mar dubhairt cailín ruadh bréagach na mbráthar.'
["'I was going to do it," as the lying, red-haired maid of the brothers said.']
County Mayo
Ó Máille 1948 No. 1585 with the comment: ['the servant girl who was always about to do it when she was asked to do any piece of work'] and references, for instance, to a little story about this character in the magazine *An t-Éireannach*, May 1939

cf the proverbial simile 'chomh dona le cailín ruadh bréagach na mbráthar' ['as bad as the lying red-haired maid of the brothers'] Co. Galway Ó Máille *ibid.*

dusta (ceo)/cuileóg (cuileog)   Part A 69
B 71.1 "'Nach mise a thóg an dusta?" ars' an chuileóg i ndiaidh an chóiste.'
["'Didn't I raise the dust?" said the fly behind the coach.']
County Monaghan
Ua Muirgheasa 1907 No. 992/1976 No. 1185 with the comment: 'This saying has had a classic origin. It satirizes the vanity of small-minded people whom chance happens to place in positions of importance.' Cited in [Carson] Williams 1992 p. 75/2000a p. 73

.2 "'Nach mise a thóg an ceo?" mar dúirt an chuileog i ndiaidh an chóiste.'
["'Didn't I raise the dust?" as the fly behind the coach said.']

de Bhaldraithe 1959 under 'fly': 'F[amiliar]: to play the fly on the wheel, cúnamh an dreoilín don fharraige ['the wren's help to the sea']; "Nach mise a thóg an ceo?" mar dúirt an chuileog i ndiaidh an chóiste.'

see also Part B 22.

E

eadraibh/fear

B 72.1 '"Eadraibh féin bíodh sé," mar dubhairt an fear a chaith an tuirnín i measg na ngéanna.'

['"Sort it out yourselves!" as the man who threw the spinning wheel amongst the geese said.']

County Mayo

IFC 114:340 collected along with other sayings in 1935 by SPÓP from his mother [aged 53] and published in Ó Máille 1952 No. 4677 with the comment: [[said] 'in a place where a group is in dispute to leave them to settle it amongst themselves'].

eadrainn/cat (sionnach)

B 73.1 '"Eadrainn féin atá sé," mar adubhairt an cat leis an iasg.'

['"It's just you and me," as the cat said to the fish.']

Galway City

Ó Máille 1952 No. 2686, with the comment for **.1** & **.2**: ['If there's good there it's for ourselves'] and a ref. to a Manx item — Morrison & Roeder No. 9 — which is not, however, a wellerism

.2 '"Eadrainn féin atá sé," mar adubhairt an sionnach leis an ngé.'

['"It's just you and me," as the fox said to the geese.']

County Galway

Ó Máille 1952 No. 2686, for his comment see **.1**.

eangach/fíogaigh

B 74.1 'Dubhairt an fíogaigh leis na fleangaigh, "Téanam ag déanamh bundún eangaighe."

['Said the smooth-skinned dogfish to the rough-skinned dogfish, "Come and we'll ?entangle the net."']

County Mayo

226

Stockman 1974 No. 419 with the comment: 'old fishermen used to say this when they saw two *bundúns?*'
bundún=a tiresome person; bundún leice=a greyish fish with a sucker which enables it to cling to rocks defs. Stockman p. 363

Note: 'bundún leice' is more usually 'sea anenome.' The wellerism was collected from a shoemaker, email 14/6/2002 from Gerry Stockman. I thank Ruairí Ó Bléine for examining this wellerism.

éascaidheacht/fear
B 75.1 "'Chuile shórt ar éascaidheacht," mar dubhairt an fear a thóig an fata as an mbainne le n-a mhéara.'
["Anything for convenience," as the man who lifted the potato from the milk with his fingers said.']
County Mayo
Ó Máille 1952 No. 2621 with the comment: ['Do it any way at all to save yourself trouble'].

Éire (Dia)/bean   *cf Ger
B 76.1 "'Nach fada fairsing í Éire?" ers' an bhean nuair a sheasaimh sí ag Mám an Chlasaigh fudó.'
["Isn't Ireland long and extensive?" said the woman when she stood at Mám an Chlasaigh long ago.']
County Kerry
Almqvist *Collection of proverbs ...* ts, collected by **BA** from **MÓG** between 1966 and 1974, with the comment: 'M. an Chl. is the highest point on the hill road between Dunquin and Ventry. **M[ÓG]** maintains that the woman was Cáit' [his older sister, who went off to work in Dingle town and later the USA]

.2 "'A Dhia ghleigil, nach fada fairsing í Éire?" arsa an bhean nuair a chonaic sí an radharc ó Bharra an Chlasaigh i nDún Chaoin.'
["'Oh great God, isn't Ireland long and extensive?" said the woman when she saw the view from Barra an Chlasaigh in Dunquin.']
Munster
'An Seabhac' 1984 No. 972

cf Muiris Ó Súilleabháin 1933, 1976 ed., Mac Tomáis, Editor, p. 70, ref. via Almqvist *Collection of proverbs ...* ts. Context from Llewelyn Davies & Thomson's translation [O'Sullivan 1941]: 'When we [two schoolboy islanders] came in sight of the parish of Ventry Tomás was lost in astonishment. "Oh, Maurice, isn't Ireland wide and spacious?"

"Upon my word, Tomás, she is bigger than that. What about Dingle [town] where I was long ago?" "And where is Dingle?" "To the south of that hill." "Oh Lord, I always thought there was nothing in Ireland, only the Blasket, Dunquin and Iveragh' [the peninsula visible from the Great Blasket Island to the south of the Dingle peninsula] Ch. 5 'Ventry Races' p. 53

*cf Ger, for example, '"Moder, wat ist die Welt doch grot?" sad de Jung,' donn keek hei achter 'n Tuun ruut.' ['"Mother, isn't the world big?" said the boy looking over the fence.'] Neumann Q No. 20

Note: Mám an Chlasaigh *or* Barra an Chlasaigh, marked on maps as Mám Clasach, is a pass from which there is a magnificent view of Dunquin and the Atlantic Ocean to the west and the rest of Ireland to the east. I thank Paul Tempan for the place-name details.

Éire/maighistir
B 77.1 '"Tá Éire fada fairsing a's ní'l claidhe ar bith ar Albain," mar dubhairt an maighistir nuair a bhí sé ag tabhairt an tuarastail do Ghiolla na Leisce.'
['"Ireland is wide enough and there's no fence around Scotland," as the employer said when he was paying the Ghiolla na Leisce his wages.']
County Donegal
Mac Meanman *Rácáil agus Scuabadh.* 1955 Dublin p. 34, in a section titled 'Natháin agus Abraidhe atá leighte i ndearmad.' ['Neglected Sayings and Expressions.'], pp. 30–35, in which five wellerisms [this and Part B 19.2, 24, 52 & 141] are listed together, with the comment that they are still to be heard amongst the over fifties

cf 'Tá Éire fada fairsing agus fál thart timcheall uirthi' ['Ireland is spacious and has no hedge around it'] Ó Máille 1952 No. 4596 with the comment: ['That's what the man whose horse was lost said']

Note: 'an Giolla na Leisce' literally means 'the Lazy Fellow' so the employer was probably paying him off.

eùn (neach, nígh)/cuach (traona, tréana)
B 78.1 '"Gach eùn mur óiltear è," ars' an chuach a' dul 's a neanntàig.'
['"Every bird as it's been reared," said the cuckoo going into the nettles.']
Ulster 1830s
Mac Adam 1858 No. 289

228

.2 & .3 '"Gach 'n neach mar oiltear é," ars' a' traona ag dul 'sa' neantóig.'
['"Everyone as he's been reared," said the corncrake going into the nettles.']
Counties Armagh & Monaghan
Ua Muirgheasa 1907 No. 233a/1976 No. 270a with the following: 'When the birds were surprized some took to their wings, some took to the water and some found shelter in the trees, but the corncrake sought refuge in the nettles, consoling himself, as he did so, with the above sapient reflection'

.4 '"Gach nígh 's a nádúir féin aige," arsan tréana nuair a ?chuir sí féin i bhfolach i gcrapán cualfaith.'
['"Everything as its own nature," said the corncrake when she hid herself in a pile of nettles.']
County Donegal
IFCS 1080:288 in a list, mainly of proverbs

cf the proverb 'Gach eùn mur oiltear è a's an uiseag chun na mòna.' ['Every bird as it's been reared and the lark to the bog.'] Mac Adam 1858 No. 290; this, and similar variants, is common in Irish.

F

fad/fear
B 79.1 '"Ní bheidh mé i bhfad ann," mar dúirt an fear a bhí ag damhsa ar an mbóthar.'
['"I won't be here long," as the man dancing in the middle of the road said.']
County Mayo
Q 1973 IFC 1888:123 C m+ with the comment: ['A person says this if he is in a hurry to leave a house or company. It is said in fun']. For Correspondent's further comment see Part B 169

Note: There may be a pun as the quote could mean that the man may not live long.

fad/pilibín
B 80.1 '"Ní hé sin féin ach an fad atá ann," mar dubhairt an pilibín leis an bpiastóg.'

["It's not that, it's the length of it," as the lapwing [or plover] said of the worm.']
County Mayo c. 1900
Ó Máille 1952 No. 4603. I thank Ruairí Ó Bléine for examining this wellerism.

fada/moncaí   Part A 182
B 81.1 '"Ní bheidh sé rófhada anois," mar dúirt an moncaí nuair a gearradh an ruball dó.'
['"It won't be too long now," as the monkey said when his tail was cut off.']
County Donegal
Q 1973 IFC 1888:12 C m+ with the comment: 'another that I heard but I wouldn't say it is native.'

faitchíos/táilliúir
B 82.1 '"Faitchíos atá ort, a tháilliúir?"
"Ní headh," ars an táilliúir, "ach b'fhearr liom a bheith amuigh."'
['"Are you afraid, tailor?"
"No," said the tailor, "but I prefer to be outside."']
County Galway
Ó Máille 1952 No. 4606.

faobhar/Cailleach Bhéarra
B 83.1 '"Faobhar a bhaineas féar," arsa Cailleach Bhéarra.'
['"An edge reaps grass," said the Hag of Beara.']
County Galway
Ó Máille 1952 No. 3860

Note: for information on the Cailleach Bhéarra see Part B 50 where she is also the speaker, as she is in Part B 129.

fear/Conán
B 84.1 '"Cumhduigheadh 'chuile fhear é féin," arsa Conán.'
['"Let every man protect himself," said Conán.']
County Galway
Ar Aghaidh, June 1936 as cited in Ó Máille 1952 No. 2684

Note: for information on Conán see Part B 33 where he is also the speaker, as he is in Part B 85.

fear/Conán

B 85.1 '"**Ní hé 'n fear ós chóir is measa dhuit ach an fear er do chúl," a ndúirt Cunán fudó.**'
['"It's not the man who's facing you who's worst for you but the man behind you," said Conán long ago.']
County Kerry
Almqvist *Collection of proverbs* … ts, collected by **BA** from **MÓG** between 1966 and 1974, with the comment: 'There was nobody behind, but C. said so in order to trick his adversary to turn round'

Note: for information on Conán see Part B 33 where he is also the speaker, as he is in Part B 84.

fear/Éamonn

B 86.1 '"**Nach é an fear é?**" **arsa Éamonn leis an reithe.**'
['"Isn't he some man?" said Éamonn of the ram.']
Munster
'An Seabhac' 1926 No. 835/1984 No. 1000

see also Part B 87.

fear/madaruadh

B 87.1 '"**Arú! Nach é an fear é an báirneach?**" **mar adubhairt an madaruadh.**'
['"Wow! Isn't the limpet some man?" as the fox said.']
Munster
'An Seabhac' 1926 No. 836/1984 No. 1001 with the comment: ['This is said of a show-off']. Cited in Rosenstock 1993 p. 54/translation and tale p. 55 & Williams 1999 p. 366

.2 '"**Arú! Nach tú an fear agam?**" **a ndubhairt an madaruadh leis an mbáirneach.**'
['"Wow! Aren't you some man?" said the fox to the limpet.']
Munster
'An Seabhac' 1926 No. 836/1984 No. 1002. For his comment see .1

cf the folktale *TIF 105 The Cat's Only Trick*, of which this is a by-form. For some comments on this see Williams 1999 pp. 365–66

see also Part B 86.

fear a' tuí/bean an tuí
B 88.1 '"Fear a' tuí ar meisge agus a bhean chéile ag ól uisce," arsa bean an tuí nuair a tháinig an fear abhaile ag am codlata.'
['"The husband drunk and his wife drinking water," said the housewife when the husband came home at bed time.']
County Donegal
Q 1973 IFC 1888:22 C m+.

fearr/Colmcille
B 89.1 '"Go mba fearr i mbárach thú!" mar dubhairt Colmcille le n-a mháthair.'
['"May you be better tomorrow!" as Colmcille said to his mother.']
County Mayo *c.* 1900
Ó Máille 1952 No. 3770 with his alternative meaning: may you be 'a man' tomorrow

.2 as .1
County Galway
Ó Máille 1952 No. 3770. For his comment see **.1**

.3 '"Go mba seacht míle fearr i mbárach thú!" mar dubhairt Colmcille le n-a mháthair.'
['"May you be seven times better tomorrow!" as Colmcille said to his mother.']
County Galway
Ó Máille 1952 No. 3770

Notes: for information on Colmcille/Colm Cille see Part B 14. He is also the speaker in Part B 23 & 164.

féasóg/sionnach   Part A 19
B 90.1 '"Is faide do chuid féasóige ná do chuid intleachta," mar dúbhairt an sionnach leis an ngabhar.'
['"Your beard's more extensive than your intellect," as the fox said to the goat.']
Connacht
Ó Máille 1948 No. 1431. Cited in [Carson] Williams 1992 p. 67/2000a p. 66.

féin/mada beag   Part A 132
B 91.1 '"Bhí mé féin ann," mar a dúirt an mada beag.'
['"I was there myself!" as the little dog said.']
County Mayo
Q 1973 IFC 1888:123 C m+ with the comment: ['A person talking about some place he had been where a fight or disturbance was going on but he himself was not participating']. For Correspondent's further comment see Part B 169.

féin/tincéaraí
B 92.1 '"Sinn féin atá ann," mar dubhairt na tincéaraí i mBalla.'
['"It's ourselves," as the tinkers in Balla said.']
County Mayo *c.* 1900
Ó Máille 1952 No. 3112 with the comment: ['People who are bold and independent(?)'].

fill/droch-ghnó(tha)
B 93.1 '"Fill orm!" deir an droch-ghnó.'
['"Come back to me," says the botched job.']
County Cork
Irisleabhar na Gaedhilge, 4, No. 46 (July 1893), in a list on the front page titled 'Popular Irish Proverbs.'

.2 as .1
County Cork
Irisleabhar na Gaedhilge, 4, No. 46 (July 1893), in a list titled 'Popular Irish Proverbs From Skibbereen —' pp. 209–10, p. 209

.3 '"Fill orm," adeir an droch-ghnó.'
Munster
'An Seabhac' 1926 No. 822/1984 No. 987

.4 '"Fíll oram," adeir an dro-ghnú.'
County Kerry
Almqvist *Collection of proverbs …* ts, collected by **BA** from **MÓG** between 1966 and 1974

.5 '"Fill orm agus dein arís mé," adeir an droch-ghnó.'
['"Come back and do me again," says the work ill-done.']
Dinneen 1934 ed., 1970 rpt. under 'droch-ghnó'

.6 '"Fill orm," adeir an droch-ghnó, "agus dein arís mé."'

["Come back to me," says the badly-done work, "and do me again.""]
Munster
'An Seabhac' 1926 No. 822/1984 No. 987

.7 '"Fill orm," adeir droch-ghnótha.'
['"Come back to me," says badly-done work.']
County Galway
Ó Máille 1952 No. 3729

cf 'the *Cm*. [= Co. Waterford] saying is: a dhroch-ghnó dein ath-ghnó, botching worker do the work again,' Dinneen *ibid.*, where it is used to illustrate 'droch-ghnó.'

fios see *chonaic*

fírinne/Cloch Labhrais
B 94.1 '"Bíonn an fhírinne searbh," adubhairt Cloch Labhrais ag preabadh.'
['"The truth's bitter," said Cloch Labhrais jumping.']
Munster
Ua Donnchadha 1902 p. 4. Cited in 'An Seabhac' 1926 No. 803/1984 No. 966 with a comment similar to O'Rahilly's, see **.2**

.2 '"Bíonn an fhírinne searbh," arsa Cloch Labhrais ag preabadh.'
County Waterford
O'Rahilly 1922 under No. 52 with the comment: '"Cloch Labhrais" (*i.e.* speaking-stone?) being the name of a huge boulder which lies near Stradbally, [Co. Waterford] and which is cleft in a remarkable manner. Local tradition accounts for the fissure by relating that the boulder burst asunder on a certain occasion on which a falsehood was uttered upon it'

cf the motif *MI* D 1318 *Magic object reveals guilt*, & similar motifs.

Note: the proverb 'Bíonn an fhírinne searbh' is common in Irish and English.

fuaduigh/Fómhar
B 95.1 '"Fuaduigh mé," arsan Fómhar.'
['"Steal me away," said Autumn.']
Munster
'An Seabhac' 1926 No. 834/1984 No. 999.

234

fuinneog/amadan
B 96.1 '"Briseadh gach uile dhuine fuinneog dó féin," mur a dubhairt an t-amadan.'
['"Let everyone break a window for himself," as the fool said.']
Ulster 1830s
Mac Adam 1861–62 No. 565.

G

glac/firín
B 96a.1 '"Glac nuair gheobhair," mar a dúirt an firín buí.'
['"Take it as you get it," said the little yellow man.']
County Kerry
Ó Criomhthain *Allagar na hInise*, autobiographical, 1928 Dublin, 1977 ed. p. 8.

<u>game</u>/fear
B 97.1 '"<u>I'll never again play this game of</u> 'An bhfuil agut tá,'" ers' an fear fudó.'
['"I'll never again play this game of 'Have you got yes,'" said the man long ago.']
County Kerry
Almqvist *Collection of proverbs* … ts, collected by **BA** from **MÓG** between 1966 and 1974, with the comment: 'He knew only English and had been playing cards with two Irish speakers who had cheated him out of all of his money. "An bhfuil agut" means "Have you (a certain card or suit)?" and "Tá" "Yes," but the English speaker took it to be the name of the game'

cf the folktale *TIF* 1699 *Misunderstanding Because of Ignorance of a Foreign Language*. At least ten versions of the cardplaying senario, including one collected by **MÓG** in 1960 IFC 1603:252–54 and one recorded from him in 1973 by James Stewart, exist, see Stewart 1977–79 'The Game of "An bhFuil Agat? — Tá"… ,' where texts are respectively Appendix 3A and 3B.

gaol/mada rua   *cf Am Eng
B 98.1 '"Is múr é mo ghaol leat, a uain," ers' an mada rua.'
['"I'm closely related to you, lamb," said the fox.']
County Kerry

Almqvist *Collection of proverbs* … ts, collected by **BA** from **MÓG** between 1966 and 1974

*cf Am Eng '"Thou knowest that I love thee!" as the cat said to the mouse.' *DOW* 781.

garrdha/Tadhg Beag
B 99.1 '"Chugad mé, a gharrdha!" mar adeireadh Tadhg Beag.'
['"Here I come, [vegetable] garden!" as Tadhg Beag [ie. little Tadhg] said.']
County Galway
Ó Máille 1948 No. 1587 with the comment: [said] 'About a person who would be boasting about what he would do but who would be unable to accomplish it']. Ó Máille *ibid.* refers to a related story in *Sgéala Éireann*, April 13–16, 1938.

geal/sweep
B 100.1 '"Go n-éirighidh leat go geal!" mar adubhairt an sweep le n-a mhac.'
['"May you have a bright future!" as the sweep said to his son.']
Munster
'An Seabhac' 1926 No. 820/1984 No. 985

.2 as .1
County Galway
Ó Máille 1948 No. 25

.3 as .1
Mac Con Iomaire 1988 p. 212 with a photographic illustration.

gearánta (g'ránta)/fear (bacach)
B 101.1 '"Ní gearánta dhom," arsa fear na coise briste.'
['"I shouldn't complain," said the man with the broken leg.']
Munster
Irisleabhar na Gaedhilge, 5, No. 11 (OS 50) (1 Feb. 1895), in a note in a list titled 'Proverbs — Munster Mr P. M'Carthy, Clohane Castle,' p. 172. This wellerism is added by Padruig O'Laoghaire in a note to item No. 4, 'Ní gearánta dhom, ar nós fhir na coise briste. I shouldn't complain, like the man with the broken leg. ('"Ní gearánta dhom," arsa fear na coise briste,' ['"I shouldn't complain," said the man with the broken leg'] that is, though matters are bad enough, yet they might have been worse')

236

.2 '"Ní gearánta dhom," a ndubhairt fear na coise briste.'
Munster
'An Seabhac' 1926 No. 813/1984 No. 978 with the comment: ['Both legs could be broken']

.3 '"Ní g'ránta dhom," a ndúirt an bacach lena chois mhaide.'
['"I shouldn't complain," said the cripple to his wooden leg.']
County Kerry
Almqvist *Collection of proverbs* ... ts, collected by **BA** from **MÓG** between 1966 and 1974 with the comment: 'He might have had two wooden legs.'

geárrtha/Crochúr a' Chasuir
B 102.1 '"Fágaim geárrtha 'gat é," ars' Crochúr a' Chasuir leis a' mada ruadh.'
['"I've curtailed you," said Crochúr a' Chasuir [Crochúr of the hammer] to the fox.']
County Kerry
IFC 797:513 C TÓM m+ followed by a version of *TIF* 67**, in summary: Crochúr a' Chasuir is one of the 'Casurs' of Crois a' Chárta. A fox was taking all the hens, one by one, from inside his house until there was only one left. Crochúr a' Chasuir blocked the fox's escape but the fox put one new shoe on the fire. When Crochúr a' Chasuir was rescuing his shoe the fox ran out with Crochúr shouting, '"Ó, fágaim geárrtha 'gat é!" ["Oh, I've curtailed you!" and ever since it has been a saying, '"I've curtailed you,' said Crochúr a' Chasuir to the fox"']

see also Part A 196 & Part A 224 where the same tale, *TIF* 67** *The Fox Caught by the Butcher* [96 versions], occurs with different wellerisms.

glaine(eacht)/bean   Part A 38
B 103.1 '"Is deas an rud a' ghlaine," mar dubhairt an bhean nuair thionntuigh sí a léine i ndiaidh seacht mbliadhna.'
['"Cleanliness is a fine thing," as the woman said when she turned her shift after seven years.']
County Monaghan
Ua Muirgheasa 1907 No. 1105/1976 No. 1325 with the comment: 'This is an instance of that exaggeration — the climax of absurdity — so beloved of Irish humourists.' Cited in [Carson] Williams 1992 p. 111/2000a p. 97

.2 '"Is mór is fiú an ghlaineacht, ach a déanamh go hannamh," mar dubhairt an bhean a thionntuigh a léine i gcionn seacht mbliadhan.'
['"Cleanliness is worthwhile if it doesn't need to be attended to often," as the woman who turned her shift after seven years said.']
County Mayo
Ó Máille 1952 No. 3738

see also Part B 104.

glaineacht/Máire Shalach
B 104.1 '"Is mór is fiú an ghlaineacht," mar dubhairt Máire shalach.'
['"Cleanliness is worth a lot," as dirty Máire said.']
County Galway
Ó Máille 1952 No. 3738

see also Part B 103.

glaineacht/straoill (bean a' tighe)   Ger, Sc Gae & *cf Fin,
    †cf Swe, ‡cf Nor
B 105.1 '"Is deas í an ghlaineacht," ars an straoill 's í a' glanadh an phláta le iorball an chait.'
['"Cleanliness is a fine thing," said the slattern cleaning the plate with the cat's tail.']
County Galway
Ó Máille 1952 No. 3738

.2 '"Is mór is fiú an ghlaineacht," mar dubhairt bean a' tighe nuair a ghlan sí mias an ime le iorball an mhadaidh.'
['"Cleanliness is worth a lot," as the housewife said when she cleaned the butter dish with the dog's tail.']
County Galway
Ó Máille 1952 No. 3738

Meek No. 651
*cf Fin '"Konstit on monet," sano akka, ku kissala pöytää pyhki.' ['"You just have to know how to do it," said the woman wiping the table down with the cat.'] Sallinen p. 106 (522) No. 39
†cf Swe from Sallinen
‡cf Nor from Sallinen.

238

gléas ceóil & *gléus ceoil* see *glèus ceòil*
gleo see *glór/Aidhbhirseoir (Maonus, bean, caora)*

glèus ceòil (gléas ceóil, ceól, gléus ceoil, ceóil)/fear (bean)
Part A 142
B 106.1 '"Is iomadh glèus ceòil a bhìos ann," ars' an fear a robh a trumpa maide aige.'
['"There are many musical instruments," said the man with the imitation [*lit.* wooden] trump.']
Ulster 1830s
Mac Adam 1861–62 No. 566. Cited in Ua Muirgheasa 1907 No. 1051a/1976 No. 1242

.2 '"Is 'omaí gléas ceóil a bhíonns ionn," arsa'n fear a raibh an trompa maide aige.'
County Cavan 1931–33
Ó Tuathail 1934 'Text III Sean-fhocla agus Sean-Ráité.' ['Proverbs and Old Sayings.'] pp. 26–27, No. 13 p. 26, a list of 30 items, mainly proverbs

.3 '"'S iomdha gléus ceoil a bhíonns ann," arsan fear a raibh an trumpa maide aige.'
County Donegal
IFCS 1059:375 in a list+, mainly of proverbs

.4 '"Is iomdha sórt ceól," mar dubhairt an fear a raibh an trompa maide aige.'
['"There are many kinds of music," as the man with the imitation trump said.']
West Connacht
Irisleabhar na Gaedhilge, 5, No. 5 (OS 53) (1 Aug. 1894), in a list titled 'Popular Proverbs, West Connaught' pp. 71–73, item No. 5 p. 71/translation p. 72. Cited in Ó Máille 1948 No. 1269 with the comment: ['People are not all alike']

.5 '"Is iomdha seórt ceóil a bhíonns ann," mar dubhairt an fear a rabh an trompa maide aige.'
['"Many sorts of music exist," as the man with the imitation trump said.']
County Armagh
Ua Muirgheasa 1907 No. 1051b with the comment: 'a wooden trump would be an altogether hopeless attempt at producing music. This saying is used by way of apology for any poor makeshift'

.6 "'Is iomaidh gléas ceoil a bhíos ann," ars an bhean a raibh trumpa maide aicí.'
[''There are many musical instruments," said the woman with the imitation trump.']
County Donegal
Q 1973 IFC 1888:7 C m+ [E & Ir] with the comment: 'can be said by someone who is doing something in an unacceptable way'

.7 "'Is iomdha gléas ceoil a bhíos ann," mar adúirt fear an trumpa maide.'
[''There are many musical instruments," as the man of the imitation trump said.']
County Donegal
Q 1973 IFC 1888:18 C m+

Notes: in the English of the north of Ireland, at least, *trump=Jew's harp* def. Ua Muirgheasa 1907, see **.5** above.
The proverb quoted is common in Irish see, for example, Ó Dónaill under 'gléas 2.'

glór (scaladh, gleo, torann)/Áidhbhirseoir (Maonus, bean, caora) Part A 48
B 107.1 "'Glór mór ar bheagán olna," mar adubhairt an tÁidhbhirseoir nuair a bhí sé ag bearradh na muice.'
[''Great noise for little wool," as the Adversary [ie. Devil] said when he was shearing the pigs.']
Munster
'An Seabhac' 1926 No. 801/1986 No. 963

.2 "'Glór mór ar bheagán olla," mar a dúirt an t-áibhirseoir agus é ag bearradh na muice.'
Mac Con Iomaire 1988 p. 215 with a photographic illustration

.3 "'Scaladh mór agus beagán olna," mar adubhairt Maonus is é ag lomadh na muice.'
[''Great clamour [*or* scalding] and little wool," as Maonas said when shearing the pigs.']
Munster
'An Seabhac' 1926 No. 801/1986 No. 964

.4 "'Is mór an gleo na an t-olainn," mar dubhairt an bhean nuair a bhí sí ag bearradh an gabhair.'

240

["'The noise is greater than the wool," as the woman said when she was shearing the goat.']
County Clare
IFCS 624:146 in a list, mainly of proverbs

.5 "'Is mó an torann ná an olann," mar a dúirt an chaora leis an ngabhar a bhí á lomadh.'
["'More noise than wool," as the sheep said of the goat being shorn.']
Ó Dónaill 1977 under 'olann' — the sole wellerism in this dictionary out of 614 different proverbs in Irish, several hundred in English and one in Latin, as well as many other expressions

.6 Irish lacking
["'A lot of noise but little wool," as the Devil said while clipping the pig.']
Q 1973 IFC 1888:58 C m+. The Correspondent's address is Co. Galway. After listing some proverbial comparisons in English he writes '--- agus ón Ghaeilge:' ['and from Irish:'] and then gives the above [Part B 107.6] and [Part B 44.6 & 143.12 & .13]. He then adds, in Irish, that he knows scores of them in Irish.

glór/madadh ruadh (madaruadh)
B 108.1 "'Is 'mó glór díomhaoin id' cheann," mar dubhairt an madadh ruadh leis an gclog.'
["'You've many idle noises in your head," as the fox said to the bell.']
Dinneen 1934 ed., 1970 rpt. under 'glór'

.2 "'Is mó glór díomhaoin id' cheann," a ndubhairt an madaruadh leis an gclog.'
Munster
'An Seabhac' 1926 No. 830/1984 No. 995 with the comment for both of his variants, this and **.3**: ['said to an overtalkative person']

.3 "'Is mó glór díomhaoin id' cheann," a ndubhairt an madaruadh le clog an teampaill.'
["'You've many idle noises in your head," said the fox to the church bell.']
Munster
'An Seabhac' 1926 No. 830/1984 No. 995. For comment see **.2**

gnó an Earraigh/fear
B 109.1 '"Seadh, tá an méid sin do ghnó an Earraigh déanta agam!" a ndubhairt an fear nuair a chuir sé a bhean.'
['"Well, I've that much of the Spring work done!" said the man when he buried his wife.']
Munster
'An Seabhac' 1926 No. 837/1986 No. 1003 with the comment: ['said when part of the spring work has been completed'].

gnoithe/reithe
B 110.1 '"Deán do gnoithe duit féin," arsa'n Reithe le Eibhlinn.'
['"Do your business yourself," said the ram to Eibhlinn.']
County Donegal
IFCS 1078:94 in a list, mainly of proverbs

Mieder & Tóthné Litovkina p. 140 [but no wellerism].

grá/Mac an Bháird
B 111.1 Mar dubhairt Mac an Bháird le h-Ó Domhnaill i bhfad ó shoin, "Foluigheann grádh gráin."'
['As Ward said to O'Donnell long ago, "Love is blind to uncomliness."']
County Donegal
Mac Meanman *Crathadh an Phocáin*, short stories, 1955 Dublin p. 75, line 20

Note: Bháird and Ó Domhnaill represent clan leaders. One Mac an Bháird head was renowned for finely-honed insults. I thank Ciarán Ó Duibhín for this information. See Part B 24 for another wellerism with Mac an Bháird as speaker.

grádh/fear
B 112.1 '"Más é sin an ghrádh, tá mo sháith agam de," mar adubhairt an fear nuair a fáisgeadh a lámh.'
['"If this is love I've had enough of it," as the man said when his hand was wrung.']
County Mayo
Ó Máille 1952 No. 2547

Note: a custom for sealing bargains, such as an engagement, was for the couple to stand on either side of a holed pillar stone and clasp hands together through it; is it possible that it is this to which the wellerism

242

refers, rather than a firm handshake. I thank Ruairí Ó Bléine for examining this wellerism.

g'ránta see *gearánta*

I

iasc/fear

B 113.1 '"Sin é an t-iasc, ach cá bhfuil an salan?" a ndúirt an fear, nuair a dh'imig an túin as an saighne.'
['"There's the fish, but where's the salt?" said the man when the bottom fell out of the seine net.']
County Kerry
Almqvist *Collection of proverbs* … ts, collected by **BA** from **MÓG** between 1966 and 1974.

im/cat

B 114.1 'Deir an cat, "Cé d'ith an t-im? Na mná."'
['Said the cat, "Who ate the butter? The women."']
County Donegal
Quiggin 1906 No. 13 p. 195, in a list of 24 items titled 'Seanfhocla.' ['Proverbs.']

cf the proverb 'Ní ólann ná mná leann, acht imthigeann sé len-a linn' 'The women never drink beer, but it disappears when they are around' *Irisleabhar na Gaedhilge*, 9, No. 101 (Nov. 1898), p. 271 No. 20, and another in Irish to the same effect — as FCW remembers it — 'Only the women and the tailor were there but the butter disappeared.'

inughnín/cat

B 115.1 'Arsan cat leis an choinín, "Ná bí in mo inughnín."'
['Said the cat to the rabbit, "Don't get into my claws."']
County Donegal
IFCS 1059:374 in a list+, mainly of proverbs.

ísleán/fear (madaruadh)

B 116.1 '"Ní lia ísleán sona ann ná árdán dona ann," mar adubhairt an fear agus é ag ithe píobáin an ghanndail.'
['"Pleasant hollows are no fewer than bleak heights," as the man said when he was eating the gander's neck.']

County Kerry
'Duilleacán an Irisleabhar,' a grammar leaflet published by *Irisleabhar na Gaedhilge*, Jan. 1899, 'Simple Lessons in Irish Part V Cont'd. Ex. CLXXVI' pp. 31–34, Section 1452 p. 33, in a short list titled 'Proverbs'

.2 '"Ní liachta isleán sona ann ná árdán dona ann," mar dubhairt an fear le píobán an ghanndail.'
['"Pleasant hollows are no fewer than bleak heights," as the man with the gander's neck said.']
County Kerry
Seosamh Laoide 'Mac Tíre na Páirce' [Joseph Henry Lloyd 1865–1939, editor, for a time, of *Irisleabhar na Gaedhilge*] *Tonn Tóime Tiomargadh ... ó Chiarraighe Luachra*, a collection of folklore, 1915 Dublin. Section XLIX, in a list titled 'Seanráidhte 'na leathbheannaibh: leathchéad a líon,' pp. 113–16, consisting mainly of proverbs, collected by Liam Ó Lúing [William Long] and others, p. 113 No. 9

.3 & .4 '"Ní lia ísleán sona ná árdán dona ann," mar adubhairt an fear (*or* madaruadh) agus é ag ithe píobán an ghanndail.'
['"Pleasant hollows are no fewer than bleak heights," as the man (*or* fox) said when he was eating the gander's neck.']
Munster
'An Seabhac' 1926 No. 814/1984 No. 979 with the comment: ['the same thing could be said of many aspects of life']

cf 'tá oiread í. sona ann is árdán dona is tá ar scluig an ghandail, it has as many pleasant hollows and bleak ridges as a gander's neck' Dinneen under 'ísleán.'

L

lá/dreoilín
B 117.1 '"Ní'l aon lá riamh ná bíonn an gruas ag déanamh cos ar bolg ar an éagcruas," mar adubhairt an dreoilín leis an bhfiolar.'
['"Never a day passes in which the strong doesn't oppress the weak," as the wren said to the eagle.']
Dinneen 1934 ed., 1970 rpt. under 'gruas'; 'gruas' is not defined and only this wellerism appears under it.

244

lá/Peadar a' Gharraí
B 117a.1 '"Lá mór in Eccleston amárach," mar a dúirt Peadar a' Gharraí Aird.'
['"A great day in Eccleston tomorrow," as Peadar of Garraí Aird said.']
County Mayo
i Tony Catherine Antoine William 'Fear Pholl a' Bhroic'+ [b. *c.* 1930s] *Seanfhocail as Acaill*, a collection of 368 items, mainly proverbs, from this farm labourer and psychiatric nurse. 1995 Indreabhán, Conamara. 1997 ed., No. 363.

lá/sglábhuidhe
B 118.1 '"Is dóigh liom go ndeaghaigh an lá i mbreaghthacht," mar adubhairt an sglábhuidhe nuair d'ól sé an pigín praisge.'
['"I think the day has just got better," as the labourer said when he drank the piggin [= vessel] of gruel.']
Munster
E[ugene] O'Growney [editor for a period of *Irisleabhar na Gaedhilge*], Prescott, Arizona, USA 'Connlach' [= 'stubble' ?ie. 'remnants'], a glossary, pp. 269–70 *Irisleabhar na Gaedhilge*, 9, No. 101 (Nov. 1898) in the Munster section of the glossary on p. 270 under No. 16: 'For *ríobún, sríobún* is said in some places, a mixture of skim milk and raw oatmeal. When milk was scarce, a cooked mixture of meal was used called *praisge*. Hence the proverb: *Is dóigh liom go ndeaghaigh [= ndeachaidh] an lá ... pigín praisge*. Also the retort on boasters, *do dhéanfadh gaisge ar phigín praisge*' ['who would do great things after a vessel of gruel'].

lá/sionnach
B 119.1 '"Ach go dtigidh an lá breágh, déanfaidh mé teach," mar adubhairt an sionnach, ach nuair tháinig, dheamhan teach ná teach.'
['"As soon as a good day comes, I'll make a house," as the fox said, but when it came, nary a house.']
County Mayo
Ó Máille 1952 No. 2918 where he gives a ref. to *Reliquiae Celticae* Vol. II, 479, 'An girrfhiadh adubhairt' ['The hare said']; see also *ibid.* another similar item

cf the folktale AT 81 (formerly 72**) *Too Cold for Hare to Build House in Winter*, & similar motif *MI* A 2233.2.1 *Too cold for hare (dog) to build house in winter, not necessary in summer.*

léan/gé
B 120.1 '"Mo léan géar!" adeir an ghé bhí ar deireadh, "bhí mise lá a mbínn chun tosaigh."'
['"Cruel misfortune!" said the hindmost goose, "there was a time when I used to be at the front."']
County Galway
IFC 101:546 in a list, mainly of proverbs, collected by SUaM in 1934. Published in Ó Máille 1948 No. 1685c.

léan/sean-bhean   Part A 302
B 121.1 '"Ní thig an léan leis féin," mar dubhairt an tsean-bhean nuair cailleadh a fear 's rug an chearc amuigh.'
['"Misfortune doesn't come on its own," as the old woman said when her husband died and the hen laid out.']
County Galway
Ó Máille 1952 No. 3315. Cited in [Carson] Williams 1992 p. 136/2000a p. 114.

light/cailleach   Part A 170
B 122.1 '"More light," ars an chailleach nuair a bhí an teach le thine.'
['"More light," said the hag when the house was on fire.']
County Armagh
Ua Muirgheasa 1907 No. 1545/1976 No. 1794. Cited in [Carson] Williams 1992 p. 5/2000a p. 16.

luas/gabhar
B 123.1 'Mar dubhairt an gabhar bacach, "Níl fhios agam cé acu is fearr, luas nó moilleas."'
['As the lame goat said, "I don't know which is better, speed or slowness."']
Connacht
An Claidheamh Soluis, 28/3/1903 as cited in Ó Máille 1948 No. 79

.2 'Mar adubhairt an gabhar bacach, "Ní fheadar ciaca is fearr, luas nó moilleas."'
Munster
'An Seabhac' 1926 No. 833/1984 No. 998

cf 'Níl fhios agam cé is fearr, luas nó moill ach dubhairt an sean-ghabhar bacach go mb'fhearr an mhoill, 's dubhairt an coinín go mb'fhearr an luas' ['I don't know which is better, fastness or slowness but the old goat said that slowness is better and the rabbit that speed is better'] Ó Máille 1948 No. 79

Note: 'Níl fhios agam cé is fearr, luas nó moill' is common.

luigh(e)/madadh rua(dh)

B 124.1 '"Luighe gan éirghe chugat!" ars' a madadh ruadh leis an chaoirigh.'
['"Lying down without rising to you!" said the fox to the sheep.']
County Monaghan
Ua Muirgheasa 1907 No. 946b/1976 No. 1124b with the observation: 'in which case he'd come in for [= obtain] a good meal'

.2 '"Luigh gan éirí!" dúirt an madadh rua leis an chaora.'
['"Lying down without rising!" said the fox to the sheep.']
County Donegal
Lúcás 1986 under 'luí v[erbal] n[oun] 3,' designated 'proverb,' collected from SÓB m b. 1906

Note: '"Luí gan éirí chugat!" ie. "Death!"' was collected as a curse in Counties Donegal and Monaghan, Ua Muirgheasa 1907 No. 946a/1976 No. 1124a.

M

mac see *duine uasail*
macántas see *cneastacht*

maidin/ceannaidh Ghort an Charnáin (c. Phort an Charnáin)
B 125.1 '"Seo libh go maidin é," mar deir Ceannaidh Ghort an Charnáin.'
['"Here you are till morning," as the dealer of Ghort an Charnáin said.']
County Galway
Ó Máille 1952 No. 4456 with the explanation, p. 440, that Gort an Charnáin lies between Moycullen and Uachtarard, and the comment for both variants: ['Said at the start of a night's revelry(?)'] and a ref. to a similar saying in Mac Craith [Rev. Michael McGrath] 1936–37 *Cinnlae Amhlaoidh Uí Shúileabháin (1829–32)*

.2 '"Seo libh go maidin é," mar deir Ceannaidh Phort an Charnáin.'

Connacht
Ó Máille *ibid.* For his comment see **.1.**

'máireach/oifigeach
B 126.1 '"Mair go dí 'máireach is geói' tú scilin," ers' an t-oifigeach leis an sighdiúir fudó.'
['"Live until tomorrow and you'll get a shilling," said the officer to the soldier long ago.']
County Kerry
Almqvist *Collection of proverbs* ... ts, collected by **BA** from **MÓG** between 1966 and 1974.

máistir/tincéar
B 127.1 '"Más máistir mise agus máistir tusa cé thiomáinfidh an t-asal?" arsan tincéar lena mhac.'
['"If I'm master and you're master who'll drive the ass?" said the tinker to his son.']
County Clare
Q 1973 IFC 1917:9 C m with the following: ['One day a pair of tinkers were going along the road. They were a father and son and they were arguing. Finally the father said to his son — "If I'm master ... ass?" said the tinker to his son.']

maith/An Dálach
B 128.1 '"Mar dubhairt an Dálach i bhfad ó shoin leis an Bhaoigheallach, "Tá mé is maith le charaid agus mar is olc le mo námhaid."'
['As The Ó Dálach said long ago to The Ó Baoigheallach, "I am as my friends would wish me to be and as my enemies would not."']
County Donegal
Mac Meanman *Fear Siubhail*, short stories, 1924 Dublin, 1931 ed., p. 11, line 23

Note: The Ó Dálach and The Ó Bhaoigheallach stand for clan chiefs.

maith (cóir)/Cailleach M(h)uigheo (Cailleach Bhéar(r)a, Cailleach Thír Eoghain)
B 129.1 'Arsa Cailleach Mhuigheo le Chailligh Thíre Eoghain, "An té bhidheas go maith duit bí go maith dó."'
['Said the Hag of Mayo to the Hag of Tyrone, "Be good to the one who's good to you."']
County Monaghan

248

Irisleabhar na Gaedhilge, 8, No. 95 (Mar. 1898), in a list titled 'Farney (Co. Monaghan) Proverbs and Sayings.' pp. 177–80, signed Eanraoi Ua Muirgheasa, item No. 58 p. 178/translation p. 180. Cited in Ua Muirgheasa 1907 No. 169/1976 No. 193, but with the quote first

.2 'Arsa Cailleach M(h)uigheo le Chailleach T(h)ír Eoghain, "An té bhéidheas go maith duit bí go maith dhó."'
County Mayo 1903
Hyde ms Notebook V, 15, University College Galway, written by Douglas Hyde [1860–1949], which pertains to a competition which was part of Feis Mhuigheo in 1903, as published in Ó Máille 1953(1954) No. 33. Note: such 'feiseanna' [= 'festivals'] were held to promote the Irish language etc.

.3 'Arsa Cailleach Bhéara le Cailligh Mhuigheo, "An té bhíonn go maith dhuit bí go maith dhó."'
Munster
'An Seabhac' 1926 No. 828/1984 No. 993

.4 '"An té ghníos maith duit, déan maith dó," mar adubhairt Cailleach Bhéarra le Cailligh Mhuigheo.'
['"Do good to whoever does good to you," as the Hag of Beara said to the Hag of Mayo.']
County Galway
Ó Máille 1948 No. 2206

.5 '"An té atá go maith duit, bí go maith dó," arsa cailleach Thír Eoghain le cailleach Mhaigh Eo.'
['"Whoever's good to you, be good to him," said the Hag of Tyrone to the Hag of Mayo.']
County Mayo
i Tony Catherine Antoine William 'Fear Pholl a' Bhroic'+ [b. *c.* 1930s], *Seanfhocail as Acaill*, a collection of 368 items, mainly proverbs, from this farm labourer and psychiatric nurse. 1995 Indreabhán, Conamara. 1997 ed., p. 49 No. 306. Illustrated p. 51 with a cartoon by Fearghas Mac Lochlainn

?.6 & .7 ''Sé dubhairt Cailleach Bhéarra le Cailligh Mhuigheo, "An té bhíos go maith dhuit, bí go maith dhó."'
['As the Hag of Beara said to the Hag of Mayo, "Whoever's good to you, be good to him."']
County Galway

Ó Máille 1948 No. 2206; the exact number of versions and the order of the two parts is unclear in Ó Máille, see also **?.8**

?.8 '"An té bhíos cóir, bí cóir leis," 'sé dubhairt Cailleach Bhéarra le Cailligh Mhuigheo.'
['"Show kindness to whoever's kind to you," as the Hag of Beara said to the Hag of Mayo.']
County Galway
Ó Máille 1948 No. 2206; the exact number of versions and the order of the two parts is unclear in Ó Máille, see also **?.6 & .7**

Mieder & Tóthné Litovkina pp. 66–67 [but no wellerism]

Note: for information on the Cailleach Bhéara see Part B 50, where she is also the speaker, as she is in Part B 83.

maith/cat see *deireadh*

ma(i)th/fear
B 130.1 '"Ba mhaith iad san féin ann," mar deireadh an fear le Cuan Cromdha.'
['"It was good that they at least were there," as the man said of Cuan Cromdha.']
County Kerry
Ó Criomhthain *An tOileánach*, autobiographical, 1929 Dublin p. 77, ref. via Almqvist *Collection of Proverbs* … ts. Context from Flower's translation [Ó Crohan 1937, 1974 rpt.]: 'You see how soon we were scattered! The merriment, the jokes, the fun that never ceased — before meals, at meals, and after meals — it was all gone now, and not a sound was to be heard but the voice of the old hag opposite and the droning of Bald Tom: but, "It was some comfort that even they were there," as the man said of Cuan Croumha.' Ch. 8 'Marriage, Our Family Scattered' p. 65

.2 '"Is math ann é," ers' an fear le Cuas Crommtha.'
['"It's good that it's there," as the man said of Cuas Cromtha.']
County Kerry
Almqvist *Collection of proverbs* … ts, collected by **BA** from **MÓG** between 1966 and 1974

cf 'Is maith ann é Cuan Cromtha' ['It's good that Cuan Cromtha's there'] with a story of its origin, in summary, said by one of Failbhe Ua Ráthaigh's men on reaching Cuan Cromtha after a stormy night at sea

250

heading for Valentia Harbour 'An Seabhac' 1926 No. 889/1984 No.
1060, ref. via Almqvist *Collection of Proverbs* ... ts

Note: Cuan Cromtha is a bay near Caherciveen on the north of the
Iveragh Peninsula, Co. Kerry. I thank Paul Tempan for the place-name
information.

maith/Ó hIarlaithe
**B 131.1 '"Is beag an mhaith fairis sin í," a dúirt Ó hIarlaithe
leis an roilleogach.'**
['"It's little good otherwise," said Ó hIarlaithe of the bog myrtle.']
Munster
'An Seabhac' 1984 No. 973

cf the expression 'Is beag an mhaith fairis sin é' Ó Dónaill under 'fara 2'

Notes: bog myrtle [*Myrica gale*] was believed to have been used to
scourge Christ, see Dinneen under 'roideog.' In the 18th century in
Múscraí/Muskerry, West Cork, there was a noted family of clergy and
poets called Ó hIarlaithe to whom this wellerism may be related. I thank
Ciarán Ó Duibhín for this information.

mála/bacach
**B 132.1 '"Gluais, a mhála, is go n-eirghe an t-ádh leat!" arsan
bacach ar maidin.'**
['"Advance, bag, and good luck!" said the tramp in the morning.']
Munster
'An Seabhac' 1926 No. 802/1984 No. 965

**.2 '"Gluais, a mhála, is go n-éirí an t-ádh leat!" mar a dúirt an
bacach ar maidin.'**
['"Get going, bag, and good luck!" as the tramp said in the morning.']
Mac Con Iomaire 1988 p. 217 with a photographic illustration 'Tramping
in Co. Wicklow.'

mallacht/cailleach
**B 133.1 '"Mallacht chnâ an teammpail er an té ghoid mo
sp'ráinín," ers' an chaileach fudó.'**
['"The curse of the church bones [ie.?relics] on the person who stole my
little purse," said the old woman long ago.']
County Kerry
Almqvist *Collection of proverbs* ... ts, collected by **BA** from **MÓG**
between 1966 and 1974.

marbh-fáisg/bean
B 134.1 '"Marbh-fáisg ar a' h-áilneacht!" ars' an bhean nuair a tharraing sí na stócaí bána ar na cosaibh dubha.'
['"Bad luck to beauty!" said the woman when she pulled the white stockings onto her black feet.']
County Donegal
Morris 1918 No. 187.

marcuigheacht/bean   Part A 308
B 135.1 '"Is olc an mharcuigheacht nach fearr é ná'n dubh-choisidheacht," ars' an bhean a bhí ag marcuigheacht ar an tor tromain.'
['"It's poor riding that's not better than walking," said the woman who was riding on the elder bush.']
County Londonderry
Morris 1918 No. 186

Note: the woman was even oblivious to the ubiquitous belief that elder [*Sambucus nigra*] was unlucky!

math see *ma(i)th/fear*

méadú/dreoillín
B 136.1 '"Sin méadú ort," ars an dreoillín nuair rinne sé a mhún sa bhfairrge.'
['"That'll add to you," said the wren when he urinated in the sea.']
County Galway
Ó Máille 1948 No. 403

see also Part B 22 & 44 and the converse Part A 164.

mill/bean
B 137.1 '"Mé féin a mhill mé féin," mar dubhairt an bhean a thuit ar a tóin san im.'
['"It was I who ruined myself," as the woman who fell on her backside in the butter said.']
County Mayo *c.* 1900
Ó Máille 1952 No. 4785.

252

min/fear

B 138.1 "'Chití, mara bhfuil tuilleadh mine agat, beidh do bhrothchán lom," mar dubhairt an fear fadó le n-a mhnaoi nuair thuit an sac mine sa lán mara air.'

["'Cití, unless you have some more meal, your porridge is going to be thin," as the man long ago said to his wife when he let the flour sack fall into the sea.']
County Mayo
Ó Máille 1952 No. 4171.

mná/gabhar

B 139.1 "'A' lorg mná," a ndubhairt an gabhar.'

["'Looking for women," said the goat.']
Munster
'An Seabhac' 1926 No. 831/1984 No. 996

see also Part B 1 where the story is also given.

moill(iú)/fear

B 140.1 "'Níl aon mhaith dhí mhoill," arsan fear do bhí ag baint na móna fáoi Fhéil' Mhichíl, deireadh na bliadhna.'

["'There's no good in delaying it," said the man who was drawing turf at Michaelmas, at the end of the year.']
Fhéil' Mhichíl [Michaelmas], 29th Sept.
Connacht
Irisleabhar na Gaedhilge, 15, No. 2 (OS 181) (Oct. 1905), in a list titled 'Seanfhocail IV Tomás Ó hEidhin do bhailigh' ['Proverbs IV collected by TÓhE'+] pp. 19–21, item No. 492, p. 21, note p. 21: 'Ni raibh aon mhoill le deanamh aige, acht an mhóin do chaitheamh suas. "There's no good in delaying it." Do chaitheamh suas, "to throw up," "to give up."' This long list of 653 items won first prize at the Oireachtus of 1902, Competition 18. It was published in 7 parts, the first section being in Vol. 14, No. 178 (July 1905) pp. 827–31. The list consists mostly of proverbs but contains four wellerisms [this and Part B 11.2, 41.5 & 56]

.2 "'Níl gar dhá mhoilliú," mar dubhairt an fear a bhí a' baint na móna fá Fhéil' Mhichíl.'

["'There's no good in delaying," as the man who was drawing turf at Michaelmas said.']
County Galway
Ó Máille 1952 No. 2955

Note: the proverb 'Níl gar dhá mhoilliú' ['There is no good in delay'/'Delays are dangerous'] is well-known in Irish and is also known in English.

móin/fear

B 141.1 '"Mur' bhfuil móin agat féin déan do ghoradh le gréin!" mar dubhairt an fear a tháinig ar a chomharsain ag goid na mónadh.'
['"If you've no turf, warm yourself with the sun," as the man said when he came on his neighbour stealing his turf.']
County Donegal
Mac Meanman *Rácáil agus Scuabadh.* 1955 Dublin p. 34, in a section titled 'Natháin agus Abraidhe atá leighte i ndearmad.' ['Neglected Sayings and Expressions.'] pp. 30–35, in which five wellerisms [this and Part B 19.2, 24, 52 & 77] are listed together, with the comment that they are still to be heard amongst the over fifties

Note: the proverb 'Mur' bhfuil móin agat féin déan do ghoradh le gréin!' and similar is fairly common in Irish and in English.

muiltín/fear

B 142.1 '"Is mairg a mhuirbhfinn mo mhuiltín fóghmhar is tusa 'do luighe ar do leic go modhmhar," ars' an fear leis an bháirneach.'
['"Alas, that I should kill my little autumn wether and you reposing quietly on your rock," said the man to the limpet.']
County Donegal
Morris 1918 No. 159.

N

neach see *eùn*

neart/dreoil(l)ín   Part A 277

B 143.1 '"Is mór an ní an neart!" arsa an dreóilín nuair a chaith sé an chiaróg leis an bhfaill.'
['"Strength's a great thing!" said the wren when he threw the beetle over the cliff.']
Munster

'An Seabhac' 1926 No. 816/1984 No. 981 with the comment there for all three variants: ['This would be said when you'd see a small, weak person undertaking a strenuous task']

.2 '"Is mór an ní an neart!" mar a dúirt an dreóilín nuair a chaith sí an chiaróg leis an bhfaill.'
['"Strength's a great thing!" as the wren said when she threw the beetle over the cliff.']
Q 2000 i JC(ii) m+ [E & Ir], b. Cork *c*. 1930, retired professor of literature: 'A well-known one is "Is mór an ní ..." --- 'I'm afraid I cannot offer a single source for that wren proverb. At school we were encouraged to learn many such and to lard our Irish essays with them! They were offered to us in isolation from any literary work, and presented as little nuggets of wit and wisdom of a generic kind. The wren proverb was clearly intended to puncture the pomposity of the little bird and one would be encouraged to fit this concept appropriately into one's own prose efforts.' Emails of 6th & 7th Mar. 2000. JC(ii) attended an Irish-medium school in Cork city

.3 '"Is mór an ní an neart!" arsa an dreóilín nuair a tharraing sé an phiast as an sioc.'
['"Strength's a great thing!" said the wren when he pulled the worm out of the frost.']
Munster
'An Seabhac' 1926 No. 816/1984 No. 981. For his comment see **.1**

.4 '"Is mór an ní an neart!" arsa an dreóilín nuair a tharraing sé an fhrig as an mbualtach.'
['"Strength's a great thing!" said the wren when he pulled the mite out of the midden.']
Munster
'An Seabhac' 1926 No. 816/1984 No. 981. For his comment see **.1**

.5 '"Is mór an ní an neart!" arsa an dreoilín nuair a chaith sé ciarog leis an bhfaill.'
['"Strength's a great thing!" said the wren when he threw a beetle over the cliff.']
County Cork
Q 1973 IFC 1911:72 C f+ [E & Ir], a nun

.6 '"Is mór an rud an neart!" mar dubhairt an dreoillín nuair mharbhuigh sé an phéist.'
['"Strength's a great thing!" as the wren said when he killed the worm.']

County Mayo
Ó Máille 1952 No. 3128

.7 '"Is iontach an rud é an neart!" mar a dúirt an dreoilín nuair a tharraing sé an phéist as an sioc.'
['"Strength's a wonderful thing!" as the wren said when he pulled the worm out of the frost.']
Mac Con Iomaire 1988 p. 210, in a short introduction to a set of wellerisms titled 'Quotation Proverbs': '...The quotation itself is always serious but becomes humorous when attributed to a certain speaker in a certain situation; '"Strength is a great thing,' — as the wren said when he pulled the worm out of the frost" (*"Is iontach ... an sioc)*'

.8 'Mar a dúirt an dreoilín fadó nuair a tharraig sé an phiast as an sioc, "Á, is breá é an neart!"'
['As the wren said long ago when he pulled the worm out of the frost, "Ah, strength's a fine thing!"']
County Kerry
Muiris Ó Súilleabháin *Fiche Blian ag Fás*, autobiography, 1933, 1976 ed., Mac Tomais, Editor, p. 143, ref. via Almqvist *Collection of proverbs* ... ts. Context from Llewelyn Davies & Thomson's translation [O'Sullivan 1941]: The Blasket Islanders are salvaging and Muiris and his schoolfriend Tomás see two women trying to roll a barrel above high water mark: 'We stopped to help them. "Musha, love of my heart for ever," cried Peg, "youth is good. And as the wren said long ago when he pulled the worm out of the frost ..." "What did he say, Peg?" "'Ah,' said he, 'strength is fine,' and that is the way with the two of us."' Ch. 13 'The Shipwreck' p. 169

.9 '"Is múr is fiú an neart," ers' an dreóilín nuair a chaith sé an ciarhóg leis an bhfaill.'
['"Strength's worth a lot!" said the wren when he threw the beetle off the cliff.']
County Kerry
Almqvist *Collection of proverbs* ... ts, collected by **BA** from **MÓG** between 1966 and 1974

.10 '"Neart!" ars an dreoillín nuair thuit sé ar a thóin a' tarraing péiste as an talamh.'
['"Strength!" said the wren when he fell on his rear pulling a worm out of the ground.']
County Galway

256

Ó Máille 1952 No. 3128. Cited in [Carson] Williams 1992 p. 69/2000a p. 69 [*sic*]

.11 '"Is mór an rud an neart!" ars an dreoillín.'
['"Strength's a great thing!" said the wren.']
County Mayo
Ó Máille 1952 No. 3128

.12 & .13 Irish lacking
['"Strength's a great thing," as the wren said when he (she) pushed the beetle over the cliff.']
Q 1973 IFC 1888:58 C m+. The Correspondent's address is Co. Galway. After listing some proverbial comparisons in English he writes 'agus ón Ghaeilge:' ['and from Irish:'] and then gives the above [Part **B 143.12 & .13**] and Part B 44.6 & 107.6. He then adds, in Irish, that he knows scores of wellerisms in Irish

see also Part B 144.

neart/dreoilín
B 144.1 '"Och, car imig mo neart?" ers' an dreóilin nuair ná féadfach sé an meacan a straca as an dtalamh.'
['"Alas, where's my strength gone?" said the wren when he couldn't pull the carrot out of the ground.']
County Kerry
Almqvist *Collection of proverbs* ... ts, collected by **BA** from **MÓG** between 1966 and 1974

see also Part B 143.

nígh see *eùn*

'nois (anois)/bean (céile)
B 145.1 '"Mar dubhairt bean a' tseanduine dhóighte, "Mur déanann tú 'nois é, ní dhéanfaidh tú choidhche é!"'
['As the wizened old man's wife said, "If you don't do it now, you'll never do it."']
County Donegal
'Máire' *Nuair a Bhí Mé Óg*, autobiographical, 1924 Dublin p. 227, line 22

.2 '"Mar dubhairt a chéile chaoin leis a' tseanduine dhóighte, "Mura ndéana tú anois é, ní dhéanfaidh tú choidhche é!"'

['As his gentle spouse said to the wizened old man, "If you don't do it now, you'll never do it."']
County Donegal
'Máire' *Saoghal Corrach*, autobiographical, 1945 Dublin p. 218, line 6

Note: The part quoted is a line from a ribald song called *An seanduine dóighte,* still current in Donegal. For a version of the song see Ó Baoill agus Ó Baoill 1997 *Ceolta Gael*, pp. 84–85. I am grateful to John Moulden for this ref.

now (diail)/cail(l)each
B 146.1 '"Now for it!" mar adubhairt an chailleach agus í ag rith le na scáth.'
['"Now for it!" as the hag said when she was running with her shadow.']
Munster
'An Seabhac' 1926 No. 807/1984 No. 970

.2 '"Seo chút mé, a dhiail!" ers' an chaileach fudó is í á' rith i ndiaig a scáth.'
['"Here I come, you devil!" said the hag long ago when she was running after her shadow.']
County Kerry
Almqvist *Collection of proverbs* ... ts, collected by **BA** from **MÓG** between 1966 and 1974

cf the motif *MI* J 1790 *Shadow mistaken for substance*

Note: 'ag rith le do scáth' also means 'chasing dreams.'

'Nuighidh/sgadán
B 147.1 '"Is fada siar ''Nuighidh Dia' ionnad," mar dubhairt an sgadán leis an míol mór nuair shluig sé é.'
['"You have to look far into you to find a friendly greeting," as the herring said to the whale when it swallowed him.']
County Mayo *c.* 1900
Ó Máille 1948 No. 1923 with the comment: 'a surly person.'

O

ochón see *cúis gháire*

258

ocras/táilliúir   *cf Mediaeval Latin
B 148.1 '"Rud ar bith leis an ocras a mhaolú," arsa an táilliúir agus é ag ithe míoltóige.'
['"Anything to assuage the hunger," said the tailor eating midges.']
míoltóg/midge [Ceratopogonidae or *Chironomidae]=very small fly*
Rosenstock 1993 p. 52/translation p. 53

cf 'Rud ar bith leis an ocras a bhodhradh, agus é ag ithe míoltóige' ['Anything to bother the hunger, and he eating midges'] Co. Mayo Ó Máille 1952 No. 4822. Cited in [Carson] Williams 1992 p. 105/2000a p. 93

cf 'Anything to bother the hunger, like the tailor when he swallowed the midge' Co. Sligo IFCS 167:637, with a story. Published in [Carson] Williams 1992 p. 105/2000a p. 93

*cf Mediaeval Latin '"Something is better than nothing," said the wolf when he swallowed the louse' Taylor 1962 fac., 1985 rpt., p. 205. Cited in *DOW* 1226

Note: I thank John Prenter for discussing species.

oineach na bainríoghna/Frainc 'ac Confhaola
B 149.1 '"Is fada ó oineach na bainríoghna thú," mar deir Frainc 'ac Confhaola le Doire Thuirc.'
['"You're far from the queen's hospitality," as Frainc 'ac Confhaola said to Doire Thuirc.']
County Galway
Ó Máille 1948 No. 1922a with the comment: ['this is said of a miserly or stingy person].'

ól/luchóg
B 150.1 '"Ag ól a bhí muid annsin," mar dubhairt an luchóg leis an gcat.'
['"We were drinking then," as the mouse said to the cat.']
County Mayo c. 1900
Ó Máille 1952 No. 2513 with the following: ['a broken promise. This refers to the story where a cat rescues a mouse from a vat of ale on condition that he may eat her. The mouse escaped and this is her excuse for breaking her promise'].

ól/ól

B 151.1 '"Ná hól an t-ól," ars an t-ól, "gur eol duit go n-ólfar é.'

['"Don't drink the drink," said the drink, "until you know that it'll be drunk."']

County Galway

Ó Máille 1952 No. 3240 with the comment: ['Don't drink a drop until it's ready for drinking'].

olann/fear bocht

B 152.1 '"Is deacar olann a bhaint de ghabha(i)r," arsa an fear bocht nach raibh i ndán a chuid fiacha a dhíol.'

['"It's difficult to get wool from a goat," said the poor man who wasn't able to pay his debts.']

County Donegal

Q 1973 IFC 1888:22 C m+

Note: the proverb 'Is deacar olann a bhaint de ghabhar' is common in Irish and also in English.

P

paidreacha/gasúr

B 153.1 'Mar dubhairt an gasúr leis an sagart nuair dubhairt sé leis a phaidreacha a rádh, "Níl na paidreacha agam ach tá an tiúin agam."'

['As the boy said to the priest when he told him to say his prayers, "I don't know the prayers but I know the tune."']

County Galway

Ó Máille 1948 No. 1483.

páirt/sionnach   Part A 306

B 154.1 '"Beidh mise i bpáirt leat," mar adubhairt an sionnach leis an gcoileach.'

['"I'll assist you," as the fox said to the cock.']

County Galway

Ó Máille 1948 No. 851 with the following: '["It is for his own benefit that the strong (or crafty) person helps out the weak person"] … Ecclus. XIII 17.'

peac(h)ach/fear

B 155.1 '"Is iomdha seórt rud a leanas a' peacach," mar dubhairt an fear a rabh an ganndal 'na dhiaidh.'
['"Many sorts of thing follow the sinful," as the man with the gander after him said.']
County Armagh
Ua Muirgheasa 1907 No. 512/1976 No. 623

.2 '"Is iomdha seort rud a leanas an peachach," mar adubhairt an fear agus ganndal 'na dhiaidh.'
County Mayo
IFC 210:140 in a list, mainly of proverbs, collected by BNíC in 1930 from Bean uí S. Published in Ó Máille 1948 No. 1482a.

pósfaidh see *bean*

R

rabhadh/bean

B 156.1 '"Is mairg a thugann rabhadh dá chomharsain," mar a dúirt an bhean ar thóg an barra taoide í.'
['"Woe to the one who forewarns his neighbour," as the woman taken by the neap tide said.']
Munster
'An Seabhac' 1984 No. 959 with the comment: ['Talkative women from then on have been forewarned by her example']

cf 'Mairg do bheir r.[abhadh] dá chomharsain, woe to the man who tells others what he is going to do, as, in bidding at an auction, *etc.*, *al*[ternatively] woe to him who is a warning to others' Dinneen under 'rabhadh.'

rannaigí/fear

B 157.1 '"Rannaigí eadraibh féin é," mar a dúirt an fear a bhí i lár an phlaincéid.'
['"Divide it between you," as the man in the middle of the blanket said.']
County Donegal
Ó Muirgheasa 1931, 1976 ed. No. 1638

see also Part B 184.

rath/mac

**B 158.1 "'Ní bhíonn aon rath ach mar a bhíonn an smacht,"
mar a dúirt an mac agus é ag bualadh a athar.'**

['"There isn't any luck except where there's discipline," as the son said
while beating his father.']

Mac Con Iomaire 1988 p. 210, in a short introduction to a set of
wellerisms titled 'Quotation Proverbs': 'The most humorous Irish
proverbs by far are those known as "quotation proverbs." They not only
lack the seriousness and solemnity of ordinary proverbs, but they turn
some of them about and hold them up to ridicule: "'There is no luck
without discipline' — as the son said while beating his father" (*"Ní
bhíonn aon rath ... ag bualadh a athar*). ...'

cf Mieder & Tóthné Litovkina pp. 183–84

Notes: one of the four examples on Q 1973 was *'Ní bhíonn an rath ach
mar a mbhíonn an smacht,' mar dúirt an maicín nuair a bhuail sé a
athair.* ['There's no luck except where's there's discipline,' as the little
son said when he beat his father.] See Appendix 1 for the English-
language version used on Q 1973
The proverb *'Ní bhíonn aon rath ach mar a bhíonn an smacht'* is
common in Irish and is also found with this wording in English.

réi(dh)teach/ Tadhg na Spréach (dochtúir)

**B 159.1 "'Ag réidhteach chuige!" mar adubhairt Tadhg na
Spréach leis an bhfiacail.'**

['"Clearing the way for it," as Tadhg na Spréach [= Tadhg of the sparks]
said about the tooth.']

Munster

'An Seabhac' 1926 No. 825/1984 No. 990 with the comment: ['He had
pulled out the wrong tooth by mistake and this is what he said he had
been doing when he was questioned as to why he hadn't pulled the right
one']

**.2 "'A' réiteach chúihe," mar dúirt an dochtúir le fear an déid
thinis fudó.'**

['"Preparing the way for it," as the doctor said to the man with the sore
tooth long ago.']

County Kerry

Almqvist *Collection of proverbs* ... ts, collected by **BA** from **MÓG**
between 1966 and 1974 with the comment: 'This was the answer when
the patient complained that the dentist had pulled the wrong tooth.
M[ÓG] maintains that the patient was MÓC, a Blasketman, and that he

himself witnessed the incident in Dingle [town]. The joke, however, is international and of considerable age.' Ó Duilearga 1948 notes that as a folktale it is found in Kerry, Ulster and Denmark, and collected an example from Kerry in 1926, text p. 283 No. 84 (ii)/notes p. 434 & p. 483

cf 'Making preparations as Tadhg na Spréach was with the tooth' with its explanatory story is given in the section titled 'Proverbs' pp. 20–21 in Ó Súilleabháin 1937 — the 'mini *Handbook*' for use in schools — as an example of the sort of local story of the origin of expressions which was sought and is defined there as 'a lame excuse.' As a humorous folktale it is summarised in the *Handbook*, Ó Súilleabháin 1963, p. 634 No. 49 'A dentist (smith) pulls a patient's wrong tooth. Explains that he was only preparing the way.' Alerted to Ó Duilearga and *Handbook* refs via Almqvist *Collection of Proverbs* ... ts.

Rí na n-Éan/dreoilín
B 160.1 '"Is mise Rí na n-Éan," ers' an dreoilín is é er dhromm an iolair.'
['"I'm King of the Birds," said the wren when he was on the eagle's back.']
County Kerry
Almqvist *Collection of Proverbs* ... ts, collected by **BA** from **MÓG** between 1966 and 1974

cf the folktale *TIF* 221 *The Election of Bird-king.* [98 versions] & similar, and the motif *MI* K 25.1 *Wren hides in eagle's wings*

Note: a different wellerism with the same motif has been recorded in Sc Gae Nicolson p. 75 No. 3.

rod see *rud/Súisín Triopallach (ean, gabhairín)*

roinnigí/fear
B 161.1 '"Roinnigí eadraibh í!" mar dubhairt an fear a thug leith-phighinn do lucht an dreoillín.'
['"Divide it between you!" as the man who gave the halfpenny to the wrenboys said.']
County Mayo
Ó Máille 1948 No. 2244

Note: Both Ruairí Ó Bléine and Ciarán Ó Duibhin suggest that 'lucht an dreoillín,' lit. 'wren's clutch,' may refer to wrenboys, groups of youths

who, on St. Stephen's Day, 26th Dec., went from house to house
collecting money. The ambiguity may be intended.

rómhat (romhatsa)/bríste córda
B 162.1 '"Raghad-sa rómhat-sa!" adeir an bríste córda.'
['"I'll go in front of you!" say the corduroy breeches.']
Dinneen 1934 ed., 1970 rpt. under 'roimh' with the comment: 'from the
illusion one wearing such has of being followed.' Used to illustrate the
meaning with '*teighim*, I precede, come or pass in front of'

.2 '"Raghadsa romhatsa!" adeir an bríste corda.'
County Kerry
Q 2000(4/3/02) i **BA** who heard it in the 1970s from **SÓD** who explained
to him that: 'corduroy trousers made a sound when one leg brushed
against the other that could be interpreted as "raghadh-romhatsa" ["I'll
go before you"].'

ruaim/bean bhuidhe-dhubh
**B 163.1 '"Is mise fuair an chéad tomadh 'san ruaim," arsa
bean (ars' an bhean) bhuidhe-dhubh.'**
['"It was I who was first dipped in the wool-dye," said a (the) tawny
woman.']
Dinneen 1934 ed., 1970 rpt. under 'ruaim' with the second version under
'tomadh.' Used to illustrate 'ruaim' and 'tomadh.'

rud/Col(ui)m Cille
**B 164.1 'Mar dubairt Coluim Cille — agus b'fhíor dó (é) —
"An té a bheir rud duit tabhair rud dó."'**
['As Colm Cille said — and he was right — "Whoever gives you
something, give something to him."']
County Tyrone
The Ulster Herald, a weekly newspaper published in Omagh, 15th Feb.
or 14th Mar. 1908 as cited in Ó Tuathail 1933a No. 53, p. 147, in section
LVIII titled 'Sean-ráití Ghleann Aichle.' ['Old Glenelly Sayings.'], a list
of 84 items, mainly proverbs, collected by PMhacC m

**.2 'Mar dubhairt Colm Cille, "An té a bheir rud duit tabhair
rud dó."'**
['As Colm Cille said, "Whoever gives you something, give something to
him."']
County Donegal
IFCS 1060:310 in a list, mainly of proverbs, collected from SMacU m+

264

Note: for information on Colm Cille/Colmcille see Part B 14. He is also
the speaker in Part B 23 & 89.

rud (rod)/Súisín Triopallach (ean, gabhairín)
**B 165.1 'Adeireadh an Súisín Triopallach, "Bíodh rud agat
féin nó bí 'na uireasbha."'**
['The Súisín Triopallach said, "Have a thing yourself or be without."']
súisín=a coverlet or mophead; triopallach=neatly-shaped
Munster
'An Seabhac' 1926 No. 827/1984 No. 992

**.2 '"Bíodh rod agut féin, nú bí dá uireasa," a ndúirt an
gabhairín triopaileach.'**
['"Have a thing yourself or be without," said the neat little goat.']
County Kerry
Almqvist *Collection of proverbs* ... ts, collected by **BA** from **MÓG**
between 1966 and 1974

**.3 'Mar a dubhairt an t-ean, "Bíodh rud agat fhéin, sin no bí
follamh."'**
['As the bird said, "Have a thing yourself, that, or be without."']
County Donegal
IFCS 1059:360 in a list, mainly of proverbs

cf the riddle 'Cad dúirt an damhaisín triopalach? "Bíoch rud agat féin,"
adúirt sé, "nú bí á eireasa."' ['What did the neat little ox say? "Have a
thing yourself," he said, "or be without."'] Co. Kerry IFC 858:448 ref.
via Almqvist *Collection of Proverbs* ... ts. The riddle was collected in
1942 by **SÓD** from Peig Sayers

Note: the proverb 'Bíodh rud agat féin nó bí 'na uireasbha' is common in
Irish, as it is in English.

S

sála/fear
**B 166.1 '"Bímis ag súgradh ach seachnaímis sála a chéile," a
dúirt fear na sáile tinne.'**
['"We were playing but we avoided heels together," said the man with
the fire-speckled heels.']
Munster

'An Seabhac' 1984 No. 958.

saoghal/fear

B 167.1 **"'Is maith an saoghal é má mhaireann sé i gcomhnaidhe ach mairfidh sé fhad 's mhairfeas mo chuid dlighidh,"** **mar adubhairt an fear a raibh an pota feola ar an teinidh aige.'**
["'It's a good life if it lasts for ever but it will last as long as my law lasts," as the man with the pot of meat on the fire said.']
County Galway
Ó Máille 1952 No. 4890

Note: 'Is maith an saoghal é má mhaireann sé i gcomhnaidhe' is a common expression.

saoghal/Páidín

B 168.1 **"'Saoghal corrach,"** **arsa Páidín agus é a' rith anuas le fánaidh.'**
["'It's an uneasy life," said Páidín running down the slope.']
County Galway
Ó Máille 1948 No. 1573a.

saol/Sean-Mhicheál

B 169.1 **"'Níl sa saol seo ach ceo,"** **mar dúirt Sean-Mhicheál.'**
["'This life is but mist," as Sean-Mhicheál [= old Micheál] said.']
County Mayo
Q 1973 IFC 1888:123 C m+ with the comment: ['People often make use in their speech of sayings or proverbs of another person. For example "'Níl sa saol seo ach ceo," mar dúirt Sean-Mhicheál.' Often the person speaking does not know the originator of the old saying and in that case he says "--- as the person who said it said." Here are examples of such old sayings: ' [see also Part B 41.2, 58.1, 79 & 91]]

Note: the proverb 'Níl sa saol seo ach ceo,' from the biblical Job, is very common.

sáthach/bodach

B 170.1 **"'Beidh tú sáthach luath,"** **mar dubhairt bodach na gcos mall.'**
["'You'll be soon enough," as the tramp with the slow feet said.']
County Mayo
Ó Máille 1952 No. 2926.

266

scaladh see *glór/Áidhbhirseoir (Maonus, bean, caora)*

scéal/cat
B 171.1 '"Is olc an sgéal é," ars an cat nuair cuireadh an bainne in san gcomhra uaidh.'
['"It's a sorry tale," *or* "That's bad news," said the cat when the milk was put away from him in the cupboard.']
South Connacht, probably County Galway, not before 1864
Royal Irish Academy mss, in a list, mainly of proverbs, as published in Ó Máille 1952 No. 3033.

scéal/cat see also *chonaic*

sean-chnáimh/dreoillín
B 172.1 'Mar dubhairt an dreoillín, nuair bhí sé fhéin 's a dhá'rdhéag mac a' bualadh coirce, "Is maith é an sean-chnáimh."'
['As the wren said when he and his twelve sons were threshing oats, "The old carcass is good."']
County Mayo *c.* 1900
Ó Máille 1948 No. 301 with the comment for all five variants there: ['The wren's offspring failed to pull a maggot out of the ground until the father came along'] and a ref. to the folktale in, for example, IFC 113:13–23 collected in 1935 in Connacht

.2 as .1
County Galway
Ó Máille 1948 No. 301. For his comment see **.1**

.3 'Mar dubhairt an dreoillín, "Mo cheol go deo an sean-chnáimh."'
['As the wren said, "Bless the old carcass!"']
Connacht
An Claidheamh Soluis, 7/11/1903 as cited in Ó Máille 1948 No. 301. For his comment see **.1**

.4 'Mar dubhairt an dreoillín, "Go neartuighidh Dia an sean-chnáimh!"'
['As the wren said, "God strengthen the old carcass!"']
County Galway
Ó Máille 1948 No. 301. For his comment see **.1**

.5 '"Is maith é an sean-chnáimh féin," mar dubhairt an dreoillín.'
['"Even the old carcass is good," as the wren said.']
County Galway
Ó Máille 1948 No. 301. For his comment see **.1**

cf the folktale *TIF* 232C* *Which Bird is Father?* [18 versions].

seasamh/fear
B 173.1 '"Seasamh fada ar chosa laga agat!" mar dubhairt an fear fadó.'
['"A long stand on weak legs to you!" as the man said long ago.']
Connacht
An Claidheamh Soluis, n.d., but not after 1918, as cited in Ó Máille 1948
No. 1557 with the comment: ['one of the worst things for the body']

.2 as .1
County Galway
Ó Máille 1948 No. 1557. For his comment see **.1**

Note: 'Seasamh fada ar chosa laga!' is a common curse, also known in English, see, for example, entries under Ó Máille *ibid.* Here he also cites a related proverb from Co. Galway: 'Ní féidir seasamh fada ar chosa laga' ['A long stand on weak legs is not possible'].

seo/píobaire
B 174.1 & .2 '"Ní hé seo ach é siúd," mar adubhairt an píobaire, "ach cá mbeidh muid san oidhche i mbárach?"'
['"It's not that, but this," as the piper said, "where'll we be this time tomorrow night?"']
both County Galway
Ó Máille 1948 No. 2156 with the comment: ['It's right to start work immediately and not to waste time. It is said that a group of people were getting ready for a certain occasion but they wasted much time talking and whispering until someone said the above'].

seo/tuata
B 175.1 '"Tá sé mar seo nú mar siúd," adeir an tuata tuisceanach.'
['"It's either this way or that," said the knowing country person.']
County Kerry

Almqvist *Collection of proverbs … ts*, collected by **BA** from **MÓG** between 1966 and 1974.

sgread/fiach dubh   Scots

B 176.1 '"Sgread maidne ar an gcúpla!" mar adubhairt an fiach dubh lena chrúba.'
['"Confound the pair of them!" as the raven said of his claws.']
County Sligo *c.* the end of the 19th century
Ó Máille 1948 No. 1286

DOW 1177

see also Part B 195.

siúlann/seanbhean

B 177.1 '"Is mairg ná siúlann," fé mar a dúirt an tseanbhean fadó nuair a thug sí a chéad turas amach go Dún Chaoin.'
['"It's a pity of those who don't travel," as the old woman said long ago on her first journey over [lit. out] to Dunquin.']
Dún Chaoin/Dunquin=the customary landing place on the mainland for the Blasket Islanders
County Kerry
Muiris Ó Súilleabháin *Fiche Blian ag Fás*, autobiography, 1933 Dublin, 1976 ed., Mac Tomais, Editor, p. 216. Context from Llewelyn Davies & Thomson's translation [O'Sullivan 1941]: 'We stopped at cross-roads near the castle [in Dublin] to wait for a bus. … There were many others like ourselves going to the pictures ... Isn't it a great pity entirely for the poor lads back in the Island with nothing for them to see or hear but the big rollers coming up through the sound and the rough noise of the wind blowing from the north-west across the hills, and often for four weeks without news from the mainland! Musha, woe to him who travels not, as the old woman said long ago on her first journey out to Dunquin. I felt a prod on my shoulder. "The bus is coming," said George.' [Thomson] Ch. 23 'The City of Dublin.' p. 298
cf Mieder & Tóthné Litovkina p. 217 [but no wellerism].

sliabh/bean

B 178.1 '"Ní sliabh an baile nach bhfuil cailín eile le fághail," mar dubhairt an bhean nuair a bhí a cailín ag imtheacht uaithi.'
['"? The town is not [like] a mountain where another maid can't be found," as the woman said when her maid left her.']

County Mayo
Ó Máille 1952 No. 3470 with the comment: ['if a servant girl departs another will be found'].

snáth/bean

B 179.1 'Mar adubhairt a' bhean leis a' gcailín sníomhacháin, "Tá an snáth dócra(ch) caol i n-áiteacha."'
['As the woman said to the girl spinner, "That thread is terribly thin in places."']
Ulster written *c.* 1830
Robert Mac Adam [1808–95] ms xxxi, or, same collector, on a loose leaf, Mac Adam-Bryson Collection, Belfast Central Library, as published by Ó Tuathail 1933b in 'A Northern Medley,' section 'XIV Sean-Ráidhte.' ['Old Sayings.'] p. 212 No. 30.

socair/gaoth
B 180.1 '"Fan socair!" arsan ghaoth.'
['"Keep calm!" said the wind.']
Munster
'An Seabhac' 1926 No. 821/1984 No. 986 with the comment: ['And it blowing its hardest!']

.2 '"Fan socair!" arsan ghaoth, "go gcuirfead mo chosa fúm."'
['"Keep calm!" said the wind, "until I put my legs under me."']
County Kerry
Almqvist *Collection of proverbs* … ts, collected by **BA** from **MÓG** between 1966 and 1974.

soirbhighe/*Bhaitear* Brídean
B 181.1 '"Go seacht soirbhighe Dia na rún duit," mar dubhairt Bháitear ([ie.] Walter) Brídean le n-a bhean nuair a bhí sí ag 'ul dá báthadh féin.'
['"God speed your intention sevenfold," as Walter Brídean said to his wife when she was going to drown herself.']
Ulster written *c.* 1830
Robert Mac Adam ms xxxi, or, same collector, on a loose leaf, Mac Adam-Bryson Collection, Belfast Central Library, as published by Ó Tuathail 1933b in 'A Northern Medley,' section 'XII Beannachta' ['Blessings'] p. 209 No. 20.

solas/bodach

B 182.1 '"Is mairg a d'ith cuid an tsolais!" mar dubhairt an bodach nuair bhí se ag 'ul go hIfreann.'
['"Woe to the one who ate the money for the light!" as the churl said when he was going to hell.']
County Galway
Ó Máille 1952 No. 3826 with the comment: ['There is no comfort in a house without light and it is not right to spend the money for tallow on anything else']

cf 'Is mairg a duaith cuid an tsolais, it is a mistake to eat the material for light (i.e., tallow, of uneconomical acts)' Dinneen under 'solas'; there are also several versions of this proverb in Ó Máille *ibid.*

sólás/mongcaidhe   Part A 233
B 183.1 & .2 '"Níl aon tsólás ná go leanann a dhólás féin é," fé mar dubhairt an mongcaidhe nuair a thug sé póg do'n ghrainneóig (do'n ngrainneoig).'
['"There's no joy without its sorrow," as the monkey said when he kissed the hedgehog.']
Ó Dálaigh 'Common Noun' *Clocha Sgáil* 1939 Dublin pp. 126–27 and p. 137, ref. via Almqvist *Collection of Proverbs … ts*

cf the riddle 'Cad dúirt an <u>ass</u> leis an ngráineóig fudó nuair a phóg sé sa tor í? Mhuise, níl aon tsólás gan a dhólas féinig.' ['What did the ass say to the hedgehog long ago when he kissed her in the bush? Well, there's no joy without its sorrow.'] Almqvist *Collection of Proverbs … ts* Collected by **BA** from **MÓG** between 1966 and 1974

Notes: Ó Dálaigh was **SÓD**'s father.
The proverb 'Níl aon tsólás ná go leanann a dhólás féin é' is common in Irish.

stracaigh (straicaidh, tarraingí)/fear
B 184.1 '"Stracaigh ó chéile é!" arsa fear láir a' tsúsa.'
['"Pull it asunder!" said the man in the middle of the blanket.']
Irisleabhar na Gaedhilge, 6, No. 4 (OS 64) (1 July 1895), in a list of set phrases etc., titled 'Thall 's i bhfus' complied by E[ugene] O'G[rowney] pp. 59–60, p. 60: '"Pull it asunder," said (ironically) the man in the middle of the blanket (to those on either side of him)'

.2 '"Stracaidh ó chéile é!" arsa fear lár an tsúsa.'

An Connacht, Oct. 1907 as cited in Ó Máille 1952 No. 2704 with the following, which also applies to .4: ['He himself would be sure of being covered as long as the two others were pulling].' Ó Máille adds that folklore attached to this can be traced back to the poet Tadhg Dall Ó hUiginn [1550–91] *Filíocht Thaighd Dhaill*, II 282 (notes)

.3 '"Tarraingidh ó chéile é!" arsa fear láir an tsúsa.'
['"Pull it away from each other!" said the man in the middle of the blanket.']
Munster
'An Seabhac' 1926 No. 818/1984 No. 983 with the comment: ['Three were in one bed and the blanket wasn't wide enough and the two on the outside were pulling it away from each other. This didn't matter to the man in the middle. It is said of things besides a blanket']. The 1984 ed. has, in addition: ['... until they tore it. Then he himself was left bereft']

.4 '"Tarraingigí ó chéile é!" arsa fear lár na leabtha.'
County Galway
Ó Máille 1952 No. 2704. For his comment see **.2**

see also Part B 157.

suig/bean an doihil
B 185.1 '"Suig má shuíon tú, ach is dócha ná suífir, mar bíon deabhadh er do leithéid chuíhe," ersa bean an doihil fudó.'
['"Sit, if you wish to sit, but I suppose you won't, for people like you are always in a hurry," said the inhospitable woman long ago.']
County Kerry
Almqvist *Collection of proverbs* ... ts, collected by **BA** from **MÓG** between 1966 and 1974

cf '"Suig, ó is dócha ná suífir, ith greimm ó is dócha ná híosfair, dá mbein-se aiget thíg-se, fé mar taoi-se aigem thig-se, ní stadfain don ruith sin go raghaim im' thig féin' ['Sit, as it is certain you won't, eat your share as it is certain you won't, if I were at your house as you are at my house I wouldn't cease running until I got to my own house']. Almqvist *Collection of Proverbs* ... ts, collected in Co. Kerry by **BA** from **SÓD**.

T

tarraingidh & tarraingigí see *stracaigh*

272

teannam/Bás
B 186.1 '"Teannam ort," ars' an bás le Síle.'
['"Come along," said Death to Síle.']
County Cork
Irisleabhar na Gaedhilge, 6, No. 6 (OS 66) (1 Sept. 1895), in a list titled 'Proverbs (Continued). From D. J. Galvin+, Glashakinleen, N[ational] S[chool], Newmarket,' pp. 90–91, No. 33, p. 90. Galvin's list begins in Vol. 6, No. 4, (OS 64) p. 60 and is in four parts with three wellerisms in all [this and Part B 11.1 & 46.1]

.2 as .1
Munster
'An Seabhac' 1926 No. 811/1984 No. 976 with the comment: ['An invitation that can't be refused']

see also Part B 7.

teach/fear   Part A 134
B 187.1 '"Is fearr teach folamh nó droch thionanntaí," ars an fear nuair a lig sé brim.'
['"An empty house is better than a bad tenant," said the man when he broke wind.']
County Donegal
IFCS 1072:102 in a list, mainly of proverbs, with a comment by the teacher, PMacC m, to the effect that the majority were collected twenty years ago, ie. *c.* 1918, in Na Rosa/The Rosses and the remainder from the same place over the past 20 years

Note: the proverb '"Is fearr teach folamh nó droch thionanntaí," is fairly common in Irish and English.

teagasc/seandaoine   Dan, Bel &/or Dut, Fin, Swe & *cf E Eng
B 188.1 '"Lean a dteagasc ach ná bac lena mbealach," a déaradh na seandaoine i dtaobh na sagart.'
['"Follow their teaching but don't bother with their ways," said the old people about the priests.']
County Galway
IFC 1833:76 [vol. and page no. as given in DIF card index, however, there is no wellerism on this page] collector **CB** 1973

*cf E Eng '"Do as I say and not as I do," as the parson said when they wheeled him home in a wheelbarrow.' *DOW* 317

Mieder & Tóthné Litovkina pp. 174–75.

t(e)ine/sionnach (madarua) Part A 83

B 189.1 '"Nuair a lasfas tú déanfaidh tú teine," ars an sionnach nuair chac sé ar an sneachta.'

['"When you light up you'll make a fire," said the fox when he defecated on the snow.']
County Mayo
Ó Máille 1952 No. 5000 with the comment: [[?said of] 'a bad fire or a fire that won't light']

.2 '"Beidh tine anseo ar ball," mar a duirt an madarua nuair a mhún sé ar an gcarraig.'

['"We'll have a fire here yet," as the fox said when he urinated on the rock.']
County Cork
Q 2000 i DÓM m 60s in a letter 14/2/2000: 'I remember one from my father S, who was from Ballyvourney in West Cork. Reading of some T.D. blathering on about some grandiose scheme, he'd say: Beidh tine anseo ... ar an gcarraig.'

tigh an diail/Diarmaid na Bolagaí

B 190.1 '"Is a' dol ó thig an diail go tig an deamhain dhom é," ersa Diarmaid na Bolagaí fudó.'

['"It's [a case of] going from the devil's house to the demon's house for me," said Diarmaid na Bolagaí long ago.']
County Kerry
Almqvist *Collection of Proverbs* ... ts, collected by **BA** from **MÓG** between 1966 and 1974, with the comment: '**M[ÓG]** relates the saying to a story about how D. na B. was refused lodging [on] a stormy night. Essentially the same story is found in SB [Jackson 1938 'Aoir an Tailliúir' *Scéalta ón mBlascaod* No. 38, pp. 81–83 & Note p. 93], though the satirical poem about the inhospitable house is not there ascribed to D. na B.'

.2 '"Ag dul ó thigh an diabhail go tigh an deamhain dom é," fe mar dúirt Diarmaid na Bolagaí fadó, nuair a cuireadh amach sa ghleann é.'

['Going from the devil's house to the demon's house for me," as Diarmaid na Bolagaí said long ago, when he was put out into the glen [= valley].']
County Kerry

Ó Gaoithín *Beatha Pheig Sayers*, biography of his mother, 1970 Dublin p. 52: '"… agus más ag dul ó thigh an diabhail go tigh an deamhain dom é, fe mar dúirt Diarmaid na Bolagaí fadó, nuair a cuireadh amach sa ghleann é' ['and if it is going from the devil's house to the demon's house for me, as Diarmaid na Bolagaí said long ago, when he was put out into the glen']; Peig describes how the wind had destroyed the roof of his house, which had been in poor shape anyway

Note: Diarmaid 'na Bolagaí' Ó Sé [*c.* 1760–1846] was a Kerry folk poet see Ó Súilleabháin 1937 *Diarmuid na Bolgaighe agus a Chomharsain* and Ó hÓgáin 1982 *An File*.

tine see *t(e)ine*

tiompán/ceoltóir

B 191.1 '"Is mairg dhóighfeadh a thiompán leat," mar adubhairt an ceoltóir le n-a bhean.'

['"It's a pity of the one who would burn his tiompán for you," as the musician said to his wife.']
Munster
'An Seabhac' 1926 No. 839/1984 No. 1005 with the following story which is summarised here: A tiompán player and his wife were crossing a hill on their way to a fair when they were caught by bad weather. The woman was dying of cold so the man saved his wife by breaking up and burning his tiompán. At the fair the man was unable to earn any money and when his wife began to complain about this he said the above and left her

cf 'Is mairg loiscfeadh a thiompán leat, only a fool would sacrifice himself for you (said by a tympanum-player to his wife who grumbled after he had burnt it to warm her)' Dinneen under 'tiompán'

cf 'Is mairg a loiscfeadh a thiompán leis, it would be a pity to waste one's last resource on it' Ó Dónaill under 'tiompán'

cf 'A well-known Scottish proverb runs "Mairg do loisgfeadh a thiompán leat." … The story goes that a harper once, having nothing to make a fire with, burned his harp in order to make a fire for his wife who was benumbed with cold; but she repaid his sacrifice immediately afterwards by eloping with another man cf Nicolson p. 267. This proverb was formerly well-known in Ireland too ---' O'Rahilly 1922 under No. 341

Notes: **MÓG** knew [?of] a poem with this story, p.c. from **BA** 1987. The musician Derek Bell recreated the obsolete tiompán on the lines of the dulcimer.

tobac/fear
B 192.1 '"An te nach fuil tobac aige cacadh sé ina phíp!" arsa an fear ná raibh aon easpa air féin.'
['"He who hasn't tobacco will have to defecate in his pipe!" said the man who wasn't short of anything himself.']
Munster
'An Seabhac' 1984 No. 974.

tobac/madaruadh
B 193.1 '"Tobac!" arsan madaruadh is é 'Tráigh Mhór soir.'
['"Tobacco!" said the fox when he was heading east to Tráigh Mhór.']
Munster
'An Seabhac' 1926 No. 826/1984 No. 991 with the comment: ['When a person or thing is moving fast this is said of him/it'].

torann see *glór/Áidhbhirseoir (Maonus, bean, caora)*

tosnú/bithiúnach   Am Eng, Bel &/or Dut, Ger
B 194.1 '"Bíonn gach aon tosnú lag," mar aduairt an bithiúnach nuair a thosnaigh sé ar an inneoin a ghoid ón ngabha.'
['"Every single beginning is difficult," as the criminal said when he started to steal the anvil from the blacksmith.']
County Cork
IFC 43:237 in a list, mainly of proverbs, written *c.* 1933

DOW 69 & 70
Note: the proverb 'Bíonn gach aon tosnú lag' is very common in Irish and is mirrored in English in the form 'Every beginning is weak.'

tubaiste/gabhar   Scots
B 195.1 '"Tuilleadh tubaiste chughaibh!" ar san gabhar le n-a chosaibh.'
['"More bad luck to you," said the goat to his legs.']
Dinneen 1934 ed., 1970 rpt. under 'tubaiste' which it is used to illustrate

DOW 1176
see also Part B 176.

276

U

uan/ministir
B 196.1 '"Uan dubh ag cuíora bhán agus uan bán ag cuíora dhubh, a dhritháireacha," a ndúirt an ministir fudó, "nach múr an t-iúntas é sin?"'
['"A white sheep having a black lamb and a black sheep having a white lamb, bretheren," said the minister long ago, "isn't that a great wonder?"']
County Kerry
Almqvist *Collection of proverbs* ... ts, collected by **BA** from **MÓG** between 1966 and 1974

cf 'O the wonderful Works of Nature! that a black Hen should have a white egg.' Swift ... *Polite Conversation* ... 1738, 1963 ed., p. 83, spoken by the colonel.

urchóid/fear
B 197.1 '"Is caol a thig an urchóid," ars' an fear a raibh an gander ag siubhal air.'
['"Misfortune comes from small things," said the man on whom the gander was walking.']
County Monaghan
Irisleabhar na Gaedhilge, 8, No. 95 (Mar. 1898), in a list titled 'Farney (Co. Monaghan) Proverbs and Sayings.' pp. 177–80, signed Eanraoi Ua Muirgheasa, item No. 8, p. 177/translation p. 179. Cited in Ua Muirgheasa 1907 No. 1356/1976 No. 1599.

W

water/Sasanach
B 198.1 '"More water!" arsan Sasanach agus é á bháthadh.'
['"More water!" said the English person when he was drowning.']
Munster
'An Seabhac' 1926 No. 806/1984 No. 969

.2 as .1
County Cork
IFC 43:249 collected in 1921 by CNíL+ who wrote down the list, mainly of proverbs, *c.* 1933

.3 & .4 '"More water!" ars an Sasanach 's é dhá bháthadh.'
both County Galway
Ó Máille 1952 No. 3704 and *An Stoc* undated citation, but not later than 1932, in Ó Máille *ibid.* with the comment: ['the Sasanach is impossible to satisfy']

.5 '"More water!" arsan Sasanach agus é báth.'
['"More water!" said the Protestant when he was drowning.']
County Kerry
Flower *The Western Isle, or the Great Blasket.* 1944 Oxford, 1978 ed.: 'As I went [crawling in fear back along a sheep track above a cliff], I remembered the story of the Skelligs [other steep-sided islands]. From the side of the Great Skellig a point of rock juts out over the sea, with the mark of a cross inscribed on its extremity. It is a piece of devotion to crawl out along this rock and kiss the cross. An Englishman, they say, once attempted this feat in mockery of the people's devotion. But the vengeance of Heaven overtook him halfway, and, slipping on the rock, he went down into the sea. There used to be a proverb on the opposite mainland: '"More water!" arsan Sasanach agus é báth' — '"More water!" cried the drowning Protestant' — and the interpretation of this was that he took so long in falling through the air that he prayed to the water to hasten to meet him and end his misery. Thinking fearfully of this I, lately come from London, prayed to all that was Irish in me to save all that was Irish from that horrible descent, and my prayer was heard.' Ch. titled 'The Sorrowful Slope' p. 73.

ABBREVIATIONS & SYMBOLS

LANGUAGES

Am Eng=the English of the United States of America
Aus Eng=the English of Australia
Bel=Belgic [Fyvie Mayo's description]
E Eng=the English of England
Can Eng=the English of Canada
Dan=Danish
Dut=Dutch
E=English
E Ara=the Arabic of Egypt
E Eng=the English of England
Est=Estonian
Fin=Finnish
Fri=Frisian
Geo=Georgian
Ger=German
Gr=Modern Greek
Hun=Hungarian
Ind Eng=the English of India
Ir=Irish
Lat=Latvian
Lit=Lithuanian
M Ara=the Arabic of Morocco
Nor=Norwegian
NZ Eng=the English of New Zealand
Pol=Polish
Rus=Russian
Sc Gae=Scottish Gaelic
Sp=Spanish
Wel=Welsh

OTHER

Acadamh Ríoga na hÉireann=Royal Irish Academy.
Addenda='Welleristic Addenda ... ,' *see* 'Bibliography, Reference
  Works, Mieder 1997.
AT=*The Types of the Folktale* see Bibliography, Sources, Aarne &
  Thompson
Aug.=August
b.=born

b. & r.=born and reared

Bean=with a person's initials indicates a married woman

Byers Papers=Byers Papers, Ulster Dialect Archive, National
Museums & Galleries of Northern Ireland, Ulster Folk and
Transport Museum.

c.=about

C=questionnaire correspondent

Ch.=chapter

cited in=this version is cited in the location named.

Co=Company

Co.=County

COED=The Compact Edition of the Oxford English Dictionary
see Bibliography, Reference Works, The Compact ...

Cont'd=Continued

d.=died

Dec.=December

Def. and def.=definition

DIF=The Department of Irish Folklore, University College
Dublin, The National University of Ireland.

DOW=Dictionary of Wellerisms see Bibliography, Reference
Works Mieder & Kingsbury.

E & Ir=both English-language and Irish-language wellerisms
received from that contributor.

ed.=edition

EKM=Eesti Kirjadusmuuseum [Estonian Literary Museum].

ERA=Eesti Rahvaluule Arhiiv [Estonian Folklore Archives].

f=female

f+=female from whom there is more than one wellerism.

fac.=facsimile

Feb.=February

ff=and following pages

GB=Great Britain, ie. England, Scotland and Wales.

(H)=the collection, begun 1880, of Henry Chichester Hart (1847–
1908), included in Traynor see Bibliography, Sources.

i=informant

IFC=Irish Folklore Collection Main Manuscript, DIF.

IFCS=Irish Folklore Collection School Manuscript, DIF.

Jan.=January

lit.=literally

LTR= Lietuviu Tautosakos Rankra_tynas/Lithuanian Folklore
Archive, Institute of Lithuanian Literature & Folklore.

m=male

m+=male from whom there is more than one wellerism.

MI=Motif Index see Bibliography, Sources, Thompson
ms(s)=manuscript(s)
n.a.=not after
n.d.=no date
n.p.=no pagination
Ní in a person's initials indicates a female, as do 'uí' and 'Uí,' with
the exception of Part B 36.3.
NMGNI=National Museums & Galleries of Northern Ireland.
No(s).=Number(s)
Nov.=November
Oct.=October
OS=Old Series
p.=page
p.c.=personal communication
pp.=pages
Phr. and phr.=phrase
Pt.=Part
pub.=publication
published=first time in print for that version.
Q 1973=Questionnaire 1973 — returns until 1978.
Q 1973(74)=Questionnaire 1973, returned in 1974, and so on.
Q 2000=Questionnaire 2000, used from Jan. 2000 for almost two years.
Q 2000(01)=Questionnaire 2000, returned in 2001, and so on.
QUA=Queen's University of Belfast, Armagh Campus.
QUB=Queen's University of Belfast.
ref.=reference
ref. via=alerted to ref. by the source mentioned and then the
original was consulted.
ref. at=ref. as cited by the source mentioned is used rather than the
original.
Rev.=Reverend
RIA=Royal Irish Academy
RKM=folklore collection of the Folklore Department of the State
Literary Museum, Tartu, mostly 1945–95.
rpt.=reprint
RTE and RTÉ=Raidió Teilifís Éireann.
'S & P'='Sayings and Proverbs.'
Sept.=September
Taoiseach=leader of Dáil Éireann, the parliament of the Republic
of Ireland.
T.D.=Teachta Dála, political representative in Dáil Éireann, the
parliament of the Republic of Ireland.
TIF=The Types of the Irish Folktale see Bibliography, Sources,

Ó Súilleabháin & Christiansen.
ts=typescript
Ua in a person's initials indicates a male.
UFTM=National Museums & Galleries of Northern Ireland, Ulster
Folk and Transport Museum.
uí or Uí in a person's initials, with the exception of Part B 36.3,
indicate a female, as does 'Ní.'
USA=United States of America.
UU=University of Ulster, York Street Campus, Belfast.
voc.=vocative case

+ indicates that there was more than one wellerism from that
Correspondent or from that informant

(rann) informant's word(s), that is, a word or words in bold in round
brackets.
[rann] editor's word(s), that is, a word or words not in bold in square
brackets.

Where contexts are quoted only the page number containing the
wellerism is given, although the quotation may extend to the previous or
next page.

APPENDIX 1

Q 1973 Below is the questionnaire circulated in 1973 by the Department of Irish Folklore. This was bilingual with English on one side and Irish on the other side of a single sheet. The same wording exactly, including the same examples of wellerisms, was used in both languages.

UNIVERSITY COLLEGE DUBLIN
DEPARTMENT OF IRISH FOLKLORE

WELLERISMS

Proverbs and pithy sayings contain the accumulated wit and wisdom of the ordinary folk. They are thus of the greatest interest to the folklorist. A special type of proverb — much discussed in international scholarship, but rather neglected in Ireland — is the so-called quotation proverb or wellerism. The term wellerism is derived from Sam Weller in Dickens' Pickwick Papers [*sic*], who was in the habit of scattering such proverbs around. As the term implies these 'quotation proverbs' are made up of remarks ascribed to certain personages:

"I see," said the blind man.

"Again to it," said the bull to the butcher.

Sometimes wellerisms parody ordinary proverbs:

"Everyone to his taste," said the farmer when he kissed the cow.

"There is no luck where there is no discipline," said the son when he was beating his father.

As the popularity of the wellerism may vary considerably from place to place the collector should not be discouraged if he finds but few examples. Even a couple may be of great value in determining the distribution of the wellerism and how it spread.

In making enquiries it may be helpful to ask for sayings attributed to certain characters. The following is a list of 'speakers' known to have had such sayings attributed to them:

Named persons, varying from locality to locality;

The man, the old man, the good man, the boy;

The baker, the farmer, the miller, the smith, the tailor and other craftsmen;

The bull, the fox, the lamb, the monkey, the crab, the heron, the wren and other animals and birds.

We would be grateful if you would write down any wellerisms you find about these and other personages.

If possible state where and when you, or your informant, heard them and give examples of how they are used.

*****

Q 2000 Below is the questionnaire circulated by FCW from Jan. 2000 for almost two years. At the start of this period a version on which these and five more examples were included was used.

An interesting kind of proverb which circulates orally and is also found in literature is the quotation proverb, such as:

'"I see," says the blind man.
"You're a liar," says the beggar'

and

'"I saw you before," as the cat said to the boiling milk,'

meaning that a wise person is not deceived twice.
Sometimes the circumstances are added, making it comical, as in the following:

'"That'll be the end of it," as the monkey said when the train ran over his tail'.

Others found are '"**More haste, less speed,**" as the tailor said to the long thread' and '"**Great cry and little wool,**" as the devil said when he was shaving the pig'.

While this type plays an important part in speech and literature — James Joyce, Dean Swift and Samuel Lover, not to mention Charles Dickens, particularly in his character Sam Weller, often included them — few have been recorded locally and I would like to invite you to send me any that you **use** or have **heard** or **read**. Please include the examples above if you know them too.

....

....

....

....

....

Contributor:

Please give any details possible such as **when** (eg. 1990s, or by my father) and **where** (eg. in a shop in Comber) the proverbs were used, or, if from a book, the book's title.

Sheets can be returned to   or direct to me:

Fionnuala Carson Williams, The Institute of Irish Studies, 8 Fitzwilliam Street, The Queen's University of Belfast, BT 9 6 AW, email: fionnuala.williams@qub.ac.uk

APPENDIX 2

Below are transcripts of radio broadcasts. The five wellerisms that were broadcast, along with four of the others that the programme received by email and letter were forwarded in an email list to me on 17/1/2002 by the show's researcher. The researcher's email variants are used in the catalogue for the four that the presenter John Creedon broadcast in slightly different ways, cf Part A 8.1, 46.1, 67.1 & 249.1.

'Eh, Fionnuala, Fionnuala was on to us — Fionnuala Carson Williams isn't it? She was on to us about wellerisms. She is er, compiling a book of wellerisms. She's almost there. She wanted a handful more and we invited you to help her out and you did, in huge numbers — and they're awful. They're god-awful. They really are awful, these wellerisms. Em, these are the best two: "'See you at the corner,' as one wall said to the other." I don't see anyone falling around the place holding their sides at that one. Or here's another one from H. in Walkinstown "'You go on ahead, I'll hang around,' as the scarf said to the hat." I think I'm about to have one of my dizzy spells.'

Break for advertisements

From 'The John Creedon Show' RTÉ Radio 1 Wednesday 16th January 2002.

'You might remember Fionnuala Carson Williams was on to us yesterday. She's compiling a book of wellerisms. Those little, eh, clichés I suppose is what they are really. You know the format — when somebody says something and then they, they, they, they eh, they respond "as so and so said to so-and-so." Look, I'll put it to you this way, a letter arrived on my desk today, a sealed envelope and written on the cover was "'Drilling is a bit boring,' said the woodwork teacher to the class" and then in brackets "and there's worse inside." And, sure enough, I opened it and he's right. There's worse inside. It's a note from PJ — he's a stack of them for us like "'You're in for a long wait,' as the train said to the bridge," and DK in Dublin said, well he emailed me this morning, and D. said "Good luck with the show today, John, remember "'We'll all be rooting for you," as the seedling said to the nurseryman.'" Will you stop?'

From 'The John Creedon Show' RTÉ Radio 1 Thursday 17th January 2002.

BIBLIOGRAPHY

Baile Átha Cliath/Dublin; Corcaigh/Cork.

SOURCES

NON-PRINTED

Bo Almqvist. *Collection of proverbs from Mícheál Ó Gaoithín, Dunquin, (formerly Great Blasket), Co. Kerry, undertaken between 1966 and 1974*, annotated typescript. Copy in The Department of Irish Folklore, University College Dublin.

— *Irish Wellerisms* 1973– [*c*. 1994]. File, at present with FCW.

Armagh Miscellanea see *Paterson*

Byers Papers, especially 'Sayings and Proverbs.' Box T4 typescript T-4-6, Ulster Dialect Archive, NMGNI, Ulster Folk and Transport Museum.

Electronic Database, Ulster Dialect Archive, NMGNI, Ulster Folk and Transport Museum.

Main Manuscript Collection, Department of Irish Folklore, University College Dublin, IFC 1888, IFC 1911, IFC 1917, IFC 2027 and IFC 2154:279 which contain the responses to Questionnaire 1973, and other selected pages.

Ciarán Ó Duibhín. 2002 *Tobar na Gaedhilge.* http://www.smo.uhi.ac.uk/~oduibhin/tobar/

Domhnall Ó Lubhlaí. 1976 *Múineadh Labhairt na Gaeilge gColáistí Samhraidh*. Desktop publication.

T. G. F. Paterson. 1920s– *Armagh Miscellanea*. Vols. I–XXV [except XIX, which is not in the museum] T. G. F. Paterson's typescripts of his notebooks. NMGNI, Armagh County Museum.

Schools' Collection, Department of Irish Folklore, University College Dublin, 1938–39 (IFCS), manuscripts for counties Cavan, Donegal, Dublin, Galway, Kildare, Monaghan, Leitrim, Louth, Sligo, Wexford and Wicklow.

Ulster Folk and Transport Museum Notebook 1959, National Museums & Galleries of Northern Ireland, UFTM.

PRINTED

'A Real Paddy' [Pierce Egan]. [1829] *Real Life in Ireland: The Day and Night Scenes, Roving, Rambles, and Sprees, Bulls, Blunders, Bodderation, and Blarney* or *Brian Boru, Esq., and his elegant*

288

friend Sir Shawn Dogherty Exhibiting a Real Picture of characters, manners Etc., in High and Low Life in Dublin and various parts of Ireland. London: William Evans & Co.

'ac Grianna *see* 'Máire'

'An Seabhac' [Padraig Ó Siochfhradha], Collector & Editor. 1926 *Seanfhocail na Muimhneach.* Corcaigh: no publisher given. Also New ed., 1984 Pádraig Ua Maoileoin, Compiler & Editor *Seanfhocail na Mumhan.* Dublin: An Gúm.

Anon. 1913 *National Proverbs: Ireland.* London: Frank Palmer.

Brendan Behan. 1980 ed. *Borstal Boy.* London: Corgi.

— 1962 *Brendan Behan's Island: an Irish Sketch-book.* London: Corgi.

— 1978 *The Complete Plays The Quare Fellow, The Hostage* ... introduced by Alan Simpson. London: Eyre Methuen.

Francis Joseph Bigger. 1926 'Canon Abraham Hume Famous Hillsborough Scholar, Cleric and Antiquary.' *Belfast News-letter* 3/8/1926, p. 5.

Rev. John Boyce, D[octor of] D[ivinity]. 1853 *Shandy M'guire; Or Tricks Upon Travellers, Being a Story of the North of Ireland.* Boston: Patrick Donahoe.

William Carleton. 1833 *Traits and Stories of the Irish Peasantry. Second Series.* Vol. I. Dublin: William Frederick Wakeman.

Selwyn Gurney Champion. 1938 *Racial Proverbs: A Selection of the World's Proverbs arranged Linguistically.* London: George Routledge & Sons, Limited.

Cloughherney Presbyterian Church Quotation Calendar 1945. n.d. [?1944] ?Privately published and ?locally printed.

Eric Cross. 1970 ed. *The Tailor and Ansty. With an Introduction by Frank O'Connor and a Postscript giving the Tailor's views on the banning of this book.* Cork: Mercier.

Tomás de Bhaldraithe, Editor. 1959 *English-Irish Dictionary.* Baile Átha Cliath: Oifig an tSoláthair.

Seán de Búrca. 1958 *The Irish of Tourmakeady, Co. Mayo. A Phonetic Study.* Dublin: Dublin Institute for Advanced Studies.

Rev. Patrick S. Dinneen, Compiler & Editor. 1970 rpt. of 1934 ed. *Fóclóir Gaedhilge agus Béarla/An Irish-English Dictionary ... Modern Irish Language.* Dublin: The Irish Texts Society.

Egan *see* 'A Real Paddy'

Robin Flower. 1944, 1978 rpt. *The Western Island, or the Great Blasket.* Oxford *et al*: Oxford University Press.

— 1957 [1959] 'Measgra ón Oileán Tiar.' *Béaloideas*, 25, 92–97.

Isa Fyvie Mayo, Compiler. n.d. [early 20th century] *Old Stories & Sayings of Great Britain & Ireland* No. 1 in a series of 6 *Old Stories and Sayings from Many Lands.* London: C. W. Daniel.

Gaelic Journal see *Irisleabhair na Gaedhilge*

Henry Glassie. 1982 *Passing the Time, Folklore and History of an Ulster Community.* Dublin: The O'Brien Press.

Oliver St John Gogarty. 1982 ed. *Rolling down the Lea: a pageant of legendary Irish people and places.* London: Sphere Books Ltd.

'H' 1854 'Rustic Proverbs Current in Ulster.' *Ulster Journal of Archaeology*, 2, 126–29.

Christopher Holinshed. 1979 ed. *Holinshed's Irish Chronicle The Historie of Irelande from the first inhabitation thereof, vnto the yeare 1509.* Collected by Raphaell Holinshed, & continued till the yeare 1547 by Richarde Stanyhurst 1577. Dublin: Dolmen Editions 28; North America: Humanities Press Inc.

Hume *see* 'M'Cart'

Irisleabhair na Gaedhilge/The Gaelic Journal, 1882–1909, initially fortnightly, later monthly, all lists of proverbs.

James Joyce. 1989 rpt. of 1986 ed. *Ulysses.* Hans Walter Gabler, Editor, with Wolfhard Steppe & Claus Melchior, and with a new Preface by Richard Ellmann. London: The Bodley Head.

Patrick Weston Joyce. 1988 rpt. of 1979 ed. *English as we speak it in Ireland.* With Introduction by Terence Dolan. Dublin: Wolfhound Press.

Alice Kane. 1983 *Songs and Sayings of an Ulster Childhood.* Edith Fowke, Editor. Dublin: Wolfhound.

Patrick Kennedy, Editor. 1891 ed. *The Book of Modern Irish Anecdotes, Humour, Wit and Wisdom.* Dublin: M. H. Gill & Son.

Maggi Kerr Peirce. 1983 ed. *Keep the kettle boiling, Rhymes from a Belfast Childhood.* Belfast: Appletree Press.

Seosamh Laoide 'Mac Tíre na Páirce,' Collector. 1915 *Tonn Tóime Tiomargadh sean-phisreog, sean-rócán, sean-sgéal, sean-cheist, sean-naitheann, sean-fhocal agus sean-ráth ó Chiarraighe Luachra.* Baile Átha Cliath: Clódhanna, Teo.

Vincent Stuckley Lean. 1969 fac. of 1903 & 1904 vols. *Lean's Collectanea.* Vol. II, Pt. 2 & Vol. IV. Detroit: Gale Research Company.

Samuel Lover. 1831. *Stories and Legends of Ireland.* Etchings by the author. Dublin: W. F. Wakeman; London: Baldwin and Cradock; Edinburgh: Oliver and Boyd. Also [?2nd Series] n.d. New Edition. London & New York: Ward, Lock & Co.

— 1844 *Treasure Trove: The First of a Series of Accounts of Irish Heirs: Being a Romantic Irish Tale of the Last Century.* London: Frederick Lover.

— 1898 ed. *Rory O'More: A National Romance.* D. J. O'Donoghue, Editor. Westminster: Archibald Constable & Co.

— n.d. *Handy Andy: A Tale of Irish Life.* 'Cheap illustrated edition' Charing Cross: W. S. Johnson.

Leaslaoi U. Lúcás. 1986 *Cnuasach Focal as Ros Goill. Deascan Foclóireachta 5.* Tomás de Bhaldraithe, General Editor. Baile Átha Cliath: Acadamh Ríoga na hÉireann.

Robert Mac Adam. 1861–62 'Six Hundred Gaelic Proverbs Collected in Ulster.' [final part] *Ulster Journal of Archaeology*, 9, 223–36.

C. I. Macafee, Editor. 1996 *A Concise Ulster Dictionary.* Oxford: Oxford University Press.

'Billy M'Cart' [Abraham Hume]. n.d. [1860 or 61] *Poor Rabbin's Ollminick for the town o' Bilfwast, 1861 containing various different things 'at ivvery body ought t' be acquentit with, wrote down, prentet, an' put out, jist the way the people spakes, by Billy M'Cart of the County Down side that uset to be but: now of the Entherim road, toarst the Cave hill.* Belfast: John Henderson; Dublin: McGlashan & Gill *et al.* Also for the following two years with '1862' & '1863' in the title and published respectively in 1861 or 62 & 1862 or 63.

Liam Mac Con Iomaire with Bill Doyle, Photographer. 1988 *Ireland of the Proverb.* Dublin: Town House.

E. J. M'Kean. 1930 'Ulster Proverbs.' *The Irish Naturalists' Journal*, 3 (Mar.), 42–44.

Joseph McKieran. n.d. [not earlier than 2000] *By Claddagh's Banks, A History of Swanlinbar and District from earliest times.* ?Privately published and ?locally printed.

Seumas MacManus. 1950 *Heavy Hangs the Golden Bough.* New York: Macmillan.

Seaghán Mhac Meanman. 1931 *Fear Siubhail.* Baile Átha Cliath: Oifig Díolta Foillseacháin Rialtas.

— 1955 *Crathadh an Phocain.* Baile Átha Cliath: Oifig an tSoláthair.

— 1955 *Rácáil agus Scuabadh.* Baile Átha Cliath: Oifig an tSoláthair.

James Allan Mair, Editor. n.d. [late 19th century] *A Handbook of Proverbs: English, Scottish, Irish, American, Shaksperean [sic], and Scriptural; and Family Mottoes, ...* London: George Routledge And Sons.

'Máire' [Séamas 'ac Grianna]. [1926] *Cioth is Dealán.* Dún Dealgain: Preas Dhún Dealgain.

— [1945] *Saoghal Corrach.* Baile Átha Cliath: An Press Náisiúnta.

— 1948 *An Teach nár Tógadh.* Baile Átha Cliath: Oifig an tSoláthair.

— 1967 *Le Clap-Sholus.* Baile Átha Cliath: Oifig an tSoláthair.

John J. Marshall. 1931 ed. *Popular Rhymes and Sayings of Ireland.* Dungannon: Tyrone Printing Company.

Llewelyn Davies *see* O'Sullivan

Lyons Marshall *see* 'Tullyneil'

Henry Morris. 1918 'Some Ulster Proverbs.' *County Louth Archaeological Journal*, 4, No. 3, 258–72.

see also Ua Muirgheasa.

Michael J. Murphy. 1975 *Now You're Talking, Folktales from the north of Ireland.* Belfast: Blackstaff Press.

— 1990 *Sayings and Stories from Slieve Gullion, Ireland's Most Mysterious Mountain.* Dundalk: Dundalgan Press.

Seamus Murphy. 1966, 1977 rpt. *Stone Mad.* London & Henley: Routledge & Keegan Paul.

'Myles na Gopaleen' *see* 'Flann O'Brien'

'Flann O'Brien' ('Myles na Gopaleen') [Brian O'Nolan]. 1976, 1988 reissue *Further cuttings from Cruiskeen Lawn.* Edited and Prefaced by Kevin O'Nolan. London *et al*: Grafton Books.

'Flann O'Brien' [Brian O'Nolan]. 1968 *The Best of Myles.* Edited and Prefaced by Kevin O'Nolan. London: MacGibbon & Kee.

— 1993 ed. *The Dalkey Archive.* London: Flamingo.

Tomás Ó Croimhthain. 1929 *An tOileanach: sceal a bheathadh féin.* 'An Seabhac,' Editor. Baile Átha Cliath: Ó Fallamhain i gcomhair le hOifig an tSoláthair. For English translation *see* Ó Crohan in 'Reference Works.'

Seán Ó Cróinín, Collector, Donnacha Ó Cróinín, Editor. 1980 *Seanchas Amhlaoibh Í Luínse.* Baile Átha Cliath: Comhairle Bhéaloideas Éireann.

Seán Ó Dálaigh 'Common Noun.' 1939 *Clocha Sgáil.* Baile Átha Cliath: C. S. Ó Fallamhain Ltd.

Niall Ó Dónaill. 1977 *Foclóir Gaeilge-Béarla.* Tómas de Bhaldraithe, General Editor. Baile Átha Cliath: Oifig an tSoláthair.

D. J. O'Donoghue. 1894 *The Humour of Ireland.* London: Walter Scott Ltd.

Padraic O'Farrell. 1980, 1983 rpt. *How the Irish speak English.* Dublin & Cork: Mercier.

Mairtin O'Griofa. 1993 *Irish Folk Wisdom.* New York: Sterling Publishing Co., Inc.

Mícheál Ó Guithín. 1953 *Is Truagh ná Fanann an Óige.* Baile Átha Cliath: Oifig an tSoláthair. For English translation *see* O'Guiheen 1982 in 'Reference Works.'

— 1970 *Beatha Pheig Sayers.* Baile Átha Cliath: Foilseacháin Náisiúnta Teoranta.

Ó Héalaí *see* William

Ó hUrmoltaigh *see* Ua Muirgheasa

Colm Ó Lochlainn. 1936 'Sean-fhoclaí ó Phartraighe an tSléibhe.' *Béaloideas*, 6, 57–60.

Tomás S. Ó Máille. 1948, 1952 *Sean-fhocla Chonnacht*. 2 vols. Baile Átha Cliath: Oifig an tSoláthair.

Ó Muirgheasa *see* Morris. *and* Ua Muirgheasa

Brian O'Nolan. *see* 'Flann O'Brien'

Thomas F. O'Rahilly. 1922 *A Miscellany of Irish Proverbs*. Dublin: The Talbot Press Ltd.

Ó Siochfhradha *see* 'An Seabhac'

Muiris Ó Súilleabháin. 1933 *Fiche Blian ag Fás*. Baile Átha Cliath: Clólucht an Talbóidigh. For English translation *see* Maurice O'Sullivan in 'Reference Works.'

Éamonn Ó Tuathail, Editor. 1933a *Sgéalta Mhuintir Luinigh/Munterloney Folk-Tales*. Dublin: Irish Folklore Institute.

— 1933b 'A Northern Medley.' *Béaloideas*, 4, No. 2, 204–13.

— 1934 *Seanchas Ghleann Ghaibhle/Glengevlin Folk-Lore, collected & edited, with introduction, notes and glossary*. Baile Átha Cliath: Institiúid Béaloideasa Éireann.

W. H. Patterson. 1880 *A Glossary of Words from Antrim and Down*. London: published for the English Dialect Society by Trübner.

Peirce *see* Kerr Peirce

John Pepper. Early 1970s 'John Pepper's Column.' *Belfast Telegraph*, Sept.

Pro Tanto Quid. 1929–73 (except 1933, 1939, 1942, 1943, 1948, 1952 & 1972) Belfast. Some vols. n.p.

P.T.Q. see *Pro Tanto Quid*

E. C. Quiggin. 1906 *Being the Speech of Meenawannia in the Parish of Glenties, Phonology and Texts*. Cambridge: University Press.

Gabriel Rosenstock. 1993 *The Wasp in the Mug, Unforgettable Irish Proverbs*. Cork & Dublin: Mercier.

George Bernard Shaw. 1934 *Too Good to be True, Village Wooing & On the Rocks. Three Plays by Bernard Shaw*. London: Constable and Company Ltd.

Stanihurst *see* Holinshed

Jonathan Swift. 1948 ed. *Journal to Stella*. Vol. I. Harold Williams, Editor. Oxford: Clarendon Press.

— 1963 ed. ... *Polite Conversation*... Eric Partridge, Editor. London: Andre Deutsch.

The Dublin Journal of Temperance, Science and Literature, 1 (1842).

Michael Traynor. 1954 *The English Dialect of Donegal, A Glossary (including Hart 1847–1908)*. Dublin: Royal Irish Academy.

'Tullyneil' [Robert Lyons Marshall]. 1944 *At Home in Tyrone: sketches and stories*. Belfast: The Quota Press.

Tadhg Ua Donnchadha, Collector. 1902 *Sean-Fhocail na Mumhan I, Leabhairíní Gaedhilge le hAghaidh an tSluaigh VI.* Baile Átha Cliath: Connradh na Gaedhilge.

Ua Maoileoin *see* 'An Seabhac'

Énrí Ua Muirgheasa, Collector, Compiler & Editor. 1907 *Seanfhocla Uladh.* Baile Átha Cliath: Connradh na Gaedhilge. Also New ed. Ó Muirgheasa 1976 Nollaig Ó hUrmoltaigh, Editor. *Seanfhocail Uladh* Baile Átha Cliath: Oifig an tSoláthair.

see also Henry Morris.

Tony Catherine Antoine William 'Fear Pholl a' Bhroic.' 1997 ed. *Seanfhocail as Acaill.* Seán Ó Héalaí, Editor, Fearghas Mac Lochlainn, Illustrator. Indreabhán, Conamara: Cló Iar-Chonnachta Teo.

REFERENCE WORKS

NON-PRINTED

Bo Almqvist. 'The questionnaire on wellerisms — problems and results.' seminar held in the Department of Irish Folklore, University College Dublin 6/4/1976, Draft in Almqvist *Irish Wellerisms* 1973– File.

Fionnuala Carson Williams. 'Quotation Proverbs in Ireland' lecture at the colloquium *Verbal Wit and Verbal Wisdom* jointly organized by Warburg Institute and the Folklore Society, 23th–24th March 2001, in the Warburg Institute University College, London, typescript in the Folklore Society Library.

Raymond Hickey. 2000 CD-ROM *Corpus* [of Irish Drama in the English language].

PRINTED

Antti Aarne, Translated and Enlarged by Stith Thompson. 1964 2nd Revision. *The Types of the Folktale, A Classification and Bibliography.* Folklore Fellows Communications No. 3. Helsinki: Suomalainen Tiedeakatemia, Academia Scientiarum Fennica.

J. R. R. Adams. 1987 *The Printed Word and the Common Man. Popular Culture in Ulster 1700–1900.* Belfast: The Institute of Irish Studies, The Queen's University of Belfast.

Aesop. 1841 ed. *The Fables of Aesop with instructive applications.* Samuel Croxall D[octor of] D[ivinity], Editor. Belfast: Simms & M'Intyre.

— 1985 rpt. of 1899 ed. *A Hundred Fables of Aesop*. Sir Roger L'Estrange, English versions. Ware: Omega Books.

— 1973 rpt. of 1954 ed. *Fables of Aesop*. S. A. Handford, Translator. Middlesex: Penguin Books.

Bo Almqvist. 1982–83 'Siúl an Phortáin, Friotalfhocal agus Fabhalscéal (AT 276).' *Sinsear, The Folklore Journal*, 35–62.

Bendt Alster. 1993 'Proverbs from Ancient Mesopotamia: Their History and Social Implications.' *Proverbium, Yearbook of International Proverb Scholarship*, 10, 1–19.

An Roinn Oideachais. 1978 *Ainmneacha Plandaí agus Ainmhithe/Flora and Fauna Nomenclature*. Baile Átha Cliath: Oifig an tSoláthair.

'An Seabhac' [Pádraig Ó Siochfhradha]. 1936 'An Sotach 's an Mháthair.' *Béaloideas*, 6, 313–28.

Anon. 2002 'Big-hearted students turning Rag to riches.' *Queen's Now, Annual Review of Queen's University Belfast*, 21.

Arciolo *see* 'Fayo'

Brendan Behan. 1965 *Hold Your Hour and Have Another*. G[reat] B[ritain]: Corgi.

—1981 *Poems and a Play in Irish*. ['An Giall.'] Proinsias Ní Dhorchaí, Editor, Introduction, Declan Kiberd. Peter Fallon, General Editor, Gallery Books. Dublin: The Gallery Press.

Mike Benny, Francis Murray, Lori Miller Fox & Joseph Rosenbloom. 1998 *Giant Book of Riddles*. New York: Sterling Publishing Company Inc.

Franz Boas. 1897 'Eskimo tales and songs.' *Journal of American Folklore*, 10:36, 109–115.

Henry G. Bohn. 1855 *A Handbook of Proverbs* … London: H. G. Bohn.

Eilís Brady. 1984 *All in! All in! A Selection of Dublin Children's Traditional Street-Games with Rhymes and Music*. Scríbhinní Béaloidis/Folklore Studies 2. Dublin: Comhairle Bhéaloideas Éireann.

Gyles Brandreth. 1980 *1000 Riddles The Greatest Book of Riddles Ever Known*. [UK]: Carousel Books, Transworld Publishers Ltd.

Asa Briggs, Consultant Editor, Alan Isaacs & Elizabeth Martin, Editors. 1985 *Longman Dictionary of Twentieth Century Biography*. London: Longman Group.

George B. Bryan & Wolfgang Mieder. 1994 *The Proverbial Bernard Shaw. An Index to the Proverbs in the Works of George Bernard Shaw*. Westport, Connecticut: Greenwood Press.

George B. Bryan & Wolfgang Mieder. 1997 *The Proverbial Charles Dickens. An Index to the Proverbs in the Works of Charles Dickens*. New York *et al*: Peter Lang.

see also Mieder & Bryan.

295

John [Johann] Lewis [Ludwig] Burckhardt. 1830, 1st paperback fac. ed. 1984 *Arabic Proverbs or the Manners and Customs of the Modern Egyptians illustrated from their Proverbial Sayings Current at Cairo* ... Introduction, C. E. Bosworth. London: Curzon Press.

Sir Bernard Burke. 1912 New ed. Revised. *A Genealogical and Heraldic History of the Landed Gentry of Ireland.* London: Harrison & Sons.

Professor [John William] Byers. 1904 *Sayings, Proverbs and Humour of Belfast.* (This publication is a fuller version of a lecture delivered to the members of the Belfast Natural History and Philosophical Society, December 1st, 1903, and also contains a reprint of 'Ulsterisms,' originally published in *The Northern Whig* newspaper 8/5/1901.) Belfast: The Northern Whig.

Campbell *see* Meek

Pack Carnes. 1981 'The Fable and the Proverb Intertexts and Reception.' *Proverbium*, 8, 55–76, also available with a commentary by Wolfgang Mieder, in Mieder, Editor, 1994 *Wise Words, Essays on the Proverb*, Garland Folklore Casebooks Vol. 6, Alan Dundes, Series Editor, Garland Reference Library of the Humanities Vol. 1638, New York & London: Garland Publishing, Inc., 467–93.

Pack Carnes, Editor. 1988 *Proverbia in Fabula. Essays on the Relationship of the Fable and the Proverb.* Sprichwörterforschung Bd. 10. Herausgegeben von Wolfgang Mieder. Bern *et al*: Peter Lang.

Fionnuala Carson Williams. 2000a *Irish Proverbs, Traditional Wit and Wisdom.* New York: Sterling Publishing Co., Inc.

— 2000b 'Irish Proverbs and *Európai Közmondások.*' *Acta Ethnographica Hungarica, An International Journal of Ethnography.* 45, Nos. 3–4, 421–37.

— 2001a 'Quotation Proverbs in Ireland.' 2 in Séamas Ó Catháin, Editor, *Northern Lights, Following Folklore in North-Western Europe, essays in honour of Bo Almqvist.* Dublin: University College Dublin Press, 9–21.

— 2001b 'Wellerism Quest.' *FLS News, The newsletter of the Folklore Society.* Jacqueline Simpson, Editor. No. 34 (June), 15.

see also Williams.

'Andrew Cheviot' [J. Hiram Watson]. 1896 *Proverbs, Proverbial Expressions and Popular Rhymes of Scotland.* Paisley & London: Alexander Gardner.

Children of the Ladybird Book Club *see* Judith Wood *et al*

Reidar Th. Christiansen. 1992 ed. *Gamle Norske Visdomsord, Norske ordspråk i utvalg.* Oslo: J. W. Cappelens.

see also Ó Súilleabháin & Christiansen.

Tom Clyde. 2002 *Irish Literary Magazines, An Outline History and Descriptive Bibliography*. Dublin: Irish Academic Press.

Jim Cooke. 1999 *Charles Dickens's Ireland, an Anthology including an account of his visits to Ireland*. Dublin: The Wolfhound Press, in association with RTE Commercial Enterprises.

Ed Cray. 1964 'Wellerisms in Riddle Form.' 'Notes and Queries.' *Western Folklore*, 23, 114–16.

Kevin Danaher & Patricia Lysaght. 1980–81 'Supplement to *A Bibliography of Irish Ethnology and Folklore*.' *Béaloideas*, 48–49, 206–27.

J. J. Evans. 1965 *Diarhebion Cymraeg (detholiad, gyda chyfieithiad i'r Saesneg)/Welsh Proverbs (a selection, with English translations)*. Gwasg Gomer: J. D. Lewis.

'Fayo' [Raphaël A. Arciolo]. n.d. [end 20th century] *3333 Proverbs in Haitian Creole, the 11th Romance Language*. Port-au-Prince: Les Editions Fardin.

Fox *see* Benny

Edward Fraser & John Gibbons, Compilers. 1925 *Soldier and Sailor Words and Phrases* ... London: Routledge & Sons Ltd.

Morrie Gallant. 1993 *The Nuttiest Riddle Book in the World*. New York: Sterling Publishing Co., Inc.

Gibbons *see* Fraser

Brough Girling, Compiler. 1998 *The Schoolkids' Joke Book Too!* London: CollinsChildren'sBooks, a division of HarperCollins*Publishers* Ltd.

Edmund I. Gordon, with a chapter by Thorkild Jacobsen. 1959 *Sumerian Proverbs: glimpses of everyday life in ancient Mesopotamia*. Philadelphia: The University Museum, University of Pennsylvania.

Francis Grose. 1785, 1785 rpt. *A Classical Dictionary of the Vulgar Tongue*. London: S. Hooper.

Paul G. Halpern. 1994 *A Naval History of World War I*. London: UCL Press.

John Hegarty. 1987 *Amazing Animal Jokes*. A Red Fox Joke Book. London: Random House Children's Books.

Andrew Henderson, Collector & Editor. 1881 ed. *Scottish Proverbs*. A new ed. with notes and glossary by James Donald. Glasgow: Thomas D. Morison.

Hippocrene Books Editors, Compilers. 1999 *Irish Proverbs*. New York: Hippocrene Books Inc.

Alexander Hislop, Collector and Editor. 1862 *The Proverbs Of Scotland Collected And Arranged, With Notes, Explanatory And Illustrative And A Glossary*. Glasgow: Porteous & Hislop.

Robert Hogan, Editor-in-Chief. 1996 *Dictionary of Irish Literature Revised and Expanded Edition A–L, & M–Z.* 2 vols. London: Aldwych Press.

Pelle Holm. 1971 ed. *Ordspråk och talesätt.* Stockholm: Bonniers.

Huchinson's Encyclopaedia. 1991 London: Random Century Group.

A. J. Hughes. 1998 *Robert Shipboy MacAdam (1808–95) His Life and Gaelic Proverb Collection.* Belfast: The Institute of Irish Studies, The Queen's University of Belfast.

Eleanor Hull. 1927 'Legends and Traditions of the Cailleach Bheara.' *Folklore*, 38, 225–54.

Gordon Irving, Compiler. 1969 *The Wit of the Scots.* London: Leslie Frewin.

Isaacs *see* Briggs

Jacobsen *see* Gordon

Kenneth Jackson. 1938 'Scealta ón mBlascaod.' *Béaloideas*, 8, 3–96.

Iris Järviö-Nieminen. 1959 *Suomalaiset Sanomukset.* Helsinki: Suomalaisen Kirjallisuuden Seura.

Annikki Kaivola-Bregenhøj. 2001 *Riddles, Perspectives on the use, function and change in a folklore genre.* Studia Fennica Folkloristica 10. Helsinki: Finnish Literature Society.

James Kelly. 1818 ed. *A Complete Collection of Scotish [sic] Proverbs, Explained and made Intelligible to the English Reader.* London: W. & J. Innys & J. Osborn.

Iver Kjær. 1971 'Wellerisms in earlier Danish tradition.' *Proverbium*, 16, 579–82.

Elizabeth Knowles. 1999 *The Oxford Dictionary of Quotations, Major New Edition.* Oxford: Oxford University Press.

C. Kruyskamp. 1965 *Allemaal mensen ... Apologische Spreekwoorden.* s'-Gravenhage: Martinis Nijhoff.

Julian Krzy_anowski, Editor. 1969 *Nowa ksi_ga przys_ów i wyra_e_ przys_owiowych polskich.* Vol. 1. Warszawa: Pa_stwowy Instytut Wydawniczy.

C. Grant Loomis. 1955 'Wellerisms in California Sources.' *Western Folklore*, 14, 229–45.

A. T. Lucas. 1961 'A Hay-rope Pack-saddle from County Louth.' *County Louth Archaeological Journal*, 15, 13–16.

Geraldine Lynch. 1977–79 'The Lore of a Wicklow Schoolgirl.' *Béaloideas*, 45–47, 46–62.

Lysaght *see* Danaher & Lysaght

T. D. Macdonald. n.d. [probably 1926] *Gaelic Proverbs and Proverbial Sayings.* Stirling: Eneas Mackay.

John McGuckian. 2002 *Talking with My Brother.* Cladnageeragh, County Donegal: Summer Palace Press.

298

Everol McKenzie. n.d. [not earlier than 1996] *Jamaica Proverbs.* London: Blue Mountain Media. n.p.

Edward MacLysaght. 1978 ed. *The Surnames of Ireland.* Dublin: Irish Academic Press.

Maurice Maloux. 1986 ed. *Références Dictionnaire des proverbes, sentences et maximes.* Paris: Larousse.

Martin *see* Briggs

Donald E. Meek, Editor, The Rev. Duncan M. Campbell, Collector. 1978 *The Campbell Collection of Gaelic Proverbs and Proverbial Sayings.* Inverness: The Gaelic Society of Inverness.

Wolfgang Mieder. 1982 'Sexual Content of German Wellerisms.' *Maledicta*, 6, 215–23.

—1989 *American Proverbs: A Study of Texts and Contexts.* Band 13 Bern, Frankfurt am Main, New York, Paris: Peter Lang.

—1997 'Welleristic Addenda to the *Dictionary of Wellerisms.*' *Proverbium, Yearbook of International Proverb Scholarship*, 14, 187–217.

Wolfgang Mieder & George B. Bryan. 1996 *Proverbs in World Literature: A Bibliography.* New York *et al*: Peter Lang.

Wolfgang Mieder & Stewart A. Kingsbury. 1994 *A Dictionary of Wellerisms.* Oxford: Oxford University Press.

Wolfgang Mieder & Anna Tóthné Litovkina. 1999 *Twisted Wisdom, Modern Anti-Proverbs.* Supplement Series of *Proverbium, Yearbook of International Proverb Scholarship* edited by Wolfgang Mieder Vol. 4. Burlington: The University of Vermont.

Mieder *see also* Bryan & Mieder.

E. H. Mikhail. 1982 *Brendan Behan: Interviews and Recollections.* Vol. I. London & Basingstoke: Macmillan; Dublin: Gill & Macmillan.

S[ophia] Morrison & C[harles] Roeder. 1905 rpt. *Manx Proverbs and Sayings.* Rpt. from the *Isle of Man Examiner.* Douglas: S. K. Broadbent & Co. Ltd.

David Murison. 1981 *Scots Saws From the folk-wisdom of Scotland.* Edinburgh: James Thin, The Mercat Press.

Michael J. Murphy. 1983 *Ulster Folk of Field and Fireside.* Dundalk: Dundalgan Press.

Murray *see* Benny

Siegfried Neumann, Compiler & Editor. 1996 *Sprichwörtliches aus Mecklenburg: Anekdotensprüche, Antisprichwörter, apologische Sprichwörter, Beispielsprichwörter, erzählende Sprichwörter, Sagte-Sprichwörter, Sagwörter, Schwanksprüche, Wellerismen, Zitatensprichwörter.* Göttingen: Otto Schwartz & Co.

Bairbre Ní Fhloinn. 'In Correspondence with Tradition: The Role of the Postal Questionnaire in the Collection of Irish Folklore.' 18 in

Séamas Ó Catháin, Editor, *Northern Lights, Following Folklore in North-Western Europe, essays in honour of Bo Almqvist.* Dublin: University College Dublin Press, 215–28.

Nicholls *see* Wood

Alexander Nicolson. [not before 1880] 1951 rpt. *Gaelic Proverbs collected and translated into English with equivalents from other European languages.* With Index, etc., by Malcolm MacInnes. Glasgow: Caledonian Press for Malcolm MacInnes.

Jess Nierenberg. 1994 'Proverbs in Graffiti: Taunting Traditional Wisdom.' Originally published in *Maledicta*, 7 (1983), 41–58. Reprinted, with Introduction by Wolfgang Mieder, in Mieder, Editor. 1994 *Wise Words, Essays on the Proverb*, Garland Folklore Casebooks Vol. 6, Alan Dundes, Series Editor, Garland Reference Library of the Humanities Vol. 1638, New York & London: Garland Publishing, Inc., 543–61.

Neal R. Norrick. 2001 'On the conversational performance of narrative jokes: Toward an account of timing.' *Humor, International Journal of Humor Research,* 14–13, 255–74.

Seán Óg agus [= &] Mánus Ó Baoill. 1997 ed. *Ceolta Gael.* Ossian published in association with Mercier Press. Cork: Ossian Publications Ltd.

'Flann O'Brien' [Brian O'Nolan]. 1986 ed. *Stories and Plays.* Introduction by Claud Cockburn. London *et al*: Grafton Books.

Tomás Ó Crohan. 1974 rpt. of 1951 ed. *The Islandman.* Robin Flower, Translator. Oxford: Oxford University Press. For original Irish *see* Ó Croimhthain in 'Sources.'

Caoimhín Ó Danachair. 1978 *A Bibliography of Irish Ethnology and Folk Tradition.* Dublin & Cork: Mercier Press. *see also* Danaher & Lysaght.

Séamas Ó Duilearga. 1948 *Leabhar Sheáin Í Chonaill.* Baile Átha Cliath: Comhairle Bhéaloideas Éireann.

Padraic O'Farrell. 1995 *Irish Toasts, Curses & Blessings.* New York: Sterling Publishing Co., Inc., originally published 1993 as *Before the Devil Knows You're Dead*, Cork *et al*: Mercier Press.

John O'Grady. 1966 *Aussie English, an explanation of the Australian Idiom.* London: Nicholas Vane Ltd.

Micheál O'Guiheen. 1982 ed. *A pity youth does not last, Reminiscences of the Last of the Great Blasket Island's Poets and Storytellers.* Tim Enright, Translator. This ed. includes a reprinted selection of O'Guiheen's poetry. Oxford *et al*: Oxford University Press. For original Irish *see* Ó Guithín 1953 in 'Sources.'

Dáithi Ó hÓgain. 1982 *An File.* Baile Átha Cliath: Oifig an tSóláthair.

300

—1990 *Myth, Legend & Romance, An Encyclopaedia of the Irish Folk Tradition.* London: Ryan Publishing Co. Ltd.

Dáithi Ó hÓgain, Editor. 2001 *Binsín Luachra, Gearrscéalta agus Seanchas le Proinsias de Róiste.* Baile Átha Cliath: An Clóchmhar Tta.

Diamaid Ó Muirithe. 2000 *A Dictionary of Anglo-Irish, words and phrases from Gaelic in the English of Ireland.* Dublin: Four Courts Press.

O'Nolan *see* 'O'Brien'

Ó Siochfhradha *see* 'An Seabhac'

Seán Ó Súilleabháin. 1937 *Diarmuid na Bolgaighe agus a Chomharsain.* Dublin: Oifig Díolta Foillseacháin an Rialtais.

—1963 fac. of 1942 ed. *A Handbook of Irish Folklore.* Hatboro, Pennsylvania: Folklore Associates.

—1976 'Oliver Cromwell in Irish Oral Tradition.' in Linda Dégh, Henry Glassie, Felix J. Oinas, Editors, *Folklore Today A Festschrift for Richard M. Dorson.* Bloomington: Indiana University, 473–83.

Seán Ó Súilleabháin & Reidar Th. Christiansen. 1963 *The Types of the Irish Folktale.* Folklore Fellows Communications No. 188. Helsinki: Suomalainen Tiedeakatemia.

Seán Ó Súilleabháin in conjunction with the Department of Education. 1937 *Irish Folklore and Tradition.* No place of publication.

Maurice O'Sullivan. 1941 ed. *Twenty Years A-Growing.* Moya Llewelyn Davies & George Thomson, Translators, The Golden Library No. 10, 1933. London: Chatto & Windus. For original Irish *see* Ó Súilleabháin in 'Sources.'

Iona & Peter Opie. 1959 *The Lore and Language of Schoolchildren.* London *et al*: Oxford University Press.

Gyula Paczolay. 1997 *European Proverbs in 55 Languages with Equivalents in Arabic, Persian, Sanskrit, Chinese and Japanese/Európai Közmondások 55 Nyelven ...* Veszprém: Veszprémi Nyomda Rt.

A. A. Parker. 1963 *The Humour of Spanish Proverbs Canning House Ninth Annual Lecture 16 May 1962.* Diamante XIII. London: The Hispanic & Luso-Brazillian Councils. Reprinted with Introduction by Wolfgang Mieder in Wolfgang Mieder & Alan Dundes, Editors, 1981, *The Wisdom of Many, Essays on the Proverb*, Garland Folklore Casebooks Vol. 1, Alan Dundes, General Editor. New York & London: Garland Publishing, Inc., 257–74.

Palmer *see* E. T. Williams & Palmer

Eric Partridge. 1977 *A Dictionary of Catch Phrases British and American from the Sixteenth Century to the Present Day.* London & Henley: Routledge, Keegan & Paul.

T. G. F. Paterson. 1945 ed. *Country Cracks*. Dundalk: W. Tempest.
Allan Ramsay. 1979 fac. of 1750 ed. *A Collection of Scots Proverbs*. Edinburgh: Paul Harris.
Sandy Ransford. 1999 *Spooky Jokes*. London: Macmillan Children's Books.
James T. R. Ritchie. 2000 ed. *The Singing Street, Scottish Children's Games, Rhymes and Sayings*. Edinburgh: Mercat Press, Mercat Classics.
Roeder *see* Morrison
Janet Rodgers. 1987 *The Crazy Joke Bag: the joke book you can actually wear (for primary school children)*. London: Beaver Books.
Rosenbloom *see* Benny
Pirkko Sallinen. 1969 & 70 'Skandinavische Entsprechungen Finnischer Wellerismen.' *Proverbium*, 14, 390–95 & 15, 106–09.
Karl Simrock, Compiler. 1988 rpt. *Die deutschen Sprichwörter*. Wolfgang Mieder, Editor. Stuttgart: Philipp Reclam Jun.
Alan Smith. 1968 'The Image of Cromwell in Folklore and Tradition.' *Folklore*, 79, 17–39.
William George Smith, Editor, F. P. Wilson, Editor. 1975 rpt. of 1970 ed. *The Oxford Dictionary of English Proverbs*. Introduction by Joanna Wilson. Oxford: Clarendon Press.
James Stewart. 1977–79 'The Game of "An bhFuil Agat? — Tá" or The uses of bilingualism.' *Béaloideas*, 45–47, 244–58.
Fredrik Ström. 1939 *Svenska ordstäv*. Stockholm: Bonniers.
Archer Taylor. 1962 fac., 1985 rpt. *'The Proverb' and 'An Index to the Proverb'* [orginally 1931 & 1934 respectively] with Introduction & Bibliography by Wolfgang Mieder Sprichwörterforschung Herausgegeben von Wolfgang Mieder Band 6. Bern *et al*: Peter Lang.
—1959 'The Use of Proper Names in Wellerisms and Folk Tales.' *Western Folklore*, 18, 287–93.
—1960 'Wellerisms and Riddles.' *Western Folklore*, 19, 55–56.
—1962, 1981 rpt. 'The Wisdom of Many and the Wit of One.' Reprinted with Introduction by Wolfgang Mieder in Wolfgang Mieder & Alan Dundes, Editors, 1981, *The Wisdom of Many, Essays on the Proverb*, Garland Folklore Casebooks Vol. 1, Alan Dundes, General Editor. New York & London: Garland Publishing, Inc., 3–9, Reprinted from *Swarthmore College Bulletin*, 54, 4–7.
The Compact Edition of the Oxford English Dictionary. 1979, micrographic reproduction of 1971 ed. Vol. II. London: Book Club Associates by Arrangement with Oxford University Press.
Stith Thompson. 1955–58 Revised & Enlarged Ed. *Motif-Index of Folk-Literature, A Classification of Narrative Elements in Folktales, ...*

302

Folklore Fellows Communications No. 184, Vols. 1–6. Copenhagen: Bagger & Rosenkilde; Bloomington: Indiana University Press.

Thompson *see also* Aarne & Thompson

James N. Tidwell. 1950 'Wellerisms in *Alexander's Weekly Messenger, 1837–1839.*' *Western Folklore*, 9 No. 1 (Jan.), 257–62.

Anna Tóthné Litovkina. 1999 '"Spare the rod and spoil the child": sexuality in proverbs, sayings and idioms.' *Proverbium*, 16, 141–65. *see also* Mieder & Tóthné Litovkina.

Ó Siochfhradha *see* 'An Seabhac'

Colin Walker, Compiler & Editor. New Ed. 2000 *Scottish Proverbs.* Edinburgh: Birlinn Press.

Watson *see* 'Andrew Cheviot'

Robert Welch, Editor. 1996 *The Oxford Companion to Irish Literature.* Oxford: Clarendon Press.

E. T. Williams & Helen M. Palmer, Editors. 1971 *Dictionary of National Biography 1951–60.* Oxford: Oxford University Press.

Fionnuala Williams. 1982–83 'Of Proverbial Birds and Beasts.' *Sinsear, The Folklore Journal*, 127–32.

—1986 '"An Seabhac" *Seanfhocail na Muimhneach* and *Seanfhocail na Mumhan.*' Review in *Proverbium, Yearbook of International Proverb Scholarship*, 3, 407–10.

—1999 'Maritime Referents in Irish Proverbs.' in Patricia Lysaght, Séamas Ó Catháin, Dáithí Ó hÓgáin, Editors, *Islanders and Water-Dwellers, Proceedings of the Celtic-Nordic-Baltic Folklore Symposium held at University College Dublin 16–19 June 1996.* Blackrock: DBA Publications Ltd., for the Department of Irish Folklore, University College Dublin, 359–70.

Fionnuala [Carson] Williams, Compiler. 1992 *The Poolbeg Book of Irish Proverbs.* Swords: Poolbeg Press Ltd.

see also Carson Williams.

Sir James Wilson. 1915 *Lowland Scotch as Spoken in the Lower Strathearn District of Perthshire.* London *et al*: Oxford University Press.

Judith Wood & Michael Nicholls with Children of the Ladybird Book Club. 1986 *You must be joking, A collection of Children's jokes in aid of Save the Children.* London: Ladybird Books. n.p.

Joseph Wright, Editor. 1970 ed. *The English Dialect Dictionary.* Vol. I A–C. *Oxford University Press.* GB: Fletcher & Son Ltd., Norwich.

Kwesi Yankah. 1989 'Proverbs: Problems and Strategies in Field Research.' *Proverbium, Yearbook of International Proverb Scholarship*, 6, 165–76.

'Zig + Zag.' 1996 *The Big Bad Joke Book.* London: Robinson Children's Books, an imprint of Robinson Publishing Ltd.

INDEX OF SPEAKERS IN PART A:
Wellerisms in English

eels, eels at Toome	A 217.1, .2
electrician	A 32.1
Ellen	A 222.1
Evans of the *Broke*	A 101.1
farmer	A 77.1; A 235.3; A 278.1; A 287.1, .6, .12, .19; A 310.1; A 25.1; A 328.7
father	A 110.1
fellow, *see also* lad	A 182.13, .15; A 266.1; A 291.2; A 328.6
fiddler	A 242.1; A 265.1
flaithiúil man	A 87.1
flea	A 307.1, .2
fly	A 69.1–.3; A 311.1
fool	A 158.1; A 318.1
fowler	A 66.1
fox, *see also* duck house raider *and* tod	A 16.1; A 19.1,.2; A 83.1–.7, .9, .19, .21, .22; A 106.1–.3; A 140.1; A 182.8–.12; A 197.2; A 233.1
Gansey, *see also* Jansy	A 259.56
geologist	A 56.1
giraffe	A 128.1
girl, *see also* city girls	A 4.1; A 40.1; A 163.1; A 204.1; A 274.1
gladiator	A 12.1
good woman, *see also* wife	A 287.22
goose	A 68.1
gráineog, *see also* graineoig *etc. and* hedgehog	A 5.6
graineoig, *see also* gráineog *etc. and* hedgehog	A 5.9
grainneog, *see also* gráineog *etc. and* hedgehog	A 5.5, .8
grainneóg, *see also* gráineog *etc. and* hedgehog	A 5.7
gráinneóg, *see also* gráineog *etc. and* hedgehog	A 5.10
graneóg, *see also* gráineog *etc. and* hedgehog	A 5.11

Old Mrs Davis, *see also*
Oul Mrs Davis
old one, *see also* old woman *and*
oul'/ould woman
Old Power, *see also* Ould Power
old woman, *see also* old one *and*
oul'/ould woman

Oul Mrs Davis, *see also*
Old Mrs Davis
oul' woman, *see also* old one *and*
old/ould woman
Ould Dunne, *see also*
Auld/Old Dunne
Ould Power, *see also* Old Power
Ould Wade
ould woman, *see also* old one *and*
old/oul' woman

Paddy Loughran, *see also* Paddy
Paddy, *see also* Paddy Loughran
Pára Ban, *see also* Párach Bhoe *and*
Porra Bawn
Párach Bhoe, *see also* Pára Ban *and*
Porra Bawn
parrot
passenger
Pat
patient
pauper
pebble
physiology professor
pig
pigeon
pilot
plumber
poacher
pop-star
Porra Bawn, *see also* Pára Ban *and*
Párach Bhoe
post office official
publican

A 103.1, .2

A 10.1; A 287.18

A 241.1–.5, .7, .8
A 34.1; A38.1; A 122.1; A 123.1;
A 148.1; A180.5; A 191.1;
A 30.1; A 287.3, .9, .15, .23;
A 326.1; A 327.1; A 328.3
A 103.3

A 202.1; A 272.2, .3

A 63.5

A 241.6
A 121.1
A 273.1

A 159.1
A 159.2
A 312.1

A 312.3

A 20.1
A, 81.1; A 175.1
A 14.1; A 158.3; A 308.1
A 246.1
A 248.1
A 28.1
A 43.1
A 119.1
A 313.1
A 232.1; A 258.1
A 33.1
A 263.1
A 236.1
A 312.2

A 179.1
A 237.1

INDEX [IN IRISH] OF SPEAKERS IN PART B:
Wellerisms in Irish

312

Cailleach Mhuigheo, Cailleach M(h)uigheo	B 129.1, .2
Cailleach Thír Eoghain	B 129.5
cailleach, *see also* caileach *and* Cailleach B *etc.*	B 32.1; B 122.1; B 146.1
caora, *see also* reithe	B 107.5
cat, *see also* sean-chat	B 41.1–.11; B 58.1–.3; B 73.1; B 114.1; B 115.1; B 171.1
ceannaidh Ghort an Charnáin, ceannaidh Phort an Charnáin	B 125.1, .2
ceannaidhe mála	B 46.3
cearc	B 31.1
céile	B 145.2
ceoltóir	B 191.1
Cloch Labhrais	B 94.1, .2
Colmcille, *see also* Coluim Cille *and* Colum Cille	B 89.1–.3
Coluim Cille, *see also* Colmcille *and* Colum Cille	B 164.1
Colum Cille, *see also* Colmcille *and* Coluim Cille	B 23.1; B 164.2
Conán	B 33.1; B 84.1; B 85.1
cor-éisc	B 67.1
Crochúr a' Chasuir	B 102.1
cuach	B 78.1
cuileog, cuileóg	B 71.2, .1
dall	B 40.1, .2
Diarmaid na Bolagaí	B 190.1, .2
dochtúir	B 159.2
dreancaid	B 26.1
dreoilín, *see also* dreóilín *etc.*	B 22.2; B 44.4, .5; B 117.1; B 143.1–.5, .7, .8; B 144.1; B 160.1
dreóilín, *see also* dreoilín *etc.*	B 44.1–.3
dreoillín, *see also* dreoilín *etc.*	B 48.1; B 136.1; B 143.6, .10, .11; B 172.1–.5
dreolan, *see also* dreoilín *etc.*	B 22.5
dreolán, *see also* dreoilín *etc.*	B 22.1, .4
droch-ghnó, *see also* droch-ghnótha *and* dro-ghnú	B 93.1–.3, .5, .6
droch-ghnótha, dro-ghnú, *see also* droch-ghnó	B 93.7, .4

duine bocht	B 62.1
Éamonn	B 86.1
éan, *see also* cearc, cor-éisc, dreoilín *etc*, fiach dubh, gé, pilibín *and* traona	B 22.3; B 165.2
fear, *see also under qualifiers*	B 12.1; B 25.1, .2; B 35.1, .2; B 45.1; B 46.1; B 51.1, B 53.1; B 55.1–.3; B 65.1; B 69.3; B 72.1; B 75.1; B 79.1; B 97.1; B 101.1, .2; B 106.1–.5, .7; B 109.1; B 112.1; B 113.1; B 116.1–.3; B 130.1, .2; B 138.1; B 140.1, .2; B 141.1; B 142.1; B 155.1, .2; B 157.1; B 161.1; B 166.1; B 167.1; B 173.1, .2; B 184.1–.4; B 187.1; B 192.1; B 197.1
fear a' tighe	B 17.1
fear an ocras	B 59.1
fear an Oileáin	B 18.1
fear bocht	B 46.2; B 152.1
fear lag	B 60.1
fear láidir	B 60.1
fear na feoirlinge, fear na feóirline	B 5.1, .2
fiach dubh	B 176.1
fíogaigh	B 74.1
firín buí	B 96a.1
Fómhar	B 95.1
Frainc 'ac Confhaola	B 149.1
gabhairín, *see also* gabhar	B 165.3
gabhar, *see also* gabhairín	B 1.1; B 27.1, .2; B 38.1–.4; B 68.1; B 123.1, .2; B 139.1; B 195.1
gadaí	B 2.1
gaoth	B 180.1, .2
gasúr	B 153.1
gé	B 120.1
iasc, *see also* fíogaigh *and* sgadán	B 10.1–.4

314

leadaidhe	B 63.1
leanbh	B 15.2, .3
luchóg	B 150.1
mac	B 158.1
Mac an Bháird	B 24.1; B 111.1
mada rua, *see also* madadh rua *etc.* *and* sionnach	B 98.1
madadh rua, *see also* mada rua *etc.* *and* sionnach	B 124.2
madadh ruadh, *see also* mada rua *etc.* *and* sionnach	B 108.1; B 124.1
madarua, *see also* mada rua *etc.* *and* sionnach	B 189.2
madaruadh, *see also* mada rua *etc.* *and* sionnach	B 87.1, .2; B 108.2, .3; B 116.4; B 193.1
maighistir	B 77.1
Máire Shalach	B 104.1
Maonus	B 107.3
Mathúin	B 34.1, .2
ministir	B 196.1
moncaí, *see also* mongcaidhe	B 81.1
Mongan	B 14.1
mongcaidhe, *see also* moncaí	B 183.1, .2
Ó hIarlaithe	B 131.1
oifigeach	B 126.1
ól	B 151.1
Pádraig	B 66.1
Páidín	B 45.2; B 168.1
Peadar	B 54.1–.3
Peadar a' Gharraí Aird	B 117a.1
pilibín	B 80.1
píobaire	B 174.1, .2
Ponncánach	B 57.1
púca	B 29.1
reithe, *see also* caora	B 110.1
sac	B 61.1
sagart	B 51.1
saidhbhreas	B 36.3, .4

INDEX [IN ENGLISH] OF SPEAKERS IN PART B:
Wellerisms in Irish

husband	B 17.1
inhospitable woman	B 185.1
Islandman	B 18.1
Jewel Eye *see* Súil Gheam	
labourer	B 118.1
lapwing [*or* plover]	B 80.1
lazy woman	B 49.1
little goat, *see also* goat	B 165.3
little Tadhg, *see* Tadhg Beag	
little yellow man	B 96a.1
loafer	B 63.1
lying red-haired maid	B 70.1
Mac an Bháird	B 24.1; B 111.1
Máire Shalach	B 104.1
man, *see also under qualifiers*	B 12.1; B 25.1, .2; B 35.1, .2; B 45.1; B 46.1; B 53.1; B 55.1–.3; B 65.1; B 69.3; B 72.1; B 75.1; B 79.1; B 97.1; B 101.1, .2; B 106.1–.5, .7; B 109.1; B 112.1; B 113.1; B 116.1–.3; B 130.1, .2; B 138.1; B 140.1, .2; B 141.1; B 142.1; B 155.1, .2; B 157.1; B 161.1; B 166.1; B 167.1; B 173.1, .2; B 184.1–.4; B 187.1; B 192.1; B 197.1
man with a farthing	B 5.1, .2
Maonus	B 107.3
master	B 77.1
Mathúin	B 34.1, .2
ministir	B 196.1
Mongan	B 14.1
monkey	B 81.1; B 183.1, .2
mouse	B 150.1
musician	B 191.1
mute	B 40.3
Ó hIarlaithe	B 131.1
officer	B 126.1

320

old cat, *see also* cat	B 19.1, .2
old crab	B 64.1, .2
old man	B 42.1; B 52.1 B 182.1
old people	B 188.1
old woman	B 39.1; B 121.1; B 177.1
Pádraig	B 66.1
Páidín	B 45.2; B 168.1
Peadar	B 54.1–.3
Peadar of Garraí Aird	B 117a.1
pedlar	B 46.3
piglet	B 15.1
piper	B 174.1, .2
plover *see* lapwing	
pooka	B 29.1
poor man	B 46.2; B 62.1; B 152.1
poor woman	B 30.1
priest	B 51.1, .2
Protestant, *see also* English person	B 198.5
ram, *see also* sheep	B 110.1
raven	B 176.1
sack	B 61.1
Seán Ó Néill	B 69.2
Seán Phaid	B 6.1
Seán the Munsterman	B 47.1, .2
Sean-Mhicheál	B 169.1
sheep, *see also* ram	B 107.5
slattern	B 105.1
smooth-skinned dogfish	B 74.1
son	B 158.1
spouse	B 145.2
Súil Gheam	B 4.1
Súisín Triopallach	B 165.1
sweep	B 100.1–.3
Tadhg Beag	B 99.1
Tadhg na Spréach	B 159.1
Tadhg Ó Séaghdha	B 69.1
Tadhg of the sparks *see* Tadhg na Spréach	
tailor	B 11.1–.6; B 82.1; B 148.1